Number Seventeen: The Centennial Series of the Association of Former Students, Texas A&M University

D0058604

7

Texas Tears and Texas Sunshine

Texas Tears and Texas Sunshine

Voices of Frontier Women

Edited by Jo Ella Powell Exley

Texas A&M University Press
College Station

Library of Congress Cataloging in Publication Data
Main entry under title:

Texas tears and Texas sunshine.

(The Centennial series of the Association of Former
Students, Texas A&M University ; no. 17)
    Bibliography: p.
    Includes index.
    1. Women pioneers—Texas—History—19th century—
Sources.   2. Frontier and pioneer life—Texas—Sources.
3. Texas—History—Sources.   I. Exley, Jo Ella Powell,
1940–   .   II. Series.
F381.T53   1984   976.4   84-40140
ISBN 0-89096-215-4, cloth
ISBN 0-89096-453-X, paper

Manufactured in the United States of America
FIFTH PRINTING, 1991

Dedicated to my parents,
Lydia Mae (Matula) and Thomas Hardy Powell,
and my husband,
James J. Exley

Contents

Illustrations

Preface

Long ago in Texas a woman sat on the floor of a log cabin arranging and rearranging bits of colored cloth. She was putting together a quilt pattern, which she was to name "Texas Tears." Later she put together another pattern, and she called it "Texas Sunshine." This pioneer woman was creating more than multicolored quilts; she was creating reflections of the multifaceted lives of herself, her husband, and her children—lives that were filled with tears and sunshine.

This book takes its name from the quilts that women of Texas have always made. But the women of Texas created more than quilts; they helped create Texas. This book allows them to tell their own stories.

First, these women tell of life in colonial Texas. Mary Crownover Rabb describes life as experienced by one of Stephen F. Austin's "Old Three Hundred" when she and her husband fled alternately from marauding Indians and voracious mosquitoes. Although Mary Wightman Helm tends to romanticize her stay in Matagorda, she vividly depicts the degeneration of the Karankawa Indians after their contact with civilization. And selfish and headstrong as Ann Raney Coleman may have been, her account of her life and loves as the "Belle of Brazoria" is a fascinating one.

The Texas Revolution brought more suffering and hardship to the women of Texas as they tried to escape the oncoming Mexican army. Dilue Rose Harris chronicles the horrors of what came to be known as the "Runaway Scrape." During the period when Texas was a republic, the Indian problem grew worse, and marauding bands of Comanches and Apaches roamed freely through much of Texas. Rachel Parker Plummer's description of her two-year captivity by a band of Comanches is one of the most gruesome true stories ever recorded. So bold were the Indians that not even towns were safe. Mary Adams Maverick tells of the bloody Council House Fight between Comanches and Texans on the streets of San Antonio.

The 1850's and the 1860's brought more hardship and death to

Texas as the Civil War broke out and later yellow fever raged in the coastal areas. Rebecca Bass Adams tells how the women struggled to keep themselves and their children clothed by learning to spin and weave and even tan hides. Eudora Moore lived in a town that was occupied by Federal troops. The most horrible experience which Eudora and Amelia Huddleson Barr suffered through, however, was the yellow fever epidemic of 1867. Amelia, using the extraordinary powers of description that made her a best-selling novelist, paints a vivid picture as she describes the deaths of her husband and two sons.

The last chapter of *Texas Tears and Texas Sunshine* presents vignettes from the 1870's through the first years of this century, when the last frontier, that of the High Plains, was being settled. Although the women still faced the danger of Indian attacks during the early part of this period, their accounts of life on the frontier are filled with hope for the future. After many years of suffering by Texas women, the tears had finally begun to lessen, and the sunshine had begun to break through. Mary Taylor Bunton, Ella Bird Dumont, and Mary Perritt Blankenship lived on ranches, and the freedom of the open range molded their spirits and made these women strong and fearless and optimistic. Mary Bunton even spent her honeymoon on a trail drive.

"Log Cabin," "Lone Star," "Texas Tears," and "Texas Sunshine" are the names that Texas women gave their quilts, and these are the names of the chapters in this book—their book. In *Texas Tears and Texas Sunshine*, the women themselves tell their stories. They are stories of a patchwork of happiness and sadness, pleasure and pain, health and sickness, and birth and death. Pioneer women helped mold Texas. As Ermine Redwine, a pioneer woman from Rising Star, Texas, writes: "I hope when the people of today shall read of all of the old veterans of the nineteenth century, that they will remember us kindly as the old tried and trusted pioneers that paved the road through the wilderness for them."

Acknowledgments

In the last five years I have learned that a book is seldom created by one person alone. Many people have helped me to compile *Texas Tears and Texas Sunshine*, and I would like to mention a few of them.

Much encouragement and advice were given to me by my husband James J. Exley and my friends Frank E. Tritico, Dr. James E. Stafford, Sally Stafford, and Dr. Charles Peavy. Others who offered suggestions were Dr. Marilyn McAdams Sibley, Polly McRoberts, Dolores Borchers, Frances Tursam, Marilyn Thibodeaux, and Eleanor Buller.

Librarians and archivists who were especially helpful were William Richter and Ralph Elder of the Barker Texas History Center at the University of Texas at Austin; Judy Eckmann and Carol Walther of the Harris County Public Library; Wendy Serba of the M. D. Anderson Memorial Library at the University of Houston; Lauren Brown of the Fondren Library at Rice University; Winston Atkins of the San Jacinto Museum of History; Mary Jo Cooper of the Austin History Center of the Austin Public Library; and Rebecca Herring of the Southwest Collection of Texas Tech University.

I would like to thank some of the many people who helped me to obtain pictures. Aiding me in my search were Davis McNeill, Jean Schmalz, Charlotte Simpson, Barbara Lorraine, Joy Delle Wolfram, Ethel Gusman, Mrs. Guy Cannon, and Paulette Hays. Among those who generously provided copies of pictures in their possession were Don E. Hutson, Robert R. Stough, Roberta Rylander, Glen Treibs, Helen Courtney, Jane Hoerster, Wini W. White, and Eve Bartlett.

I would also like to thank my patient typist Lori Tracy, my friend Cecelia Goad, and my dear mother.

I. Log Cabin: Colonization, 1821–35

The year 1821 marked a new beginning in the territory now known as Texas; Stephen F. Austin's first colonists set out by land and by sea to settle in the fertile valleys of the Brazos and Colorado rivers. The first settlers to come by sea were the twenty or so passengers of the schooner *Lively*. Around January, 1822, they gathered their possessions and jumped off the ship, each rushing to be the first to set foot on the shore. Unfortunately, the vessel had become lost, and the settlers never did find the mouth of the Colorado River which Austin had designated as the meeting point. Most returned to Louisiana. However, other settlers did come. Some were planters, who arrived with wagons filled with equipment and with slaves, but most were much like the relatives of Mary Crownover Rabb, hard-working farmers who longed for fertile land and wanted to make a new beginning.

Life for the settlers was hard. They were harassed by Indians, Mexican administrators, and clouds of mosquitoes and flies. Worst of all, disease was a threat, especially on the "fever coast," where settlers suffered from malaria and dysentery and died from cholera and yellow fever. Ann Raney Coleman lost both her father and mother in 1832.

As more and more Anglo-American settlers poured into Texas, the Mexicans began to doubt the wisdom of allowing the Americans to come into Mexican territory. As the Mexicans began to try to tighten their control over their Anglo-American colonists, skirmishes began to occur.

The details of this story are known to most Texans and to many others, but this is not the only story to be told. While the men were out settling land titles or fighting Mexicans or Indians, what were the women doing? Mary Crownover Rabb, Mary Wightman Helm, and Ann Raney Coleman describe life in colonial Texas from women's points of view.

Mary Crownover Rabb

"I kept my new spinning wheel whistling."

The reminiscence written by Mary Crownover Rabb, one of Stephen F. Austin's original "Old Three Hundred" colonists, is one of the few accounts of life in the earliest days of colonial Texas. Mary Crownover was born in North Carolina in 1805. Her parents were Mary (Chesney) and John Crownover. She was tall with dark eyes and black hair, and at the age of sixteen she married John Rabb in Jonesboro, Arkansas. Two years later in 1823, Mary and John and other members of the Rabb family decided to go to Texas, where members of her family had already moved. They rounded up their few cattle and packed up their belongings. Mary mounted her horse Tormentor and took her baby on her lap, and, as Mary says, "That horse and I rode to Texas."

After arriving in Texas, Mary and John led a nomadic life, since they could not decide which were worse, Indians or mosquitoes. The young couple first settled in what is now Fayette County. After Indians stole their horses, John decided to move to the Brazos River bottom. The family lived for a while near San Felipe and then in 1826 moved to their headright in what is now Fort Bend County. They lived for about a year on their league of land before John decided that loneliness was worse than Indians or mosquitoes. The family rejoined their relatives and eventually settled in Fayette County.

Mary and her husband became prominent citizens in Fayette County and leaders of the Methodist Church. In 1860 they made their last move and settled on Barton Springs near Austin. John died in 1861, but Mary lived on and built a fine two-story limestone house, which was a great improvement over a tent made with a quilt. She died in 1882 at the age of seventy-seven.

Mary Rabb's account of life on the Texas frontier is one of the most colorful ones because it is one of the few written in the vernacular of the frontier. Although Mary spelled phonetically and knew little about punctuation and grammar, she was a gifted storyteller. She communicates her terror of the Indians, but she also

From Mary Crownover Rabb, *Travels and Adventures in Texas in the 1820's* (Waco: W. M. Morrison, 1962).

Mary and John Rabb. (*Courtesy Barker Texas History Center, University of Texas at Austin*)

includes humorous anecdotes which reveal much about the daily life of a woman on the Texas frontier. Tying the account together is the whir of the spinning wheel as Mary spins thread for her family in her cabin, in a tent, under a tree, and even under a mosquito bar.

To clarify the complicated story that Mary tells, I have divided the account into paragraphs and have modernized her spelling and punctuation.

*   *   *

I left Jonesboro, Red River, Miller County Arkansas, with my husband John Rabb and my little babe to come to Texas. We started October 1, 1823. We also had Mr. Rabb's father and Andrew Rabb and Thomas Rabb. Mr. Rabb also had a sister with her husband, Mr. Newman, and her children. Mr. Newman's children's names was Polly, William, Eliza, Minerva, Sarah, Thomas, and Eli. All come to Texas the same time. Every family had a few cattle.

Now my children and grandchildren, I am going to try to tell you something about the way your pa and me had to do to get land for you. As I told you, every family had a few cattle. Your pa had about 16 or 18 head of small cattle being only two grown cows with them and two or three tolerable large ones that would make oxen. We also had six head of horses which was all we had without any other means whatever.

One of those horses was a large iron gray. He was very tall. His name was Tormentor, and that horse and I rode to Texas. Your pa got me a Mexican sidesaddle that is made in this way in order to carry a pack. On those Mexican sidesaddles there has to be a sack full of something to throw across the seat of those saddles or else fold up quilts and blankets enough to fill the saddle up level with the lower part of the horns. In this way we was able to carry a pretty good pack on Tormentor besides myself and the little one.

Well, we was mounted and set out for Texas. We traveled on about one hundred miles, and our cattle got sick and commenced dying, and we had to stop driving them. Your uncle Tom Rabb stayed with the cattle, and the balance of our company drove on. After we had drove on a few days, we met up with James Gilliland and his family that was on their way to Texas: a wife and little babe and John Ingram and a little orphan boy. I did remember what his name was. I took breakfast with

Mrs. Gilliland that morning, and then we drove on. We got a quantity of nice grapes on the road, and we found one bee tree. We got some nice honey.

I do not remember any more that took place until we got to the Colorado River. We come to it where La Grange now is, but there was no house there then nor nothing but a wilderness, not even a tree cut down to mark that place.

We met two gentlemen at the river. It was fordable, but it looked full and to run swift. Those men said there was no danger. Your pa took the babe and rode to the left. One of those men rode to my right, and your pa told me to take my riding switch in my teeth, and said he, "Your head will not swim." While your pa and those men had to hold their feet up out of the water to keep them from getting wet, I was riding Tormentor and the water did not come near me.

Well, we got safe over the Colorado on the south side. There we met with your grandma Rabb and your uncle Ulysses who had come to Texas in 1822. We went up about six or seven miles above La Grange to a place they called Indian Hill at Mr. Castleman's. We got there about the 15 of December, 1823. There we was got to our journey's end safe: Mr. Rabb's father and mother and two sons, Thomas and Ulysses, and Andrew Rabb and his family, a wife and child; Mr. Newman and his family, a wife and seven children.

As Mr. Rabb's father and brother had been in Texas one year before, he had a house built, but it was not large enough for all of us to live in, so your pa got John Ingram to help him to work a while and your pa and him built a house in one week.

The house was made of logs. They made a chimney to it. The door shutter was made of thick slabs split out of thick pieces of timber, and the way we fastened the door, they bored a hole in one of the logs inside close to the door shutter, and then we had a large pin or peg that was drove in hard and fast of nights, and then the Indians could not get in. We had an earthen floor in our house.

I was in my first Texas house, and Andrew Rabb made a spinning wheel and made me a present of it. I was very much pleased, and I soon got to work to make clothing for my family.

In a few days, Thomas Rabb come on with what few cattle the muren had left. We had 8 or 9 head left and with them one milk cow. Your pa and John Ingram went in the rich land in the Colorado bottom to clear land to make a field. They cleared about six acres and come to the house one Saturday evening leaving their axes and malls and iron wedges expecting to return to their work on Monday morning. But as they had made a good many rails, the Indians thought it would be a good way to make a pen out of those rails and catch our horses. When Mr. Rabb and Ingram went to their work, they found that their axes was gone and a pen was made, and our horses were also gone. All we had but Tormentor was gone, and he would have been gone, but Mr. Rabb put a chain around his neck every night and locked him to the house with a padlock.

A day or two before the Indians come down, there was a drove of buffalo come and crossed over the river about one hundred yards above our house. There was about thirty in number. They took a straight course through the prairie, not turning to the right nor to the left. On they went southward as far as we could see them.

After the Indians stole our horses, your pa said he would not stay at Indian Hill. Your grandpa was sorry for that and did not want your pa to move away from that place. He wanted to keep his children all together, but your pa told your grandma the Indians was too bad. Then your grandpa wanted to give your pa a pony, but your pa did not want to take it. Your grandpa led the pony up to the door. My babe was sitting in the door, and he put the bridle in his hand and said he gave the pony to the babe. The pony's name was Nickety Poly.

Your pa rode Nickety Poly and went off to hunt a place for us to move where the Indians would not be so bad. Your pa went over to the Brazos about 15 miles below Richmond, Texas. There he got a league of land, his headright.

He was gone about ten days. I was left alone with my little babe, and I thought that ten days and nights was so long. I could hear the Indians walking around the house many times of nights. I had to take a padlock and chain and fasten Tormentor to the house. I thought the Indians was trying to get the horse from the house. Sometimes I thought they would cut his head off just because they could not get him. Now lonely as I was, after rising early in the morning and attending to making cornmeal for the day, I kept my new spinning wheel whistling all day and a good part of the night, for while the wheel was roaring, it would keep me from hearing the Indians walking around hunting mischief.

Now my little grandchildren, I am going to tell you a funny tale about some little pigs. When we got to Texas up on Indian Hill, your great-grandma gave your grandpa a sow, and she had nine little pigs. While your grandpa was gone, after I got tired of spinning at night, there was under the bottom log of the house close in the corner of the chimney, a little place the pigs could crawl through. When I put the wheel away and got ready to go to bed, I would shell some corn over the floor and under the bed and open that little place, and by the time I got in the bed, all them little pigs would be in the house cracking corn until I would be asleep and the Indians gone and the pigs gone. In the mornings, I would get up and sweep out my little house and stop the pigs out, and get my breakfast made and make meal for the day and then to my wheel again.

Now your pa comes home. He thanks God that we was protected, and he said he thought the savage Indians had been stayed in answer to his prayers, although he was not religious.

Then your uncle John Crownover come home with your pa and brought a horse with them to pack our goods on. Your pa had been to your grandma Crownover's. He killed a bear there. He had just come to Texas and had got a camp made near to your pa's league of land.

We made quick haste and got ready to pack up and start. We put all our raiment and things on the old horse that your pa and uncle had led up to Indian Hill for that purpose. The old horse's name was Flucus. After the most delicate part of the pack was put on first, then our provision, then our little kettle which was hardly large enough to cook a boiled dinner for three persons, then the skillet and lid was put on top, then my spinning wheel was put on top, all but the bench. We had a small yoke of oxen which had a small yoke or necking stick on, and the wheel bench was tied to that. We had our few little cattle and our sow and pigs all put together, me on Tormentor, your pa on Nickety Poly, and your uncle John on his horse. He called him Shurk. We set out unmolested although the Indians in the woods was looking at us start. That day we got to Cummins Creek and camped for the night. There your pa killed a large duck or brant. It made part of our breakfast next morning. We packed up, putting everything on old Flucus in the same manner we did the morning before.

We drove on very peaceably until some one of the cattle trod on one of the pigs and broke off its hoof and made it so lame that it could not travel. We thought it would not do to leave the pig, so your pa caught it and tied it to the top of old Flucus' pack close under the wheel rim. We went on, but the pig got tired and commenced to squeal and scramble to get down, and old Flucus got scared and run off and made a complete stampede and kept pitching and kicking until he got everything off. The result was the pig's brains was smashed out, and the dinner pot broke all in bits. Then we had to pick up the balance of the furniture the best we could and lash them on old Flucus again and set out.

We got to my pa's about 4 or 5 days after we left Indian Hill. I found my father and mother well and well pleased there. We had plenty of cornbread and bear meat and venison and honey and milk and butter. We stayed there a few weeks. We had no neighbors nearer than eight miles, and the mosquitoes was so bad, it was almost impossible to do any work like sewing and churning unless we were in a mosquito bar. The flies was eating the cattle and horses up, and so we concluded we would leave there and go higher up the Brazos River. As the flies and mosquitoes was so bad, we knew we would have to travel pretty much altogether in the night.

We had everything packed up ready to start about half an hour before sunset and made a start, but the flies was still so bad, the horses cut up so, your pa had to run to me and get me off my horse, and then he run to your grandma and your aunt Lissa and get them down. We went in the camp and stayed until sundown and then made another start and got a few steps. We had everything packed on Nickety Poly: the spinning wheel rim on top and two chickens tied to the wheel and the wheel bench tied to the oxen.

We thought we could go, but we had three pups, and your pa began to think they was too young to travel through the high grass in the prairie. The pups was all one age, but one of them was larger than the other two. I told your pa to get down off his horse and go back in the camp and get a pair of old leather leggings that was left and tie each one of them at the bottom and put the two little pups in the leggings and tie them on Nickety Poly behind his pack under the wheel. Your pa said the big pup could walk.

Everything was arranged, and we made a start in the twilight. We traveled on some distance without any trouble, but at last the big pup got tired of traveling in the high grass, and it would keep running under my horse's feet. At last Tormentor trod on it, and it scared him, and he reared straight up. I thought the horse was going to fall backward on me and the child, but he careened on his hind feet and come down, and his forefeet brushed your grandma's lap as she had just got along by the side of me while Tormentor was standing on his hind feet.

We went on by moonlight without any trouble, but then the two pups got tired being confined in the leathern leggings thrown across Nickety Poly's pack, and they begin to crabble and crack to get down. Nickety Poly thought he could not stand such crackling as that, and he run off and commenced to pitch and jump until the leggings broke apart, and one pup fell on one side and the other on the other. Nick run off, and it was some time before we could find Nickety Poly. I do not think we would have got him until daylight, but we had two chickens tied to the top of the pack, a hen and a rooster, and as it began to get the time of night for chickens to crow, our little rooster had crabbled up on the wheel and gave a big crow, and then we found Nickety Poly all right. He was eating grass and had all of our goods: bedding and provisions and spinning wheel and chickens.

Then we was ready for another start. We traveled nearly all night. We stopped about six miles below San Felipe, and there your pa commenced to build a frame house, and I was spinning under a tree. He got the house up and covered.

Then your pa thought he would move about one mile and a half to the Brazos River on two labors of land he had there. There we had no camp. We put up a quilt and a sheet for a tent. I got the head of my wheel under the tent. I got to spinning again.

After we stayed there a few days, we thought we would go a visiting to see your pa's people over to the Colorado which I think was about fifty miles. We had nobody to leave our things with, so your pa took all our goods off in a thick part of a cane brake and hid them under a yearling beef hide which would protect them from the rain.

We set out on Tormentor and Nickety Poly. We found our friends all well. We spent about two weeks with them and returned and found everything all right.

As the weather was warm, we stayed there near the Brazos some time with a shelter. I was spinning under a tree. The mosquitoes and sand gnats was so bad that it was impossible to get any sleep, but at last your pa said, "Let us go to the river and sleep on the sand beach," which was some distance from the place we stayed at. The babe and the bedclothes was to have been carried down, and when we got there and got the bed made, the wind would blow the gnats off. I was afraid the alligators would come up out of the river and get my babe, and I could not sleep, and there was danger to the river taking a sudden rise and wash us off. While we stayed at this place, Tormentor died.

Before right cold weather, your pa got us a camp covered with boards. We thought we would get a house by the first of December, but I was confined before your pa could get the house done. We got to go in a camp that belonged to one of my brothers. It was a very good camp. It had a fireplace.

When Washia was about six weeks old, your pa put me and the children on a slide and hitched Nickety Poly to it and took us out to Mr. Newman's. His wife was your pa's sister. They had a house. After we stayed there a few days, one night I awoke, and I thought from the noise the river must be rising. I put my hand out, and I found the river had rose and was nearly level with the bed place I lay on. I was afraid the children would fall out and get drowned. Next day the menfolks took Nickety Poly and hauled all the house logs out of the water and built the house upon the side of the hill. I think we stayed there until March, 1825.

Then we went to the Bernard River. There your pa built a little house. Your pa got three hundred feet of plank and put a floor in it. He gave a nice heifer for it. Then your pa left me and the children and the cows and hogs and went over to the Colorado to burn off a canebrake. He raised five hundred bushels of corn that year. I got along very well with the cows, but the hogs run off as I had no corn to give them. I stayed all summer by myself with only my two little children. As your pa had no fence around his corn, he could not take his stock there, so I stayed on the Bernard while your pa raised corn on the Colorado. I would pick the cotton with my fingers and spin six hundred thread around the reel every day and milk my cows and pound my meal in a mortar and cook and churn and mind my children.

One evening while I was at the cow pen and had Gum with me to open the gate, Washia crawled off some one hundred and fifty or perhaps two hundred yards. I could not hardly find him. When I found him, one of our dogs was standing over him licking his head. I did not whip the dog because I knew he wanted to protect him. The dog was one of the pups that we packed in the leather leggings.

After your pa gathered his corn, we moved to the Colorado in the fall of 1825. We stayed all winter in a camp with just a few boards over us. All the front and sides was open to the wind.

The first of April, 1826, we went to the Brazos. (Though I forgot to tell you, your pa sold his corn very well. He got a fine American mare for some of it.) As we went on at dinner time the tenth of April, I found some ripe dewberries. Then one day as we was going on, our oxen got so warm hot, they run to a shade in spite of all your pa could do, and your pa was caught betwixt the body of the cart and the tree. As soon as I saw the trouble your pa was in, I took my babe under my left arm and jumped down and run to your pa. But as the oxen was so very hot and had their tongues out, after they got in the shade and stopped the cart on your pa, they fell back a little to pant, and your pa dropped down from betwixt the body of the cart and the tree. By this time John Ingram and me had got to him. Your pa said for us to cord his arm as soon as we could, and as your pa used to say, my garter never failed. So his arm was soon corded, and your pa took his little old pocket knife and bled hisself.

As soon as your pa was able to travel, we went on to our place, a league of land, our headright, that we got for coming to Texas, poor things how bad that was for us. There your pa got the boards that was where your grandpa Crownover and us used to live in camp where the horseflies and mosquitoes was so bad we had to leave and travel in the night. Then your pa made me a camp and covered it with those old boards. I went to spinning and spun enough thread to make forty-six yards of mosquito barring and wove it out in the open air and sun without any covering. Your pa made the loom in two days. Then I wove another piece of cloth that was good and thick for clothing before we got any shelter for the loom. Then your pa built a good house. He made it twenty feet square. He hewed the logs down to about six inches thick, and then he made a shed for the loom. Melissa was born there May 26, 1827. Your pa raised corn on the river about three or four miles off, but we had a garden at the house.

We did not stay there long. I think the fall of 1827 your pa took a notion that he could not stay there as we had no neighbors nearer than eight miles. In the first of September we left our house and loom and garden potatoes and all went to Egypt. There your pa bought one hundred acres of land from your uncle Andrew. Your pa built a house and made a field. There the Indians was a trouble again. They killed our cattle and hogs, and I was so afraid of them. When your pa was gone from home at night, sometimes I would blow out the candle and run to bed with my little ones for fear the Indians would shoot us through the cracks of our log cabin. At other times as night would come, I would take my little ones betwixt sundown and dark and go nearly a mile to your uncle Andrew's to stay the night.

One morning Gum and Wash went out to the road a few yards from the door. They took their pups with them. It was but a few minutes until I saw seven Indians coming to the children. I hollered to the children to run to the house so I could shut the door. Gum left his pup and run in, but Washia would hang on to his, and by the time he got his pup to the door, the Indians was in the house. When the Indians got pretty close to the children, the big dog stripped the old chief of his buffalo robe and left him nearly naked.

Then them Indians begged everything they could see that was fit to eat and that was not fit. It happened that the dog had treed one of those wild leopard cats close to the house, and I took the gun and went and killed it. When your pa come, he brought it in the house to look at it. On the day before, your pa chanced to kill two deer close to the house. He brought them to the house to dress them. He hung the haslett up to keep the hogs from getting them. Them Indians took them haslett and rolled them in the fire ashes and eat them and the blood was working out of their mouths. It was winter then. They got the wildcat to eat and almost all of the deer meat and some beef bones.

There was one rode up at another time on a nice American horse. He had on a American vest and had nothing else on him. He saw a turkey under a shed outdoors. I had cut the breast off to fry. It was winter. That Indian asked for it. He took it on his horse before him and struck out at a gallop.

Those was the Tonkawa Indians. After begging all they could, they went off, but was not too good to kill a man if they could get him off by hisself. After this there was a Karankawa camp found on the river, and the Tonkawas was in partnership. They was so troublesome, your pa and uncles and as many others as they could get to drive them further off in the frontier.

I think we lived there about five years. There Marion was born in 1829. Then we moved up to Rabb's Prairie where we had a mill on the Colorado River. I think the mill was built in 1831, and we moved up in 1832. In 1833 that high overflow came. I could see the water coming up. We stayed in the house until the water was over the floor. Me and some of the little ones had to be carried to the wagon as the water was over a foot and a half deep in the yard. We had to hurry to get out to the hills. Your pa and a Frenchman by the name of Bateas hurried back to try to save our goods, our beds, and clothing. They got to the house and pulled the things up in a cedar tree that was in the yard, not right in front of the house, to one side. The cedar tree is cut down, but when I go a fishing, I visit that old stump and the place where the house used to be. After your pa and Bateas got the goods put up, they tried to go to your uncle Andrew's house which was about half a mile above on the river. They had to swim nearly all the way, sometimes catching limbs and twigs of the tops of bushes. Your pa got to the house, but Bateas took the cramp and could not swim. He caught a cedar limb and pulled up on the tree and stayed all night. Your pa made a hole in the roof of the house and went down on the upper floor. There he found a cloak and a churn of cream that had been set up out of the water. So he had cream to drink, and a cloak to cover him, but poor Bateas was in the cedar tree a swinging back and forth as the water would swell and heave against the tree. Every once and a while, your pa would call to Bateas through the night to know if he was still alive, and if he still felt able to hold on the tree. He would answer, "Mighty cold." As soon as daylight come, your uncle Andrew went to work to make a canoe. He worked hard all day trying to get it done so he could go and see what had become of your pa and Bateas. Just before sundown, we saw a vessel coming in Rabb's Prairie, then going towards the house. It was Mr. Castleman. He lived where Mr. Manton lives now. He went to the house and got your pa and then went to the tree and got Bateas and brought them out to the hills where we was. Then we was all safe out of the overflow.

When the water got down low enough, Pa went back to the house and got our clothing and bed and everything out of the cedar tree and brought them out to the hill bluff on the river. There your pa wanted to settle, but then your uncle Andrew said he wanted to settle there hisself, and as your uncle Andrew was the oldest, your pa gave up to him. Your pa said he would go and hunt another place. So your pa went to the Pope place and settled there, but it was only a little while until your uncle Andrew said he wanted to settle there too. Your pa said for him to come on, but your pa did not give up his building place to him. Your uncle went two or three hundred yards along the side of the hill and rebuilt his house. We hauled our houses out of the overflow and rebuilt them. Your pa dug a well at the Pope place. It was free stone water. I used to hang sheets on them live oaks that is in the yard of the Pope place. I could bend them trees down in 1833. We stayed there some time, but was always troubled with the Indians stealing our horses and our corn out of the crib. Your pa told me that he had lost a thousand dollars worth of horses by those Indians.

I remember at one time the Indians come to our house in the night and tried to steal a horse that we had tied close to the door under the gallery roof as we had no floor in the gallery nor no shutter to the door. We brought the horse right close to the door, as your pa was gone, so the children and me could have a better chance to keep the Indians from getting him. Your uncle Andrew's black boy Frank had come to stay all night with my little boys as they thought he could protect them. At bed time I went to bed, and the little ones went to their bed. Frank spread his pallet on one side of the fireplace. As we had no shutter to the door, his little dog Trusty come in and lay down on the other side of the fireplace. We had not been still but a little while until the Indians come and was trying to get the horse. I was asleep. Frank come to me and asked me, "Where is the gun?" said he.

I said, "What do you want with the gun?"

Said he, "The Indians is here trying to get the horse." Frank got the gun, and I got up and run to the door to see. The horse was so afraid and was pulling back to get loose. As there was no shutter to the door, Trusty had nothing to do but to run out and get after them Indians. They run and got out of the yard fence and went to the corn crib and got corn. Then they went to the wash place and got a little pot and some clothing that had been left there. Then they went to your uncle

Andrew's workshop and got what they could. Your aunt Peggy and me and our children tracked them Indians a half a mile. They might have been in the thicket and killed us all.

I have went many times and took my gun and lay in the corner of the fence and helped your pa watch for Indians. One time your pa and me was a way up above here hunting bees, and I got tired and sit down close to the horses. Your pa went off some distance. After while, your pa come up to me in a great hurry. Said he, "We must be off now in a hurry." Said he, "I heard guns firing, and the smoke is just rising." Said he, "The Indians has done some mischief not far from here, and they have set the woods afire." Said your pa, "We are in danger. Now let us be off." We went on and hardly ever spoke, but when we did, we would talk low. We had not got home but a few hours until the word come that the Indians had killed Mr. Alexander. . . .

How many trials and troubles have we passed through together here in Texas, and no opportunity of going to church, yet God was mindful of us and blessed us and gave us his spirit and made us feel that we was His.

Mary Sherwood Wightman Helm

> "The cooking was done in the open air, with the wind
> blowing a gale."

Six years after Mary Crownover Rabb's overland trek to Texas,
another woman traveled to Texas, where she and her husband
founded the town of Matagorda in 1829. Mary Wightman Helm
was born in Herkimer County, New York, in 1807 to John H. and
Janet (Henderson) Sherwood. She had been teaching school for
several years when "her old teacher," Elias R. Wightman, returned from a surveying expedition in Texas. Mary describes the
courtship: "I was no longer the girl of twelve years; I admired a
something more than my old teacher. He had improved in knowledge, in his manners. His very voice was all in all to me; but he, of
course, knew not the change in my feelings, and so I made free to
encourage him to tell his strange experience of wild life." Elias
could not resist such admiration, and so they were married.

With her husband, the eighteen-year-old bride left her childhood home in 1828 to meet a group of about sixty people who
were headed for Texas. The group traveled by wagon to the Allegheny River and then set out upon what was at that time a popular
route to the West. They traveled by flatboat and raft down the
Allegheny to Pittsburgh, Pennsylvania, where they boarded a
steamboat which took them down the Ohio and Mississippi to
New Orleans. The voyage from New Orleans to the Texas coast
was usually the most difficult part of the journey. In the early
days, schooners were used because they had shallow drafts and
could usually traverse the sandbars which lined the Texas coast. In
the Gulf of Mexico the small vessels were at the mercy of hurricanes in the summer and fall and stiff north winds in the winter.
When the winds did not blow, the ships were often becalmed for
days, and travelers suffered from lack of food and water. Mary
describes her trip in *Scraps of Early Texas History*, which was
published in 1884.

Mary and Elias lived in Texas until 1841. Both taught school
in Matagorda. Elias was a surveyor for Stephen F. Austin, and the

From Mary Sherwood Helm, *Scraps of Early Texas History* (Austin: privately
printed, 1884).

Wightmans made many enjoyable trips to different parts of Austin's Colony in order to survey prospective townsites. As a reward for his services as a surveyor and the founder of Matagorda, Wightman was given a land grant on Caney Creek near the present town of Sargent. The Wightmans owned several slaves and farmed a portion of the grant. They divided their time between Caney Creek and Matagorda, frequently traveling by skiff across Matagorda Bay.

In 1841 the Wightmans sold out and moved to Covington, New York, in an attempt to improve Wightman's health, but he died two months after they arrived there. In 1843 Mary returned to Matagorda for a short visit.

Several years after the death of Elias, Mary married Meredith Helm, a native of Kentucky who was one of the founders of Connersville, Indiana. He may have been one of the soldiers in the fort when Mary first arrived in Matagorda, since Mary says one of them was "a Kentucky youth, six feet high, named Helm." Mary spent the rest of her life in Connersville, where she died in 1886 at the age of seventy-eight.

*   *   *

The usual time for sailing from New Orleans to Texas was seven days, so we only took provisions for sixty persons for seven days, and about the time that was consumed our water also became alarmingly scarce—half a pint a day to each person. Being sick, I could not drink the water, nor the tea and coffee made from it. A little vinegar and sugar, diluted with this bad water, sustained me. There were no conveniences for cooking, except a stationary sheet-iron boiler, so-called, in which we were allowed to heat water for our tea and coffee. Our Captain, one day, very kindly volunteered to make it full of vegetable soup for all the passengers, when we, or more especially the well ones, were nearly famished, and invited his sixty passengers to help themselves. And such a scrambling! It would have made a picture for Harper. Many could not procure vessels to get what they so much needed. It so happened that a small tin cup fell to my lot; it was very small at the top and took a long time to cool. I had been nine days without food and but very little to drink, because I could not eat and drink such as the vessel afforded, and having a fever did not crave much. Now came the tug of war. Those who could procure large vessels took too much. By the time I had cooled and consumed my gift of soup the boiler was empty. Looking down the hatchway I saw a family of three with a six-quart pan full, and reaching down my cup, I requested them to fill it. They parleyed and said they could not spare any. I would not report, to make trouble for my friends; but after I had retired in disgust they offered to fill my cup. I do not remember the sequel, only remember telling them of it years after, at which time, of course, they had forgotten the circumstance. After our cooked provisions had given out, crackers and hard sea bread sustained life; but when the water gave out, then real suffering commenced. And such water! I really supposed then that powder casks had been used for holding the water, not having learned then that it took time for water to become good. The well passengers could drink it made into coffee, but it so affected me that I could not endure the smell of coffee for several years. Mr. Pilgrim says that he gave his share of the water to the children, and sustained himself on whiskey and crackers.

Some of our men had the good fortune to shoot and kill a pelican, a most disgusting sea fowl that lives on fish, having a large pouch in front that holds his prey till time of need. Its flesh is black and tastes fishy. I had not tasted food for so many days, that I was constantly dreaming of soups and milk, or something to sustain life. We had a little sick boy, Laroy Griffeth, now more than sixty years of age, who also craved food. The bird was boiled and the boy promised the meat, but I not caring for the meat, craved the soup, worth more to me than its weight in gold. When, to my astonishment, the boy was in tears for fear "Aunt Mary would eat all the meat," while I was about as foolish about the soup. We had, a few days before, witnessed a burial at sea, and we naturally felt that unless relief came soon, it would be repeated. This was the first time I had ever experienced *want*—want of something to sustain life—and no wonder I worshipped the disgusting soup of the pelican, so that when a hurricane drove us into Aransas Bay, no wonder we did not think of Indians. And now, again, as we enter Matagorda Pass, Sunday morning, January 27, 1829, with all our fears of hostile Indians, whose telegraphic smokes told of our approach, a joyful thankfulness filled our hearts, for we were entering the land of promise. . . .

As no vessel had ever before entered the port [of Matagorda] great was the excitement in accomplishing that feat. The soundings of the channel had to be made so that it could not be done at once, and our

Christ Church in Matagorda, the oldest Episcopal church in Texas. This building, erected in 1859, is a replica of the one in which Mary Wightman Helm worshiped in 1841.

friends on land sent out our poor weary and worn immigrants a sumptuous dinner on board the vessel—long before she made her appearance in port—of boiled hominy, pounded in a mortar, cooked meats of various kinds, also a variety of fish and fowl, and a large bucket of sweet milk and some sweet potatoes, the first they ever saw, bread minus, for the corn only produced a small fraction of meal, when the hominy was pounded by a contrivance like an old-fashioned well sweep. We had on board plenty of flour which we had no way of cooking, also groceries, portions of which we returned to our generous donors, and I will state in passing, that requests often came with visitors from a distance for small portions of flour to show their friends who had never seen wheat flour. Our sixty starving sea-worn passengers were thus welcomed to their long sought for post, after an absence of thirty-one days from New Orleans. . . .

By the time our vessel was ready to unload passengers, our fort was vacated. I shall ever remember the kindness of its late inmates, they seemed to vie with each other in giving material aid in fish, fowl and venison — deer being in droves of hundreds in every direction which had not yet learned to fear man, but would approach him if he would sit down to see what he looked like, and thus come within gunshot. Our friends also had plenty of cows and thus we had the long coveted milk I had dreamed so much about, when starving at sea. . . .

The surroundings of our new home, as it then appears, seemed to me quite romantic. Arriving in the night, I could only see a large enclosure, some fifty feet square. In one respect it was like Solomon's temple—no sign of tools or nails being visible about our edifice. A large fire in the centre, a mosquito-net covering a rude bed at each corner of the room, the whole building being without joists or tennents, but simply forked sticks drove in the ground to support poles on which cross-poles were laid to sustain the mattress, while perpendicular poles sustained the mosquito-net—a thing quite indispensable. Our door turned on a post, the lower end of which was driven in the ground. The whole edifice was enclosed by perpendicular posts some ten or twelve feet high. At intervals the posts were forked to support horizontal poles, upon which the roof rested, and which was also supported on the inside by poles. True, there were marks of an ax, but nothing more. Long, split, dry cypress boards (so called from float timbers of some other coast cast upon the beach), formed a good substitute for shingles. . . .

For the want of material to build, as our fort let in much water in hard storms, we erected a sort of tent and covered it with long grass for a place to sleep, and the next move, was to tear down the fort, and build a smaller room to shut out the weather and rain. At last, an opportunity was offered to trade an order of five cows and calves for hewed logs sixteen feet long to build one room; we added a side porch and floored it with puncheon high and dry from the ground, and a shed kitchen from the leavings of the old fort; we had now lived one year on the ground floor, all this time the cooking was done in the open air, with the wind blowing a gale. The order of one cow and calf had by custom become a circulating medium for $10, hence the order for five cows and calves for these logs. Our relatives had all gone up the country, except the parents of my husband, E. R. Wightman, now more than seventy years of age. On June 20th, his mother died of fever; in six weeks after his father also died; those were the first graves in Matagorda cemetery—a mesquite tree marks the spot. A quantity of plank was thoughtfully taken on board at New Orleans on purpose for coffins, though no one knew the motive. Daniel Deckrow made both coffins, a yoke of oxen and a cart did the office of a hearse; kind friends dug the graves. No physician. No religious service soothed the lonely survivors, but all that sympathizing friends could do to soften the melancholy surroundings was done. . . .

At our new home everything seemed strange. We had never before traveled south of a latitude of 42°. At that time very little traveling was done; the very literature of common school books was borrowed from selections from the eminent lights of the old world. Western New York was quite a frontier, Indians being a fixture there, as also in Ohio and Indiana. . . .

The coast States, of course, had the advantage of direct intercourse with the old world, but the interior towns of all the States were so isolated that it took courage and a large stock of enterprise to make this colonization. The contrast of the idioms of language was most marked. Often when critically compared, the advantage would be in the favor of the untutored southerner, and their unassuming, free-and-easy, benevolent manners were most admirable. We did not expect such perfect Chesterfields in the garb of deerskin and mocassins, and such unselfish benevolence. All knowledge seemed practical, useful and fitted to any emergency, especially in children, which seemed so strange. They tread in the ways and manners of their elders without a rebuke, as with us, if we, when children, should presume to give our opinion to our elders; but I saw its advantages when these precocious youths were sent out on a message of fifty or a hundred miles alone through unsettled regions where he was obliged to assume the manhood he had been practicing from almost his infancy—for the very infant is expected to be introduced to every stranger and to give his little hand to everyone coming or leaving, thus cultivating the habits of social and benevolent feeling, while we northerners treat children as nonentities, and, unless business or necessity compels, the bashful youth, in consequence, shirks the society of his elders and superiors.

And then I could but notice that every boy was almost a knight errant. I noticed great deference paid to all the females: no man would remain sitting when one of us entered the house, fort or camp, and thus it was everywhere as we traveled or camped out. All the severe work on such occasions was done by the men of the company.

Flowers seemed to be the sport of the luxurious soil, instead of noxious weeds, which in other regions are ever ready without the aid of man to cover up its nakedness with the rich and variegated livery of nature. A continued and continuing variety carpeted our way for whole days together as we traveled, with scarce a sign of former traveler to mark the path, while large herds of deer in easy distance would stop grazing to look at us, and every way which the eye looked countless herds were seen in the distance. Many of these journeys, which so delighted me with their novelty and variety, were for the purpose of surveying town sites. As my husband was the founder of Matagorda, all paper town-makers made an effort to have him interested in such enterprises. Hence, my long journeys through unsettled regions to reach those sites for future cities, when we frequently fell in with large pleasure parties, who, like ourselves, had made long journeys from remote towns. On one occasion we rescued a young orphan girl from being married against her will, and gave her a home with us, at the head of the bay, forty miles distant. Another good subject for my story, without exaggeration, was when scores turned out to meet the Romans at given points to legalize the banns of matrimony. . . .

After our city of Matagorda had grown to quite a size many of our settlers still refused to have any dealings with the Indians, who were now so reduced in numbers as not to be dangerous, yet when the Indians would come to those settled on farms around the town offering to trade venison for corn or articles of clothing, the people refused to have anything to do with them, or even to be friendly.

Finally, an expedition was planned against them without Mr. Wightman's knowledge or consent, and the very day that I had fed a poor old Indian, covered with scars, he met his death at the hands of our settlers, who fell on them by surprise, and it seemed that each warrior claimed the honor of his slaughter, as he stepped forward to be a target while the women and children could have time to escape to the thicket. Of course all their goods and weapons fell into the hands of their conquerors.

After a few years a small party, evidently remembering who had fed them on the day of the fight, came to us. My husband became responsible for their good behavior, and set them to picking cotton, but before this they dared not venture into the town, only when they saw our boat coming down the Bay. There were no white settlements on the Peninsula, and the Indians had it all their own way there, but they were evidently afraid of another attack and so came and offered to work for us for protection.

I felt no fear whatever from these neighbors, but would sleep with all our doors open, with twenty-five or thirty Indians within call. It was amusing to see them parade the streets of Matagorda with their long plaid, red, blue, garments, which I had made for them, the tails tipped with ornamental feathers. One of the young women learned to speak very good English; I dressed her in my clothes, and one day thought to have some fun with her, invited her to take tea with me. But the joke turned to my own expense, for she not only used her knife and fork properly but her cup, saucer and plate like it was an every day affair. I asked her how they made out when our folks drove them off without anything. She answered that they traveled for days without food and no place to sleep, as the ground was all covered with water—which I recollected was the case. They had no means of fishing, but they kept close to the coast and at last the "Great Spirit" sent them a small vessel, after killing the crew they appropriated everything to their own use, and thus their lives were saved.

After a while they frequently had noisy nights, and upon inquiring what all this noise and dancing meant, with so many rude instruments of music, she replied that they were going west, as they had better health than with our way of living, and they were importuning the Great Spirit to give them success in stealing horses and other stock from the Mexicans who lived near the coast; and to protect them from hostile attacks. It took me a long time to become accustomed to their naked and hideous appearance, so that it did not shock me; I felt humiliated that I too was of the human species.

Their habits were idle and dirty in the extreme, but for their constant bathing in the river. The children almost lived in the water, would dive and bring up clams, etc., sometimes fighting in the water. The men would tread the water with heavy burdens on their shoulders walking erect with half their bodies dry. Our mode of living made them sickly and they were obliged often to resort to the coast. On one occasion a young wife ran off and the distressed husband applied to my husband to turn out with his skiff and help find her. They went up the river a few miles and found her at her mother's camp. She made a virtue of necessity and returned. To express his gratitude the happy husband offered to reciprocate the favor "whenever his squaw ran off."

Their few cooking utensils are made of a rude kind of pottery. Their drinking vessel is about ten inches wide at the top, coming to a point at the bottom. This is handed round for each one to take a swallow after the head man has worked it into a foam by a bunch of small sticks whirled with both hands; this serves them for their coffee cup and when all have drank the process is repeated, taking hours at a time at least twice a day. They also parch in this vessel their coffee—the leaves of an evergreen shrub resembling our garden privet. Their coffee pot in which it is boiled is of the same material, shaped like a double necked gourd, while a bunch of Spanish moss serves for a lid and a strainer.

When one of them dies his effects and his hut are burned the same day, and a corpse is never kept over night. When a chief dies the next heir to the throne, however young, marries the widow, however old. If he leaves no son after death, the nearest of kin, have periodical times of howling, generally before daylight. The women spend a great deal of time pounding a kind of root, on skins, which yields a kind of starch when washed and settled in water. Days will thus be spent in preparing what will only be a taste when divided among them. . . .

Alligator meat is a great luxury with them, and although supplied bountifully with fresh meat, they would be absent frequently, and return with pieces of cooked alligator tied between large pieces of bark swung over their shoulders. I have seen them killed. The creature is helpless when under the water and the Indians dive and stick him with a sharp knife.

They knew we did not approve of their stealing horses from the Mexicans and so when they left, they went on the sly. We got up one morning and found them all gone, and we saw no more of them for years.

In 1843, I spent some time in Matagorda when they made their appearance in a most wretched, filthy condition, few in numbers, offering to trade fish for whiskey. The young girl I had helped was dying. She formally gave away her only child to a white woman and the whole tribe formed a procession to go and deliver the child before the mother's death. I afterwards visited the child and found her at a little table with a white and a negro child, each about four years old, playing tea drinking, all speaking English together. On one occasion that summer, a stroke of lightning killed a man and his wife, but a child between them escaped unharmed, this made a profound impression upon the whole tribe. They felt it as a direct judgment from the Great Spirit for their drunkenness and bad behavior, and for days they scarcely moved or left the camp. As I left the country in 1843, I ceased to know more of these Indians. I believe that Mexico gave them a tract of land in one of her Eastern Provinces.

Ann Raney Thomas Coleman

"The country was full of bachelors."

As the farmers and ranchers of Stephen F. Austin's colony were settling near San Felipe, a different type of settlement was taking place near the coast. Wealthy planters were bringing their families and their slaves to the area around the town of Brazoria. A personal view of life in the Brazoria area is given by Ann Raney Thomas Coleman (1810–97).

Ann sailed to Brazoria, Texas, from England by way of New Orleans with her mother and sister in 1832. Ann's father, John Raney, had already arrived and was a tutor for the children of Brit Bailey, one of the planters of the area. Ann found the voyage exciting, as the ship was besieged by pirates—and she was besieged by suitors. On the last leg of the journey, Ann was pursued by the captain of the vessel, William S. Brown. She also met Sterling McNeel, a young planter. Ann describes the meeting: "One evening, on being called to supper, I saw opposite a gentleman who was extremely sober looking, who kept his eyes fixed upon myself continually. . . . I became interested in him." Although Ann protests that "I looked upon him more as a brother than a friend," she obviously was in love with him.

After Ann arrived in Brazoria, she saw McNeel frequently. Following a quarrel with her mother resulting from pressure on her to marry Captain Brown, she went to live with McNeel's sister and brother-in-law, David and Nancy Randon. While staying with the Randons, Ann contacted what she refers to as "bilious and remitting fever" and lay near death for three weeks. While she was ill, both of her parents died. She and her sister were dependent upon the charity of the people of Brazoria. Ann left the Randons after she learned that McNeel did not intend to marry her and went to live with Dr. and Mrs. Jesse Counsel. There she succumbed to pressure to marry John Thomas, a wealthy planter.

Fortunately, Ann wrote the story of her interesting life in

Reprinted, with permission, from C. Richard King, ed., *Victorian Lady on the Texas Frontier: The Journal of Ann Raney Coleman* (Norman: University of Oklahoma Press, 1971). Copyright 1971 by the University of Oklahoma Press, Publishing Division of the University of Oklahoma.

Ann Raney Coleman. (*Courtesy Manuscript Department, William R. Perkins Library, Duke University*)

seven notebooks that she sent to her niece in North Carolina. They were edited by C. Richard King and published as *Victorian Lady on the Texas Frontier*.

Ann begins her story with her early life in England. The excerpt included here begins as her boat arrives at Brazoria.

*   *   *

At five o'clock in the evening, we arrived at the town of Brazoria. A voice saluted my ear from the bank, "I am glad to see you." On looking up I saw Mr. McNeel. I felt glad to see him. He helped us one by one get out of the boat, seizing my arm first as I could only walk by the aid of a stick. My mother next. He went with us to the hotel, leaving the captain to bring my sister, which he did as soon as he gave some directions to the men in the boat. He spent the rest of the evening with us. The landlady and her daughter, who was married, Mrs. Winston, gave us a warm reception, had a good supper, our hostess making herself very agreeable. Mrs. Long was a widow, one of the early day settlers, was anxious for emigration to the country, and was very polite to strangers, kept a good table, and had a great deal of customers.

The country was full of bachelors, but very few ladies. When bed-[time] came we were ushered into a room where there were several beds. We did not like this much, as we expected a room to ourselves, but on being told that the gentlemen slept on one side and the ladies on the other side of the room, I opened both my eyes and ears and looked again at my hostess, who did not seem to be jesting. Presently several more ladies came in to go to bed. They went through the undressing operation quickly and were all in bed long before we had got over our surprise at this new fashion of sleeping. We soon undressed but did not divest ourselves of all our garments, keeping on outside garments which were calico wrappers. We had only been in bed about an hour when the gentlemen came in one by one until all had retired. I watched with breathless suspense the coming of the last one. This was something we were not accustomed to, and it was several nights before I could sleep—not until nature was completely exhausted and overcome with watching.

The ladies all laughed at us and said, "By the time you have been in Texas a few months, if you travel in the country, you will have to sleep with the man and his wife in the house you visit," as houses were only log cabins with two rooms, one for house servants, the other for the family. I found this statement correct, visiting some friends in the country two weeks after this who had a small log cabin with two rooms in it, the servants and cooking one, the other to sleep in. I had to sleep with the man and his wife. I slept at the back of the bed, the wife in the middle and the man in the front. They were settlers, had gone into the woods to make a plantation, and this was considered shelter for the present. They worked thirty hands, and several negroes lived together in one cabin. This was the way most of the wealthy planters lived when we first arrived in Texas. A double log cabin with an entry running through the middle was their residence. To make money was their chief object, all things else were subsidiary to it. . . .

[Editor's note: After quarreling with her mother over a marriage proposal she abhorred, Ann moved in with Nancy and David Randon, Sterling McNeel's sister and brother-in-law.]

Mr. Sterling McNeel was a constant visitor at his sister's, Mrs. Randon's. One evening late we were told that there was a cannon heard down the river. Everyone was in motion. "To Arms," was the cry, and in less than a few hours the men from every part of the country had gone to the scene of action. Some of our merchant vessels had passed the port, refusing to pay duties at the custom house to the Mexican authorities, and when fired on by the Mexican soldiers, this was the signal for an outbreak. In three days we took the fort, after killing one hundred and wounding two hundred, taking the rest prisoners, which I understood was some two thousand men. Mrs. Randon and myself sat the most of two nights and days moulding bullets and making bullet patches. The ladies in Brazoria were occupied in the same way for two days and nights. Captain William Brown, I was told, behaved with a reckless bravery, standing at the cannon and firing every shot himself as long as the battle lasted. The bullets flew around his person by the hundreds, yet he escaped unharmed. Colonel Williams lost his eye in the battle, Mr. Sanders was wounded in the arm. Mr. Williams of the town of Brazoria was the only man killed on our side, and some few others wounded slightly.

This battle was the beginning of the future strife, for General St.

Anna, on hearing of this massacre of his men, sent one of his generals to Brazoria to make terms with our people in a treaty, which ended in giving a dinner and ball at night. His ambassador returned to Mexico, and General St. Anna renewed his force, and in '36 he returned with a force of 10,000 men. I was invited to the ball and danced with General Urea (Mexia S.E.) and some Spanish gentlemen of note, [and] Stephen F. Austin, the Empresario of Texas. I was much complimented on my being a good dancer, and the Empresario was so much pleased with me, having been in conversation with him some time, that on learning I was the daughter of John Raney of England, next day my father received a note from him to wait on him and he would give him another league of land, his first being taken from him because father did not join him as soon as was required by Mr. Austin, as it was two years instead of one before we joined him. My father went and received his grant before the Empresario left town.

I still attended balls and places of amusement with Mr. Randon or Mr. Sterling McNeel as my escort. I met my sister once after I left home, but never with my father and mother. My sister, in tears, asked me to return, said she thought my mother was sorry for what she had said. I told her to give my love to my father, and say I still loved them as a daughter. My sister wished me to go home with her, but I did not do so. My mother's health was not good at this time. She was undergoing her acclimating and had fever quite often. My father's health declined every day and got worse. He seldom ever went out, only when his health permitted him to do so. I felt as though I had seen him for the last time. I dared not go home to see him and I was much troubled about him. I felt I should like to plead once more for her forgiveness, but this was not to be. God had determined otherwise. My sister, on parting, begged me to marry Captain Brown, but on telling her I did not love him enough to make him my husband, though she seemed displeased at the moment, she kissed me on parting.

I was so homesick to see my parents, I sank under oppression of spirits, and in a week after seeing my sister I was taken with bilious and remitting fever. For three weeks there was no change for the better. Two physicians were in attendance. They gave me up. They could do no more for me. I might linger a few days longer, but all medicine had lost its affect.

I had known no one for a week, and when the doctors left me to die, Mr. Sterling McNeel and Mrs. Randon still continued to give me medicine and at last succeeding in salivating me, which my physicians had tried to do but had not been successful. . . .

I was now an orphan with neither father nor mother to bless my return to health. It was during my illness that my mother and sister were taken sick, my father already confined to his bed. I was sent for in their dying moments, but could not go. I was also given up by my physician. Mrs. Randon would not tell me of their deaths whilst I lay low. Before life was gone, my dear mother told my sister if she lived to get well, to tell me that she forgave me, and that perhaps it was all for the best that I did not comply with her request in marrying Captain William Brown. My mother died nine days before my father. My sister, after my father's and mother's deaths, went to live with Mrs. Chase at Velasco, at the mouth of the Brazos River, remaining at the hotel with Mrs. Long until she recovered her health. Mrs. Long and her daughter were very kind to her, and she had many warm friends.

I now took a walk every day to gain strength. I was delighted with all I saw of the woods and prairies. The beautiful wild flowers of Texas cannot be surpassed. In these shades of solitude, I had leisure for reflection of past and present, but dared not look far into the perspective. I could not disperse the gloom that pervaded my whole nature, and in those seasons of retirement I alone sheltered my weary spirit.

As soon as I was able to ride, I went to the town of Brazoria to see my sister. Our meeting inflicted a fresh wound to our hearts. My sister was not strong enough to leave her room or bed. She was wasted in person and emaciated, her eyes sunk, her cheeks pale. We laid plans for us to be together. I proposed teaching a school, but in naming it to our friends they would not consent to it, saying we were too young. After staying a day or so with her, I took leave of her for a short season, telling her I would return in a few days. My sister and self were doubly dear to each other now. We were orphans. My sole thought was to make a home for my sister, who had always been my mother's favorite, being the youngest child and a delicate one. She missed my mother, and it was with difficulty I sought to console her grief. I told her we should not always be separated. I said the first chance I had of making myself a good home, she could come to live with me. She smiled sorrowfully and replied, "Do not be hasty in your choice on my account; look well before you leap." . . .

Mr. Sterling McNeel was much distressed at his father's injunction if he married he would disinherit him. Mrs. Randon had to run away and get married, also Mr. Greenville McNeel, another one of his sons, so that he was not willing for any of his sons to marry. Mrs. Randon told me, "All the rest of the family are willing for you to marry my brother, with whom you are a great favorite and with my father himself, but he was never willing for his children to marry."

I was in my room one evening when I overheard the following conversation pass between Mr. Randon and his brother-in-law, Mr. Sterling McNeel. "If you still wish to marry Miss Ann, I will make her a present of horse and saddle and you had best run off and get married, as your father will only be angry for a time, as he has been with all the rest." Mr. Sterling McNeel observed, "My father's health is very bad, and he cannot live long, and I think it best to wait awhile longer until he is dead. Miss Ann is young enough yet to marry and has a good home, and she shall not want for anything. I wish you to tell her my intentions." . . .

When Mrs. Randon informed me what her brother desired her to tell me, I was silent; seeing I did not reply, she said, "My brother Sterling loves money and does not wish my father to disinherit him, as he has always been a great favorite with him." Mr. Sterling McNeel came about once a week to see me, and sometimes, once in two weeks. This was quite a change for me who had been accustomed to seeing him once a day, and he sometimes remained all day. I felt hurt at his seeming neglect and all my former pride returned. "He does not love," I thought, "or he would not mind his father's injuction. He loves his father's money better than me." . . .

A week longer stay with my benefactors and I at last, by much persuasion, got her permission to make a visit to Mrs. Counsel in Brazoria. Had she known my intentions never to return, she would not have been willing to let me depart. It was not right that Mrs. Randon should be deprived of seeing her brother, who she thought much of, on my account. He was a great favorite in the family, and they called him Doctor as he generally doctored all the negroes on the plantation. They missed his visits more than she would acknowledge to me. My ancestral pride had returned. I was myself again. I was furnished with a horse, and a boy rode behind me to bring the horse back. A change of clothes was all I took with me to prevent suspicion. . . .

On my arrival at Dr. Counsel's they were glad to see me. In a few days after my arrival at the town of Brazoria there was a ball at Mrs. Long's. Many invitations were sent out into the country. I did not wish to attend, as my father and mother had been dead but a few months. But being overruled by my friends I went reluctantly. My dress was a white swiss muslin trimmed with black crepe, trimming of a handsome quality, and was said to be very becoming.

Mrs. Long was a lady of dignified manners, and a favorite on account of being an old settler. Her husband was killed by Indians, and she escaped by her fortitude and bravery. She was about forty at this time, had a beautiful daughter who was married, although she was very young, I think not more than eighteen. Her husband died very shortly after our arrival in the country with consumption. My sister and self were great favorites with Mrs. Long and her daughter. On the death of my mother, Mrs. Long and Mrs. Anderson attended her until her last breath was gone. She took my sister home with her, where she remained until she was well enough to go to Captain Chase's at Velasco, whose lady was very anxious to have my sister live with her, having taken quite a fancy to her.

Doctor Counsel was concocting a plan to give a ball at his house. Mrs. Counsel and self were busily occupied shopping for the occasion. After being at Mrs. Counsel's one week, my kind friend Mrs. Randon sent a boy with a horse for me to return on, but I would not see the boy who came for me and got Mrs. Counsel to plead my excuse by saying she could not spare me so soon, that I must remain sometime longer with her. Mrs. Randon did not send after me any more, and I was glad of it, as I did not wish to return. . . .

One or two weeks previous to the ball, I saw a gentleman coming down the street and go into the billiard room on the opposite side of the street. I asked Mrs. Counsel if she knew him. She replied she did not. "I think it is some stanger just come into town as he has his riding whip in his hand. I should not be in danger of falling in love with him." She asked why. I replied he was too consequential. In one hour afterwards, the Doctor came home and said, "Miss Ann, I wish you to put on your best attire this evening. I am going to bring home a beau for you. He is a rich bachelor and wishes to get married very much. You must set your cap for him; he will be a good husband for you." I laughed and told him I believed he was getting tired of me and wished to get rid of me by marrying me off to some old bachelor. "Not so, Miss Raney," he said, "unless you could do well for yourself; and I know you would if you should get Mr. Thomas. He is a man well known in the country, out of debt, and has a good home to take a wife to."

That evening after supper he came, and to my surprise, I found him the same little consequential fop I saw going into the billiard room in the morning. Mr. Thomas was a man about thirty years of age, black hair and eyes, good complexion, good looking, and a good address, a pleasant smile upon his features, and very communicative. He had one of his arms broken which turned a little out of its natural position. This gave his arm a swagger that I took for conceit of his own personal dignity. A game of whist was proposed; we went to play one, but were soon compelled to quit as Mr. Thomas was not sufficiently acquainted with the game to play.

I retired to the other end of the room to get my sewing. The Doctor and Mrs. Counsel left the room for a short time, which seemed a long time to me. Mr. Thomas drew his chair up to the table where I sat and commenced the following conversation. "I think I have been introduced to you before, Miss Raney, about six months ago at Mr. Bell's who kept the ferry across the river Brazos. I was crossing a yoke of oxen. Do you remember me? Captain Brown was with you, and I understood from Mr. Bell that you were to be married to Captain Brown." I told him I recollected the time. "I see you are not married yet, Miss Raney." "No, sir," I replied, "it isn't quite soon enough for that event." He then remarked, "How do you like this country, Miss Raney?" I replied, "I like it well enough, but we have been very unfortunate in losing our parents in a foreign land, without relations or home." "As far as home is concerned," he replied, "Miss Raney, I think I can offer as good a one as any man in the country, if you will accept it. I am not like a terrapin that carries all upon my back. I have plenty at home to make you comfortable. I know you have a great many suitors who can make many flattering speeches to you, which I cannot. I am plain as a book."

This speech brought the color to my face, and I would have given anything to have left the room. He seeing me silent, proceeded by saying, "I live thirty miles from here and the water courses are difficult to pass. If I come often to Brazoria, I shall make no crop, as I have no overseer. I should like, Miss Raney, if you could let me know if it is worth my while to come and see you again and pay my respects to you. I expect to leave town tomorrow morning, but will come back and see you before I leave." . . .

Before we had finished breakfast next morning, in walked Mr. Thomas. I was again caught for another day's courtship. I tried to excuse myself by saying I had to go and meet a friend, but he would not let me off and made himself as agreeable as possible. When evening came I could hardly believe I had been sitting all day in his company. Next day I was in hopes he would go home, but I was disappointed. He stayed this day also. He had been three days in town, notwithstanding he came in such a hurry and said he must leave the next day. He had appointed to return in one week from the time he left. I thought I would be absent, but he came in before breakfast and left me no chance to escape. It was during those visits he had been seen by Mr. McNeel coming to the house. Now Mr. Thomas had proposed marriage to me and waited my answer. . . .

After many a debate in my own mind I determined to accept Mr. Thomas's proposal. He had visited me about half a dozen times; he was well known in the country; everyone spoke well of him. This was satisfactory to me. He had given me several references as to his standing as a man in society. . . .

It was on returning from seeing [a friend] and his family one evening, I was called in the street by someone. On looking around I saw Mrs. Smith who was now keeping the same hotel as Mrs. Long used to keep, Mrs. Long having retired into private life with her daughter into the country. Mrs. Smith said, "I wish to see you a little while." I went in, took off my bonnet when Mrs. Smith remarked, "I hear you are going to be married to Mr. Thomas." "Who told you so?" I replied. "Mr. Thomas himself." "He is rather too communicative," I said. She replied, "You need not be ashamed of him. He is one of the finest men in the country. He will make you good husband." She then went on to tell all his good qualities and said nothing about the bad ones. I came out of her house to go home when I was met by Mrs. A, another friend of Mr. Thomas and one of mine also. She got hold of my arm and said, "Come take a walk with me up the street." I complied. She commenced with, "I hear you are going to be married to Mr. Thomas. Is it so?" I was silent. "If you marry him you will get a close stingy husband; and he has got a woman at home, one of his servants that will turn you out of doors before you have been home a month. He has lived a bachelor so long, he knows every grain of coffee that goes into his pot."

I listened patiently to this unpleasant news and said little in return. We did not stay long; or rather, I made my walk as short as possible without seeming rude, and bid her good evening. I was determined to tell Mr. Thomas of what his friend Mrs. A had said the next time we met, for he was a constant visitor at their house. I was looking for him to come in town daily. Had my death knell going to be sounded, I could not have dreaded it more. I was trying to summon up all my fortitude for the occasion when in walked Mr. Thomas. He came up to myself first and shook my hand and then passed on to the rest of the family. As soon as breakfast was finished Mr. Thomas and myself were left alone in the breakfast room.

He first broke the silence by saying, "I hope, Miss Ann, you have made up your answer to make me happy. It is to receive your answer I came to town today. I came near getting drowned crossing Linnville's Bayou, but I shall be repaid for the dangers I have passed if you consent to be my wife." My silence seemed to give consent, and he took my hand in his and pressed it warmly, while I burst into an agony of tears. "You shall never have cause to repent being my wife. I will do everything in my power to make you happy." I now told him what his friend Mrs. A had said. He seemed surprised and said, "Everyone is jealous of my expected happiness. You may pay no attention to anything you may hear against me. If you do not find strict obedience from every servant I have got, I will sell the first one that dares to insult or disobey you. I have a woman called Minerva who I raised from a child. She is a smart field hand and in cotton picking time she picks 300 pounds a day. In my absence she is my overseer, and though she is sometimes saucy she knows better than to give my wife any insolence." I told him I should expect perfect obedience from every one of his servants, and should they prove otherwise, he must sell them, which he said he would do. I told him I wished my sister to live with us. He said it would give him great pleasure to offer her a home.

He then went into town to make arrangements for our wedding. He was determined that no expense should be spared to make a handsome supper, which was to be provided at the hotel, Doctor Counsel's house not being large enough to entertain all that were being invited. Mr. Thomas left for home next day, and a week from that day was the one appointed for our wedding day. Mr. Thomas gave me an order on Mr. Mill's store to get anything I wanted for the occasion. I was now as busy as a bee making up my wedding suit, which was of rich white satin with blond lace, white silver artificial flowers, silver tinsel belt, black kid shoes with white satin rosettes and a gold bracelet, gold chain and no veil. This was all of my wedding dress. I had been in a fever of excitement all week, and with no appetite.

The day arrived. It rained in the morning so hard the streets were one sheet of water. Mr. Thomas arrived early in the morning bringing the girl Minerva, who I understood was such a high minded piece of humanity. He brought a boy to wait upon himself. At three o'clock in the evening I left Dr. Counsel's house for the hotel on horseback with Mr. Thomas. The streets were muddy from the recent rain. The sun shone out with all its brightness. There was a possibility that before night the water would dry up sufficiently to admit of visitors to attend our marriage. The amphibious race, the frogs, were silenced by the subduing melody of the winged tribes; all nature was bespangled with smiles. I alone seemed sad. Everyone else seemed cheerful. My intended tried to cheer me, as he saw me look thoughtful, and never left my side only when obliged to. We had a private room to ourselves, and when it was time to dress he left me and went to dress also. Crowds of persons began to flock in from the country, and by seven o'clock in the evening the hotel was filled to overflowing by two hundred persons.

Ours was the first public wedding given at the town of Brazoria. At eight o'clock my bridesmaids arrived, one a Miss Anderson, the other a Miss Bailey with whom we found our father on our arrival in Texas. Mr. Thomas had two groomsmen, one Mr. Edmond St. J. Hawkins, the other a gentleman whose name I have forgotten. At eight o'clock we entered the ball room to be married, it being the largest room in the house. The bridesmaids and groomsmen went first into the room, myself and Mr. Thomas last. I felt much abashed at the presence of so many people, and my eyes which on first entering had been cast to the ground were now raised to the face of Mr. Smith, the presiding alcalde, who was going to perform the marriage ceremony. A breathless silence pervaded the room whilst the ceremony was performed. The alcalde himself was so much excited that he paused once or twice while performing the ritual. I looked at the bridesmaids who were tastefully dressed. They looked like marble statues. As for myself, I trembled from head to foot, and when the ceremony was finished and the alcalde told Mr. Thomas to salute his bride, I saw no motion made by him to do it. At last, feeling for his embarassment, I turned my cheek to his so that he might more easily salute me, which he did. The same was done by the bridesmaids and groomsmen, the groomsmen kissing me first, then the bridesmaids. We then went out as we came in until tea and coffee were ready. Then we all assembled in the dining room where tea, coffee and cakes were handed around.

I saw a multitude of people, half of whom I was unacquainted with. The ladies were dressed very gay and in good taste and might have vied with city belles. After tea our congratulations commenced. I stood up with my husband until I was nearly exhausted, receiving one after another. At last a chair was brought me, and I sat down and only rose when obliged to. The dance had commenced and not more than half of the company had been presented to us. About ten o'clock that night I got liberty to dance for a short time. My engagements were too many to fill, so I danced but a little that I might give offense to none. About twelve o'clock at night supper was announced by our hostess, Mrs. Smith, and we retired to the supper room. Everything was tastefully arranged and the table laden with every delicacy that could be procured. Fruit from Orleans was in abundance, the cake delicious, fowl and meats plentiful, plenty of wine, also coffee. All eyes were on my husband and myself, so I ate but little; a cup of coffee was grateful to me, as it had always been my favorite beverage.

I hurried to retire where I would not be so closely observed. Everyone praised my dress, which I made myself, and said I looked charming but sad. This was a truth. I masked the feeling of my heart on this night that I might make him who I had chosen for my husband feel happy. At one o'clock I went up to my room with my servant Minerva, who, I had forgotten to state, was all obedience. I dismissed her shortly afterwards and I was left alone. My bridesmaids insisted on waiting upon me to disrobe me and see me in bed, but I would not permit them to and told them to go and enjoy themselves in the ball room. I had been sitting in one position half an hour before a looking glass that reflected my form to my view, when I thought, "I am dressed and adorned for a sacrifice." I had been sitting in one position without a motion to undress. My thoughts were on my native land with my dear brother and Henry, who I never expected to forget; my love was still his, and parted only by force of circumstances. I was disappointed in not seeing that beloved face, my sister, at my wedding.

In the midst of these reflections, someone opened the door and the alcalde put in his head. "My dear, are you not in bed? Your husband wishes to retire for the night, and it is my business, according to the Spanish law, to see you both in bed." I felt indignant to this method of the Spanish law and promised to go to bed directly. With that promise he closed the door. My face, if anyone could have seen it, was crimson with blushes. And my husband came in and I was still sitting there with all my clothes on. He was surprised at seeing me still up, and taking my hand and kissing it, he said, "My child, I will be a father as well as a husband. Do not sit there, but go to bed and take some rest, for you have need of it. Tomorrow you have a long and tiresome journey to take. The roads are bad, and without rest, you will be unfit for it. I want to start as soon as we get breakfast."

I hid my face in my handkerchief and wept bitter tears. Would he fulfill all he had promised? I had need of a father's and a husband's care. I was fifteen years younger than Mr. Thomas and a child in appearance to himself. Without saying any more he went to the other end of the room, my back being turned to him, and in a few minutes he was in bed. I slipped off my dress and all my ornaments, blew out the light, and in a few minutes I was also in bed. Shortly afterwards in came my evil genius with a light in his hand, opened a part of the [mosquito] bar and looked at us both the space of a minute and was gone without speaking. My husband laughed and so did I, though no one saw me do so for I hid my face with the cover.

Mr. Thomas was up before day, and Mrs. Smith and many of the gentlemen who had never gone to bed went to the horse lot to joke him for being up so early, and he wished himself away from Brazoria and in his quiet home. In an hour from the time he got up, breakfast was ready. I was in hopes it was too early for anyone to be up, only those laid down, but when I went to the table it was crowded. As breakfast was over, I put on my riding skirt, which was the same one I had when thrown from Mr. Sterling McNeel's horse in the pond. I had a black silk basque, green broadcloth riding cap, with a plume of black ostrich feathers, white satin rosette on one side. A great many bouquets hung in a small basket on the horn on my saddle presented me by my friends. When ready to start, everyone grasped my hand to bid me adieu until it was sore from shaking hands with so many friends. On leaving the hotel three cheers went up for us, and three more for the Caney boys, in compliment to Mr. Thomas's taking the only Belle in Brazos.

I had a nice pony of iron gray bought by Mr. Thomas expressly for me, and a natural pacer. We found the roads bad, and it was night before we reached Mr. Hensley's on Cedar Creek or Lake. They were old people, had one son, who like the Dutchman's pig, little but old. We were entertained kindly, and as we were tired, went to bed early. After supper, Mrs. Smith had put no small quantity of cake and other nice things for our lunch on the road. I slept from fatigue, the first sleep that did me any good in a week.

In the morning, we started early again. It was but thirty miles, but the roads being so bad, it took us two days to reach home. I inquired many times of Mr. Thomas if this or that place was his, being impatient to arrive at home. He replied, "No, but we will soon reach there now. We are but a few miles from my plantation." Presently we came to Caney Creek, which seemed full of water. After stopping a few minutes on the brink, Mr. Thomas observed to me, "I think Caney is swimming, but don't be afraid. It is not far across. Follow me; it has a hard bottom. There is no danger of our horses bogging down." I looked after as he went into the creek with his horse, frequently saw him swimming with him. I felt afraid and told him so. After some encouraging words from him, I whipped my horse into the creek. I was soon wet over the knees, my horse swimming but a short distance. The banks of the creek were steep and our horses found difficulty in getting up them. We were now on the opposite bank. On looking up I saw a little log cabin, a beautiful orchard of peach trees, a fine vegetable garden and lawn in front of the house. "Whose place is this?" "This is my place," said Mr. Thomas. "How glad I am," I replied. "I have got home."

On entering the enclosure, a nice, tidy mulatto woman met us at the door. She helped me off my horse and said with a polite curtsy, "I am glad, Mr., you have come home." I went into the house and as I was entering the passage through the middle of the cabin, I hit my head against the roof. I remarked to Mr. Thomas, "I think you will have to raise the roof of your house or build a new one." "Oh, my child," he replied, "I had no one to fix for when I built this house. Now I have got

a wife, I will build a better one." Every place was the essence of clean-
ness, and although a puncheon floor, it was clean enough to eat off. The
furniture was all hand made, chairs with deerskin bottoms, tables and
bedstead fixtures. Dinner was prepared and we, being very hungry,
did honor to the table, which was filled with vegetables of all kinds,
milk and butter, and the best kind of corn bread, which my husband
observing, asked me if I liked it. On replying I was not fond of it, he
said he would get some flour for me shortly. "At present, we are out."

After dinner he asked me to take a walk with him in the field,
"where my negroes are at work. I want to see how they have got along
in my absence." On coming near enough for the hands to see us, they
cheered us once or twice, and when they came up to us each one
congratulated us on our happiness with a shake of the hand. They all
appeared glad to see us, and Mr. Thomas was satisfied with the work
they had done in his absence. . . .

[Editor's note: Ann and John lived happily on the plantation
for several years. In 1835 their first child was born.]

I now had a little son about three weeks old, who my husband
named Edmond St. John Hawkins Thomas, after one of his groomsmen. One day after my sister's second marriage, my husband came
home all excited. He had sold his place and some of his negroes to a
man by the name of Russell for the sum of ten thousand dollars, which
I thought at the time was very little. He had reserved some four or five
of his Negroes for himself out of the bargain. Minerva was one he kept,
and sold Daphney, my cook and housekeeper. I remonstrated with him
for this, as I had much rather he had sold Minerva, a woman I never
liked and one I found insolent to a degree.

Part of Mrs. A's prophesy had come to pass. My husband had to
punish her many times since our marriage for her insolence to me. One
night, getting angry with her husband, one of Mr. Williams' hands, she
struck him and with an axe which nearly severed him in two and injured him so badly he was never able to work in the field any more. So,
Mr. Williams took him for his carriage driver, my husband having all
his doctor bills to pay and half of what he cost Mr. Williams, besides
five hundred exacted of my husband by Mr. Williams, which he paid. I
could not prevail with my husband to keep our cook. He said if he did

so, it would make null and void the sale of his place, and Mr. Russell knew the value of Daphney, and Mr. Russell's wife was a young and inexperienced housekeeper. This was the reason he wanted her.

Preparations were made for us to leave Caney and go on to the Brazos River to live, my husband having bought the same place where Mr. Bailey used to live, and the same gentleman we found my father staying with when we first came to the country. His daughter was one of my bridesmaids. I must state that Mr. Bailey was much addicted to drinking spiritous liquors and was insane during these times. In one of his drinking fits, he set fire to all his out houses, barn and stables. His dwelling house was only preserved by the entreaties of a favorite daughter. On getting sober and finding the mischief he had done, he determined on selling his place, which had been bought by two other gentlemen previous to my husband's purchasing it. Mr. Williams being the last gentleman who owned it, and it sold for a little less money every time, and when we got it, it was thought quite a bargain, being eleven hundred acres in the whole. Mr. Williams lived six months up-on the place and sold it to Mr. Thomas for several hundred dollars less than he gave for it.

After Mr. Bailey sold his place, he went to Brazoria to open a hotel and lived but a short time. He made a will which was a singular one. He was buried standing upright with his face to the west, and his gun in his arms, ready for a march. This was done and he requested to be buried upon the place that formerly belonged to him, which was done, in a pecan grove close to the house.

After a week's preparation, we left Caney for the Brazos River. I was sorry I did not get time to visit my sister before I left. I was told she was on a visit to Judge D. when we left, who lived some distance from us. So I was obliged to be satisfied, thinking I would visit her when I got settled in my new home. I was found in tears one day by Mr. Thomas. He asked me the cause. I told him I should not like to leave without bidding my sister goodbye. He tried to console me by saying he would send after her some day after we got settled in our new home.

On arriving there, every one of us was tired and thirsty. I took a survey of the place, which had a wild and gloomy appearance, such as you often read of in enchanted places. The dwelling house was painted red, a kitchen smoke house and some outbuildings; a pecan orchard about a quarter of a mile long lead like an avenue up to the house, having to cross a big pond of water before entering the grove. This pond was sometimes deep enough to sail a boat. Wild ducks, turkeys, cranes and other wild fowl were plentiful at this pond most of the year. In the grove close to the house was the grave of Mr. Bailey, the first occupant of the place. It was about as large around as a wash tub bottom.

I often took a walk in the grove and visited this spot. A strange whim, I thought, but a much stranger man when I visited him and his family during his life-time. I would say, "How are you today, Mr. Bailey?" "Oh, madam, I am in sack cloth and ashes." This was when he had been drinking to excess and was repenting. I often went to see them as they had been kind to my father when in bad health. They were much respected and their house was a good stopping house for travellers. He had a great many good riding horses, and Miss Sally used often to come to the town of Brazoria to get me to go and spend a day or two with her. We were sometimes accompanied by Capt. William Brown. . . .

Not many months after the war of thirty-six broke out, my husband determined to stay as long at his home as possible and work his crop, his prospects being good. My husband had one of his arms broken in two places by the fall of a tree, which disabled him so much he could not do good and efficient service, but sent his overseer, Mr. George Paine, as his substitute. Mr. Paine was about thirty and was killed in the massacre of Fannin's army. I was sorry when I heard of his death, for he was a worthy young man.

It was spring time, nature smiled, the beautiful prairie flowers put up their heads beneath the leaves of green. The jessamine covered lattice, and the atmosphere convinced me of the future resurrection of the body after death. All was sublime. I was quite happy in my home with my husband and my child, but suddenly doomed to be the reverse.

*   *   *

This idyllic spring seems to be the last happy time in Ann Raney Coleman's life. As Santa Anna's troops approached, Ann, her husband and child, and their slaves fled to Louisiana, leaving thousands of dollars worth of property behind. Fearing a Mexican victory, Thomas sold their Texas land for what Ann considered to be a ridiculously low price and went to work as an overseer. Both Thomas and their two sons died in Louisiana, and Ann was left with a young daughter and many debts. Her second marriage was even less wise than her first. She and her daughter returned to Texas, and in 1855 Ann sued for divorce. In the years that followed, Ann valiantly struggled to survive by gardening, dressmaking, and teaching. Gradually she became more and more destitute as she was shuffled from one family to another, less welcome in each home in which she lived. Ann ended her journal when her daughter died of cancer in 1890. Ann Raney Coleman died a forlorn but undefeated old woman who up to the last vainly struggled to obtain a pension for "moulding bullets in the war."

II. Lone Star: The Republic, 1836–46

Texas was the scene of great violence during its brief existence as an independent nation. The terrible threat to the Texans at the Alamo spurred the leaders of Texas to action; and on March 2, 1836, the Texas Declaration of Independence was presented to the world. Four days later the defenders of the Alamo were massacred. As General Antonio Lopez de Santa Anna advanced across Texas seemingly with the intention of exterminating the entire Anglo-American population, most of the men of Texas were serving in the army. The women, children, slaves, and old and disabled men fled from menacing Indians and tried to escape the advancing Mexican army in what came to be known as the "Runaway Scrape." When the frantic settlers abandoned their homes, they left dishes on tables, cows waiting to be milked, and hungry dogs and cats that followed them down the road for a while. Looters rode by calling, "The Mexicans are coming!" in order to lure people away from their homes even when the Mexican army was not in the vicinity.

The refugees were a pitiful sight as they struggled toward the Louisiana border. To add to their misery, rain fell continually, and soon the rivers and streams were flooded. Many of the refugees waited for days for a chance to ride the ferry across the swollen Trinity River, only to be trapped in the flooded river bottom. Disease broke out, and food and clothing were scarce. Among those who died were Dilue Harris's little sister and one of Mary Rabb's babies. Some of the settlers were on the road for six weeks.

After the victory at San Jacinto, the settlers returned to a burned and looted country to face yet another menace, Indians made desperate by the ever-increasing number of settlers.

Dilue Rose Harris

"There were fully five thousand people at the ferry."

Revolution! And soon the cry, "Remember the Alamo!" was heard. But the women who lived through those days remembered most vividly the horrors of the "Runaway Scrape" when they had fled from Santa Anna's Mexican army.

One of the best-known accounts of the "Runaway Scrape" was written by Dilue Rose Harris. Dilue Rose was born in Saint Louis, Missouri in 1825 and moved with her family to Texas when she was eight years old. The Roses first settled in Harrisburg but later moved to a farm near the present town of Sugar Land. After the Texas Revolution, the family settled on a tract of land upon which Rice University now stands.

At the age of thirteen, Dilue married Ira A. Harris, and they moved near Houston onto a farm which had been improved by the groom. The couple eventually settled in Columbus, Texas, and built a house which still stands on Washington Street. Dilue bore nine children and died at the age of eighty-eight.

Dilue's father, Dr. Pleasant Rose, kept a journal during the time that he spent in Texas. In writing her reminiscences, Dilue blended the material from her father's journal with her own memories. The result is a document filled with drama, humor, and a wealth of interesting detail.

Dilue was ten years old when she was caught up in the events which she describes in the pages which follow.

*   *   *

The people had been in a state of excitement during the winter. They knew that Colonel Travis had but few men to defend San Antonio. He was headstrong and precipitated the war with Mexico, but died at his post. I remember when his letter came calling for assistance. He was surrounded by a large army with General Santa Anna in

From Dilue Rose Harris, "The Reminiscences of Mrs. Dilue Rose Harris," *Quarterly of the Texas State Historical Association* IV (1900): 85–127; 155–89; VII (1904): 214–22. Reprinted by permission of the Texas State Historical Association.

Dilue Rose Harris. (*Courtesy San Jacinto Museum of History Association*)

command, and had been ordered to surrender, but fought till the last man died. A black flag had been hoisted by the Mexicans. This letter came in February. I have never seen it in print, but I heard mother read it. When she finished, the courier who brought it went on to Brazoria. I was near eleven years old, and I remember well the hurry and confusion. Uncle James Wells came home for mother to help him get ready to go to the army. We worked all day, and mother sat up that night sewing. She made two striped hickory shirts and bags to carry provisions. I spent the day melting lead in a pot, dipping it up with a spoon, and moulding bullets. The young man camped at our house that night and left the next morning. Our nearest neighbors, Messrs. Dyer, Bell and Neal, had families, but went to join General Houston. Father and Mr. Shipman were old, and Adam Stafford a cripple, and they stayed at home.

By the 20th of February the people of San Patricio and other western settlements were fleeing for their lives. Every family in our neighborhood was preparing to go to the United States. Wagons and other vehicles were scarce. Mr. Stafford, with the help of small boys and negroes, began gathering cattle. All the large boys had gone to the army.

By the last of February there was more hopeful news. Colonel Fannin with five hundred men was marching to San Antonio, and General Houston to Gonzales with ten thousand.

Father finished planting corn. He had hauled away a part of our household furniture and other things and hid them in the bottom. Mother had packed what bedding, clothes, and provisions she thought we should need, ready to leave at a moment's warning. Father had made arrangements with a Mr. Bundick to haul our family in his cart; but we were confident that the army under General Houston would whip the Mexicans before they reached the Colorado River.

Just as the people began to quiet down and go to work, a large herd of buffaloes came by. There were three or four thousand of them. They crossed the Brazos river above Fort Bend, and came out of the bottom at Stafford's Point, making their first appearance before day. They passed in sight of our house, but we could see only a dark cloud of dust, which looked like a sand storm. Father tried to get a shot at one, but his horse was so fractious that it was impossible. As the night was very dark we could not tell when the last buffalo passed. We were terribly frightened, for it was supposed that the Indians were following the herd. The buffaloes passed and went on to the coast, and the prairie looked afterwards as if it had been plowed.

We had been several days without any news from the army, and did not know but that our men had been massacred. News was carried at that time by a man or boy going from one neighborhood to another. We had heard that the Convention had passed a declaration of independence, and elected David G. Burnet president, and Sam Houston commander-in-chief of the army. On the 12th of March came the news of the fall of the Alamo. A courier brought a dispatch from General Houston for the people to leave. Colonel Travis and the men under his command had been slaughtered, the Texas army was retreating, and President Burnet's cabinet had gone to Harrisburg.

Then began the horrors of the "Runaway Scrape." We left home at sunset, hauling clothes, bedding and provisions on the sleigh with one yoke of oxen. Mother and I were walking, she with an infant in her arms. Brother drove the oxen, and my two little sisters rode in the sleigh. We were going ten miles to where we could be transferred to Mr. Bundick's cart. Father was helping with the cattle, but he joined us after dark and brought a horse and saddle for brother. He sent him to help Mr. Stafford with the cattle. He was to go a different road with them and ford the San Jacinto. Mother and I then rode father's horse. . . .

We camped the first night near Harrisburg, about where the railroad depot now stands. Next day we crossed Vince's Bridge and arrived at the San Jacinto in the night. There were fully five thousand people at the [Lynchburg] ferry. The planters from Brazoria and Columbia with their slaves were crossing. We waited for three days before we crossed. Our party consisted of five white families: father's, Mr. Dyer's, Mr. Bell's, Mr. Neal's and Mr. Bundick's. Father and Mr. Bundick were the only white men in the party, the others being in the army. There were twenty or thirty negroes from Stafford's plantation. They had a large wagon with five yoke of oxen, and horses, and mules, and they were in charge of an old negro man called Uncle Ned. Altogether, black and white, there were about fifty of us. Every one was trying to cross first, and it was almost a riot.

We got over the third day, and after travelling a few miles came to a big prairie. It was about twelve miles further to the next timber and water, and some of our party wanted to camp; but others said that the Trinity River was rising, and if we delayed we might not get across. So we hurried on.

When we got about half across the prairie Uncle Ned's wagon bogged. The negro men driving the carts tried to go around the big wagon one at a time until the four carts were fast in the mud. Mother was the only white woman that rode in a cart; the others travelled on horseback. Mrs. Bell's four children, Mrs. Dyer's three, and mother's four rode in the carts. All that were on horseback had gone on to the timber to let their horses feed and get water. They supposed their families would get there by dark. The negro men put all the oxen to the wagon, but could not move it; so they had to stay there until morning without wood or water. Mother gathered the white children in our cart. They behaved very well and went to sleep, except one little boy, Eli Dyer, who kicked and cried for Uncle Ned and Aunt Dilue till Uncle Ned came and carried him to the wagon. He slept that night in Uncle Ned's arms.

Mother with all the negro women and children walked six miles to the timber and found our friends in trouble. Father and Mr. Bundick had gone to the river and helped with the ferry boat, but late in the evening the boat grounded on the east bank of the Trinity and didn't get back until morning. While they were gone the horses had strayed off and they had to find them before they could go to the wagons. Those that travelled on horseback were supplied with provisions by the other campers. We that stayed in the prairie had to eat cold corn bread and cold boiled beef. The wagons and carts didn't get to the timber till night. They had to be unloaded and pulled out.

At the Trinity River men from the army began to join their families. I know they have been blamed for this, but what else could they have done? The Texas army was retreating and the Mexicans were crossing the Colorado, Col. Fannin and his men were prisoners, there were more negroes than whites among us and many of them were wild Africans, there was a large tribe of Indians on the Trinity as well as the Cherokee Indians in Eastern Texas at Nacogdoches, and there were Tories, both Mexicans and Americans, in the country. It was the intention of our men to see their families across the Sabine River, and then to return and fight the Mexicans. I must say that for the negroes that there was no insubordination among them; they were loyal to their owners.

Our hardships began at the Trinity. The river was rising and there was a struggle to see who should cross first. Measles, sore eyes, whooping cough, and every other disease that man, woman, or child is heir to, broke out among us. Our party now consisted of the five white families I first mentioned, and Mr. Adam Stafford's negroes. We had separated from Mrs. M and the other friends at Vince's bridge. The horrors of crossing the Trinity are beyond my power to describe. One of my little sisters was very sick, and the ferryman said that those families that had sick children should cross first. When our party got to the boat the water broke over the banks above where we were and ran around us. We were several hours surrounded by water. Our family was the last to get to the boat. We left more than five hundred people on the west bank. Driftwood covered the water as far as we could see. The sick child was in convulsions. It required eight men to manage the boat.

When we landed the lowlands were under water, and everybody was rushing for the prairie. Father had a good horse, and Mrs. Dyer let mother have her horse and saddle. Father carried the sick child, and sister and I rode behind mother. She carried father's gun and the little babe. All we carried with us was what clothes we were wearing at the time. The night was very dark. We crossed a bridge that was under water. As soon as we crossed, a man with a cart and oxen drove on the bridge, and it broke down, drowning the oxen. That prevented the people from crossing, as the bridge was over a slough that looked like a river.

Father and mother hurried on, and we got to the prairie and found a great many families camped there. A Mrs. Foster invited mother to her camp, and furnished us with supper, a bed, and dry clothes. . . .

The man whose oxen were drowned sold his cart to father for ten dollars. He said that he had seen enough of Mexico and would go back to old Ireland.

It had been five days since we crossed the Trinity, and we had heard no news from the army. The town of Liberty was three miles from where we camped. The people there had not left their homes, and they gave us all the help in their power. My little sister that had been sick died and was buried in the cemetery at Liberty. After resting a few days our party continued their journey, but we remained in the town. Mother was not able to travel; she had nursed an infant and the sick child until she was compelled to rest.

A few days after our friends had gone a man crossed the Trinity in a skiff bringing bad news. The Mexican army had crossed the Brazos and was between the Texas army and Harrisburg. Fannin and his men were massacred. President Burnet and his cabinet had left Harrisburg and gone to Washington on the bay and were going to Galveston Island. The people at Liberty had left. There were many families west of the Trinity, among them our nearest neighbors, Mrs. Roark and Mrs. M.

We had been at Liberty for three weeks. A Mr. Martin let father use his house. There were two families camped near, those of Mr. Bright and his son-in-law, Patrick Reels, from the Colorado River. One Thursday evening all of a sudden we heard a sound like distant thunder. When it was repeated father said it was cannon, and that the Texans and Mexicans were fighting. He had been through the war of 1812, and knew it was a battle. The cannonading lasted only a few minutes, and father said that the Texans must have been defeated, or the cannon would not have ceased firing so quickly. We left Liberty in half an hour. The reports of the cannon were so distant that father was under the impression that the fighting was near the Trinity. The river was ten miles wide at Liberty.

We traveled nearly all night, sister and I on horseback and mother in the cart. Father had two yoke of oxen now. One yoke belonged to Adam Stafford and had strayed and father found them. The extra yoke was a great help to us as the roads were very boggy. We rested a few hours to let the stock feed. Mr. Bright and two families were with us. We were as wretched as we could be; for we had been five weeks from home, and there was not much prospect of our ever returning. We had not heard a word from brother or the other boys that were driving the cattle. Mother was sick, and we had buried our dear little sister at Liberty.

We continued our journey through mud and water and when we camped in the evening fifty or sixty young men came by who were going to join General Houston. One of them was Harvey Stafford, our neighbor, who was returning from the United States with volunteers. Father told them there had been fighting, and he informed them that they could not cross the Trinity at Liberty. They brought some good news from our friends. Mr. Stafford had met his sisters, Mrs. Dyer, and Mrs. Neal. He said there had been a great deal of sickness, but no deaths. He said also that General Gaines of the United States army was at the Neches with a regiment of soldiers to keep the Indians in subjection, but didn't prevent the people from crossing with their slaves. General Gaines said the boundary line between the United States and Mexico was the Neches.

The young men went a short distance from us and camped. Then we heard some one calling in the direction of Liberty. We could see a man on horseback waving his hat; and, as we knew there was no one left at Liberty, we thought the Mexican army had crossed the Trinity. The young men came with their guns, and when the rider got near enough for us to understand what he said, it was "Turn back! The Texas army has whipped the Mexican army and the Mexican army are prisoners. No danger! No danger! Turn back!" When he got to the camp he could scarcely speak he was so excited and out of breath. When the young men began to understand the glorious news they wanted to fire a salute, but father made them stop. He told them to save their ammunition, for they might need it.

Father asked the man for an explanation, and he showed a dispatch from General Houston giving an account of the battle and saying it would be safe for people to return to their homes. The courier had crossed the Trinity River in a canoe, swimming his horse with the help of two men. He had left the battle field the next day after the fighting. He said that General Houston was wounded, and that General Santa Anna had not been captured.

The good news was cheering indeed. The courier's name was McDermot. He was an Irishman and had been an actor. He stayed with us that night and told various incidents of the battle. There was not much sleeping during the night. Mr. McDermot said that he had not slept in a week. He not only told various incidents of the retreat of the Texas army, but acted them. The first time that mother laughed after the death of my little sister was at his description of General Houston's helping to get a cannon out of a bog.

We were on the move early the next morning. The courier went on to carry the glad tidings to the people who had crossed the Sabine, but we took a lower road and went down the Trinity. We crossed the river in a flat boat. When Mr. McDermot left us the young men fired a salute. Then they traveled with us until they crossed the river.

We stayed one night at a Mr. Lawrence's, where there were a great many families. Mrs. James Perry was there. She had not gone east of the Trinity. Her husband, Captain James Perry, was in the army. Mrs. Perry was a sister of Stephen F. Austin. My parents knew them in Missouri. She had a young babe and a pretty little daughter named Emily.

After crossing the Trinity River we had a disagreeable time crossing the [Trinity] bay. It had been raining two days and nights. There was a bayou to cross over which there was no bridge, and the only way to pass was to go three miles through the bay to get around the mouth of the bayou. There were guide-posts to point out the way, but it was very dangerous. If we got near the mouth of the bayou there was quicksand. If the wind rose the waves rolled high. The bayou was infested with alligators. A few days before our family arrived at the bay a Mr. King was caught by one and carried under water. He was going east with his family. He swam his horses across the mouth of the bayou, and then he swam back to the west side and drove the cart into the bay. His wife and children became frightened, and he turned back and said he would go up the river and wait for the water to subside. He got his family back on land, and swam the bayou to bring back the horses. He had gotten nearly across with them, when a large alligator appeared. Mrs. King first saw it above water and screamed. The alligator struck her husband with its tail and he went under water. There were several men present, and they fired their guns at the animal, but it did no good. It was not in their power to rescue Mr. King. The men waited several days and then killed a beef, put a quarter on the bank, fastened it with a chain, and then watched it until the alligator came out, when they shot and killed it. This happened several days before the battle.

We passed the bayou without any trouble or accident, except the loss of my sunbonnet. It blew off as we reached the shore. The current was very swift at the mouth of the bayou. Father wanted to swim in and get it for me, but mother begged him not to go in the water, so I had the pleasure of seeing it float away. I don't remember the name of the bayou, but a little town called Wallace [Wallisville] was opposite across the bay. We saw the big dead alligator, and we were glad to leave the Trinity.

Father's horse had strayed, but we wouldn't stop to find it. He said when he got home he would go back and hunt for it.

We arrived at Lynchburg in the night. There we met several families that we knew, and among them was our neighbor, Mrs. M. She had traveled with Moses Shipman's family.

We crossed the San Jacinto the next morning and stayed until late in the evening on the battle field. Both armies were camped near. General Santa Anna had been captured. There was great rejoicing at the meeting of friends. Mr. Leo Roark was in the battle. He had met his mother's family the evening before. He came to the ferry just as we landed, and it was like seeing a brother. He asked mother to go with him to the camp to see General Santa Anna and the Mexican prisoners. She would not go, because, as she said, she was not dressed for visiting; but she gave sister and me permission to go to the camp. I had lost my bonnet crossing Trinity Bay and was compelled to wear a table cloth again. It was six weeks since we had left home, and our clothes were very much dilapidated. I could not go to see the Mexican prisoners with a table cloth tied on my head for I knew several of the young men. I was on the battle field of San Jacinto the 26th of April, 1836. The 28th was the anniversary of my birth. I was eleven years old.

We stayed on the battle field several hours. Father was helping with the ferry boat. We visited the graves of the Texans that were killed in the battle, but there were none of them that I knew. The dead Mexicans were lying around in every direction.

Mother was very uneasy about Uncle James Wells, who was missing. Mr. Roark said uncle had been sent two days before the battle with Messrs. Church Fulcher, and Wash Secrest to watch General Cos. They had gone to Stafford's Point, and were chased by the Mexicans and separated. Fulcher and Secrest returned before the battle. Mr. Roark says the burning of Vince's bridge prevented several of the scouts from getting back.

Father worked till the middle of the afternoon helping with the ferry boat, and then he visited the camp. He did not see General Santa Anna, but met some old friends he had known in Missouri. We left the battle field late in the evening. We had to pass among the dead Mexicans, and father pulled one out of the road, so we could get by without driving over the body, since we could not go around it. The prairie was very boggy, it was getting dark, and there were now twenty or thirty families with us. We were glad to leave the battle field, for it was a gruesome sight. We camped that night on the prairie, and could hear the wolves howl and bark as they devoured the dead. . . .

Early the next morning we were on the move. We had to take a roundabout road, for the burning of Vince's bridge prevented us from going directly home. We could hear nothing but sad news. San Felipe had been burned, and dear old Harrisburg was in ashes. There was nothing left of the Stafford plantation but a crib with a thousand bushels of corn. The Mexicans turned the houses at the Point into a hospital. They knew that it was a place where political meetings had been held.

Leo Roark told father while we were in the camps that he was confident Colonel Almonte, General Santa Anna's *aide-de-camp*, was the Mexican that had the horses for sale in our neighborhood on the fourth of July, '34. Father could not get to see General Almonte, for he was anxious to get us away from the battle ground before night.

Burning the saw mill at Harrisburg and the buildings on Stafford's plantation was a calamity that greatly affected the people. On the plantation were a sugar-mill, cotton-gin, blacksmith-shop, grist-mill, a dwelling house, negro houses, and a stock of farming implements. The Mexicans saved the corn for bread, and it was a great help to the people of the neighborhood.

We camped that evening on Sims' bayou. We met men with Mexicans going to the army, and heard from Brother Granville. Mr. Adam Stafford had got home with the boys, and they were all well. We heard that the cotton that the farmers had hauled to the Brazos with the expectation of shipping it to Brazoria on the steamer *Yellowstone*, then at Washington, was safe. Father said if he got his cotton to market I should have two or three sunbonnets, as he was tired of seeing me wearing a table-cloth around my head. . . .

We camped one day and two nights on Sims' Bayou. We had traveled since the twenty-first, without resting, half the time in mud and water. It was only fifteen miles home.

Early in the morning we broke camp. We were alone; the other families lived farther down the country. The weather was getting warm, and we stopped two hours in the middle of the day at a water hole. When the sun set we were still five miles from home.

We overtook our nearest neighbor, Mrs. M———. She had left

Sims' Bayou that morning with the Shipman family, but had separated from them, saying she could find the way home. One of her oxen got down, and she could neither get it up nor get the yoke off the other ox. When we drove up she had her four children on her horse and was going to walk to our house. She knew that we had started home that morning. If we had not stopped two hours we would have been with her about the middle of the afternoon. Father unyoked her oxen, and turned loose one of his that was broken down and put the other along with Mrs. M——'s stronger ox to her cart. It was now dark and we traveled slower. The oxen were tired and kept feeding all the time. One of Mrs. M——'s daughters and I rode her horse; it was a great relief to me, for I was tired of riding in the cart.

It was ten o'clock when we got home. We camped near the house.

Father said we could not go in until morning. Uncle James told mother that the floor had been torn up by the Mexicans searching for eggs. He would have put the house in order, but his shoulder and arm were so painful he could not work.

As soon as it was light enough for us to see we went into the house, and the first thing we saw was the hogs running out. Father's bookcase lay on the ground broken open, his books, medicines, and other things scattered on the ground, and the hogs sleeping on them. When Mrs. M——'s children, sister, and I got to the door, there was one big hog that would not go out till father shot at him. Then we children began picking up the books. We could not find those that Colonel Travis gave us, but did find broken toys that belonged to our dear little sister that died. Through the joy and excitement since the battle of San Jacinto, we had forgotten our sad bereavement.

The first thing that father did after breakfast was to go to the corn field. He had planted corn the first of March, and it needed plowing. He did not wait for Monday, or to put the house in order, but began plowing at once. His field was in the bottom, and he had hidden his plow.

Mother said I should ride Mrs. M——'s horse, and go to Stafford's Point and bring Brother Granville home. I did not want to go. Sister said that I could wear her bonnet. My dress was very much the worse for wear. It was pinned up the back, my shoes were down at the heels, and my stockings were dirty. I was greatly embarrassed, for I knew all the boys were at the Point. I did all the primping that the circumstances would permit, plaiting my hair, etc. I had had my face wrapped in a table cloth till it was thoroughly blanched. When I got to the Point there were more than one hundred people there, men, women, children, negroes, and Mexicans. Many of the Mexicans were sick and wounded; I had never seen such a dirty and ragged crowd. The boys were without shoes and hats, and their hair was down to their shoulders. After I had met them I did not feel ashamed of my appearance. Brother got his horse, and we went home.

When brother and I got home we found mother and Mrs. M——at the wash tub. I was shocked, for my mother always kept the Sabbath. At noon father and brother put down the floor, Mrs. M——'s girl and I scoured it, and we moved in.

Mrs. M—— took a bucket and went back to give water to her sick oxen, but found the ox dead. Brother Granville helped her to move home that evening.

Mother was very despondent, but father was hopeful. He said Texas would gain her independence and become a great nation.

Uncle James Wells came home with two Mexicans for servants, and put them to work in the corn field. There was now a scarcity of bread. The people came back in crowds, stopping at Harrisburg and in our neighborhood. A colony of Irish that had left San Patricio in February stopped at Stafford's Point.

Father had hid some of our things in the bottom, among them a big chest. Mother had packed it with bedding, clothes, and other things we could not take when we left home. After a few days, Uncle and brother hauled it to the house, and that old blue chest proved a treasure. When we left home we wore our best clothes. Now our best clothes were in the chest, among them my old sunbonnet. I was prouder of that old bonnet than in after years a new white lace one that my husband gave me.

By the middle of May our neighbors that we had parted from came home. They had got to the Sabine River before they heard of the battle of San Jacinto.

Father and the men that had cotton on the banks of the Brazos went to the river to build a flat boat to ship their cotton to Brazoria. Mother said that it would be best for them to wait a few days, but they would not stop. They said that as they had been camping for two months it would make them sick to sleep in a house. Uncle James stayed with us. He had several bales of cotton, but was not able to work. He looked after our Mexicans and helped the women in the neighborhood to get their corn worked. They all got Mexicans, but it required an overseer to make them work.

There was no prospect of a cotton crop in our neighborhood. The people had been very short of provisions, and there would have been suffering among them if the citizens of New Orleans had not sent a schooner load to Harrisburg. The provisions were distributed without cost.

There was considerable talk of a new town's being started on Buffalo Bayou about ten miles above Harrisburg by the Allen brothers. They wanted to buy out the Harris claim at Harrisburg, but the Harris brothers would not sell.

The first of June the men sent word that they had the cotton on a boat ready to start, and that Uncle Ned should be sent with the Staffords' wagon to bring home family supplies. It was more than fifty miles by land, but a long and dangerous route by water.

The new town laid out by the Allens was named Houston, in honor of General Houston. There were circulars and drawings sent out, which represented a large city, showing churches, a courthouse, a market house and a square of ground set aside to use for a building for Congress, if the seat of the government should be located there. The government had been on the move since the beginning of February, stopping temporarily at Washington on the Brazos, Harrisburg, Washington on the bay, Galveston Island, Lynchburg, Velasco, and Columbia. There was so much excitement about the city of Houston that some of the young men in our neighborhood, my brother among them, visited it. After being absent some time they said that it was hard work to find the city in the pine woods; and that, when they did, it consisted of one dugout canoe, a bottle gourd of whiskey and a surveyor's chain and compass, and was inhabited by four men with an ordinary camping outfit. We had a good joke on the boys at their disappointment. We asked them at what hotel they put up, and whether they went to church and to the theater. They took our teasing in good part and said they were thankful to get home alive. They said the mosquitoes were as large as grasshoppers, and that to get away from them they went bathing. The bayou water was clear and cool, and they thought they would have a nice bath, but in a few minutes the water was alive with alligators. One man ran out on the north side, and the others, who had come out where they went in, got a canoe and rescued him. He said a large panther had been near by, but that it ran off as the canoe approached.

While father was gone, a man came to our house trying to find a place to teach school. Mother told him that the men who had families were absent, but that she thought he could get a school, and that she expected father home in a few days. He said he was without money. He had been in the battle of San Jacinto, but as the army had gone west, he had decided to teach until he could get money to return to the United States. He offered to teach us three children for his board until he could get a school. Mother was glad to have a teacher for us, for we had been out of school since September, '35, when our teacher and the young men had gone to San Antonio, then in possession of the Mexicans under General Cos. We gathered what books we could and began work. We were well pleased with the teacher, whose name was Bennet. We were without paper and wrote on slates.

The first copy Mr. Bennet wrote seemed to amuse our Mexican servant. He picked up a pencil, wrote a few words, and handed the slate to Mr. Bennet. The Mexican wrote French, and the teacher was a French scholar, and they had a long conversation in that language. The Mexican had been a colonel under Santa Anna, and he said that he and Santa Anna were not far apart when the battle began. The Mexican soldiers were resting, and Santa Anna was asleep, not expecting an attack by the Texans. The cavalry had just finished watering their horses, and Santa Anna's servant was riding Allen Vince's fine black stallion, using a common saddle. He said the last he had seen of Santa Anna was when he was mounting the horse dressed in ordinary clothes. We had treated the Mexican like a negro servant, and had made him work, churn, wash, and do all kinds of drudgery, besides working in the corn field. He said he was well off, and had a home and family in Mexico. He stayed with us only a few days after he let us know he was a gentleman. I don't remember his name. We called him Anahuac, after the town that was the Mexican port of entry. . . .

We heard glowing accounts of the city on Buffalo Bayou. Several families from Brazoria and Columbia had moved there, among them Ben Fort Smith, his mother, Mrs. Obedience Smith, and family, Mr. Woodruff, Mr. Mann, with his wife and two step sons, Flournoy Hunt and Sam Allen, Moseley Baker, and others. Uncle James had gone to Houston to locate land. Everybody had the Houston fever. They were building a steam saw mill there. Father was going to locate land near Houston on Bray's Bayou. Mr. Smith wanted him to settle in town, and said he would give him a lot; but father could not do so, as he had to live on the land to secure title. . . .

Bray's Bayou, 1838

We enjoyed our new home very much, for we could attend church, a blessing we had been deprived of since the year 1833. Houston had improved considerably for a town not two years old. A steamboat had arrived. The captain's name was Grayson. Everybody was highly elated, as the farmers were going to plant cotton. The planters from Mississippi with their slaves were locating on the Brazos. A Mr. Jonathan Waters was going to build a cotton gin on the Brazos.

The 22nd of February, 1838, was the first time I met General Houston, the hero of San Jacinto. It was at a ball—my first ball in Houston. Sam Houston, then in his second year as president, Moseley Baker and wife, A. C. Allen and wife, a Mr. Coffee and wife, he a member of Congress from Red River County, Dr. Gazley and wife, three Misses Stockbridge and others too numerous to mention were present.

I attended school during the summer. At this time there was no church building in Houston, nor any preacher stationed there. The first sermon I heard preached in Houston was delivered by a Presbyterian minister by the name of Sullivan. He preached in the Hall of Representatives in the old Capitol. There had been a court house and jail, both of them of logs. Two men were in jail to be hanged for murder. The influx of men from the United States was not without its evils. There had been three terms of court held in Houston, but these men, Jones and Quick, were the first to be sentenced to capital punishment. With other evils, a great many gamblers had been put out of the State of Mississippi and, as it was believed that a large amount of money had been captured from the Mexicans at San Jacinto, Houston was considered the El Dorado of the West. There had been several good houses built in Houston. Mr. Andrew Briscoe, the hero of Anahuac, was living in Houston, and was judge of the probate court of Harris County. He married Miss Mary Jane

Harris in the year 1831 at Harrisburg. Mr. Woodruff's step-daughter, Miss Mary Smith, and Mr. Hugh McCrory were the first couple to marry in Houston. They married early in the year 1831, and he died a few months after.

There was to be an election this year for president, vice-president, and members of congress. The change of affairs under the Lone Star Republic may have added to the glory of statesmen and politicians, but it was a sad disappointment to the boys that were too young to vote. They never could forget the election barbecue and ball of the past. The women and girls seemed to enjoy the change.

Mr. Ben Fort Smith built a large two story house to be used for a hotel. It was opened with a grand ball on the 21st of April, the second anniversary of the battle of San Jacinto. Father, Mother, Brother, Sister and I were at the ball. The second story of the house had not been partitioned off for bedrooms, and it made a fine hall for dancing. There were three hundred people present, but not more than sixty ladies, including little girls and married women. There were but a few unmarried young ladies at that time in Texas, and as Miss Mary Jane Harris, the belle of Buffalo Bayou, was married, I, as the Rose of Bray's Bayou, came in for considerable attention. Politics ran high. General Mirabeau B. Lamar, vice-president, and a candidate for president, and Gen. Sam Houston and staff did not dance, but promenaded. One half of the men were candidates. Old Mr. Robert Wilson, "Honest Bob," was a candidate for congress. General Houston was talking with Mother and some other ladies, when Father presented Sister and me to the president. He kissed both of us and said "Dr. Rose, you have two pretty little girls." I felt rather crestfallen, as I considered myself a young lady. It had been the height of my ambition to dance with the president. At the Washington's birthday ball, Mrs. Dr. Gazley was dancing with the president. She, not feeling well, asked me to take her place, but a pretty young widow, Mrs. Archer Boyd, asked her partner to excuse her. She changed places with me, but I had the honor to dance in the same set. But as there was to be a wedding in June and I was to be first bridesmaid and General Houston best man, I didn't care. More of that wedding anon.

The second anniversary of the battle of San Jacinto had come and gone and Mother said she hoped there would be nothing else to distract us from our studies, as the school would close in June. But there was another sensation. One Monday morning in May on our arrival at the school-house, we found the town covered with play bills. A theatrical company had arrived and would give the first performance Friday night, June 11. This was the first theatrical company to come to Texas. It not only ran the young people wild, but the old people were not much better. The manager's name was Carlos, stage-manager, Curry, company, Mr. Hubert and family, Mr. Newton, Miss Hoke, Mr. and Mrs. Barker and several children. More of the Barkers anon.

The wedding came off the 15th of June. The groom was Mr. Flournoy Hunt, the bride, Miss Mary Henry. The wedding was at the Mansion House, the home of Mrs. Mann, mother of the groom. It was a grand affair, but I was snubbed again by a pretty widow. General Houston and I were to be the first attendants, Dr. Ashbel Smith and Miss Voate, second, and Dr. Ewing and Mrs. Holliday, third. At the last moment the program was changed. Mrs. Holliday suggested that I was too young and timid, and that she would take my place. General Houston offered her his arm. They took the lead, and Dr. Ewing escorted me. Everything passed off very pleasantly. As soon as congratulations were over, General Houston, who was the personification of elegance and kindness, excused himself and retired. Mrs. Holliday took possession of Doctor Ewing and left me without an escort till Mr. Hunt introduced Mr. Ira A. Harris. He was young, handsome, and had been but a few weeks in Houston; and, as I did not have the president for a partner, I was well pleased. As there was no pretty widow to interfere, we were subsequently married. Houston was at that time overrun with widows. They came from New Orleans. But it was a blessing in disguise, as all the old widowers and bachelors were thus enabled to get wives. The wedding ended with a supper and ball. The names of a few who were present and who married widows are: Thomas Earl, William Vince, owner of the Vince Bridge, and his brother Allen Vince, owner of the fine horse on which General Santa Anna made his escape from the battle field of San Jacinto.

There were no fourth of July celebrations that year. The election came off the first of September. Lamar was elected president; David G. Burnet, vice-president; Robert Wilson, senator. The condemned men, Jones and Quick, were hanged. School opened with Mrs. Robertson as teacher. President Houston had been absent in October visiting Nacogdoches. On his return the citizens arranged to give him a grand reception and banquet. The Milam Guards were to meet the president at Green's Bayou. As they marched out they came by the school house. The soldiers were a fine body of men; their uniforms were white with blue trimming. Captain Shea was in command. There were but a few girls in school. None of us was over fifteen years old, but we all had sweethearts among the Milam Guards. Soon after they left town rain began falling, and when they returned in the evening they were a sorry sight, wet and muddy, their uniforms ruined, and the president's clothing not much better. The reception was a failure, there being no ladies at the banquet. The school teacher, Mrs. Robertson, and pupils had received complimentary tickets to the theater that evening, as had also the president, his staff, and the Milam Guards. The school arrived early, found the reserved seats occupied, and was accordingly seated in the second seats. There was considerable confusion, as the house was crowded. As the president and escort entered the orchestra played "Hail to the Chief," but there were no seats vacant to accommodate them. The stage manager, Mr. Curry, came out and requested the men in front, who were gamblers and their friends, to give up the seats. This they refused to do. Then the manager called for the police to put them out. They became enraged, and drawing weapons, threatened to shoot. The sheriff called upon the soldiers to arrest and disarm them. It looked as if there would be bloodshed, gamblers on one side, soldiers on the other, women and children in between, everybody talking, women and children crying. The president got on a seat, commanded the peace, asked those in front to be seated, ordered the soldiers to stack arms, and said that he and the ladies and children would take back seats. This appeared to shame the gamblers. One man acted as spokesman and said that if their money was returned they would leave the house, as they had no desire to discommode the ladies. He said that they would have left the house at first if the police had not been called. After the gamblers left, the evening passed very pleasantly. The president addressed the audience, particularly the children, as the term for which he was elected would close soon. He admonished them to be obedient and diligent in their studies.

The first theatrical company to perform in Houston closed its engagement the next day. Mrs. Barker went home sick, Mrs. Hubbard refused to act again, and Mr. Barker took an overdose of laudanum and died, leaving his family destitute, the mother sick, with three small

Capitol of the Republic of Texas, Houston. When the Capitol was constructed in the spring of 1837, Houston was mainly a city of tents and half-finished houses. (*Courtesy Litterst-Dixon Collection, Harris County Heritage Society, Houston*)

children, in an open house without a fireplace or stove. As soon as the people buried the corpse, there was a meeting to find means to help Mrs. Barker. The gamblers gave money freely, but it was impossible to get a good house. Gen. Sam Houston came to the rescue, and said that the destitute family could have the president's mansion and that he would board. The family was moved into the mansion till Mrs. Barker was able to travel to her friends. The company returned to the United States. A few years after, Mr. Newton returned with a new company. He had married a Miss Hope. . . .

This winter, 1839, was the first cold weather I had seen in Texas. There was sleet and snow. The new congress met in December, 1838, in Houston. General M. Lamar was president; the vice-president's name I do not remember. There was as much dissension in this congress as in the Consultation of 1835. The land speculators wanted to move the seat of government from Houston. No two members could agree. Some wanted to locate it at San Antonio, others at the head of the Colorado, or at Brazoria, Nacogdoches, or San Saba—every man was for himself. Finally there was a secret session of the senate that gave some offense to Senator Robert Wilson. He exposed some transaction of the session, and this caused his expulsion. An election was ordered to fill the vacancy. "Uncle Bob Wilson," as everybody called him, was nominated and elected. As soon as he received his certificate of election the boys decided to celebrate the event. They built a throne in a wagon, seated their senator, manned the wagon, marched around town, then to the Capitol while congress was in session, hurrahing for "Uncle Bob," and shouting "Down with secret sessions," and "The seat of the Government must remain in Houston." They would have hauled the wagon into the senate chamber, but "Uncle Bob" requested them not to do so. This session of the congress passed the act locating the seat of the government on the Colorado River above the Old San Antonio Road, and naming the place Austin. All the trouble and confusion of moving is a matter of history. At this time we were harassed by Mexicans and Indians. First was General Woll's invasion. The seat of government was moved back to Houston, and then to Washington on the Brazos. Times were very hard. Texas money was down to twenty-five cents on the dollar; gold and silver disappeared from circulation; and immigration to Texas almost stopped.

On the 20th of February I was married to Ira A. Harris in a log house on Brazos [Bray's?] Bayou. The marriage ceremony was performed by Judge Andrew Briscoe, the hero of Anahuac. Mrs. Mary McCrory, now Mrs. Anson Jones, was bridesmaid, and Mr. Allen, from New York, groomsman. Among the guests were Gen. T. J. Rusk, Dr. Ashbel Smith, Louis B. and Clinton Harris, Adam Stafford, Gus and Steve Tompkins, Ben Fort Smith, Henry Woodland, Mrs. Brewster, and some friends whose acquaintance we made at Harrisburg in the year 1833, Misses Smith, Woodruff, Conklin, Ella Rose, and Peggy House, Mrs. Allen Vince, and others of cherished memory. The summer of 1839 was fraught with many incidents, some of joy, but many of sorrow, as yellow fever raged in Houston for months. My dear father died on the 27th of December of that year. My husband improved a place near Houston. We lived there till 1845, the year of annexation, and then moved to Columbus, Colorado County, where my husband died in 1869. We raised nine children, all of whom are living at this time. Two sons were born under the Lone Star of the Republic of Texas—T. P. Harris, born April 15th, 1841, at Houston; and Joe P. Harris, born Feb. 25th, 1843, who now lives in Houston. T. P. Harris is living at Luling, Texas. He was at the battle of Sabine Pass. Joe P. Harris was with the Terry Rangers. Guy C. Harris was in the Galveston storm. I am now visiting my son, Lee Harris, at Purcell, Indian Territory, but I claim dear old Texas as my home.

Rachel Parker Plummer

"Surely, surely, my poor heart must break."

The coastal plains and the Brazos River bottom were not the only areas of Texas which were being settled. Into the wilderness of East Texas went six families from Illinois. Most of them were related to Elder John Parker, a leader in the Primitive Baptist Church. In 1834 they left the last outpost behind and journeyed to the west bank of the Navasota River near the present town of Groesbeck, where they built Fort Parker, with high walls, cramped living quarters, and loopholes used for firing at Indians. At that place occurred one of the most tragic confrontations in the history of Texas.

On May 19, 1836, life in and around the fort was going on in the usual manner. Most of the men were working in the fields, and the women and children were busy inside the fort. Suddenly, a large group of Comanches, Wichitas, and Kiowas appeared. After quickly ascertaining that the settlers could easily be overpowered, the Indians drove their spears into Benjamin Parker. Thus began the Battle of Fort Parker. During the battle, Rachel Parker Plummer, her infant son, her aunt, and her two cousins were abducted. In the account which follows, Rachel tells the story of the battle and her captivity.

*   *   *

On the 19th of May, 1836, I was living in Fort Parker, on the head waters of the river Navasott. My father, (James W. Parker,) and my husband and brother-in-law were cultivating my father's farm, which was about a mile from the fort. In the morning, say 9 o'clock, my father, husband, brother-in-law, and brother, went to the farm to work. I do not think they had left the fort more than an hour before some one of the fort cried out, "Indians!" The inmates of the fort had retired to

From James W. Parker, *Narrative of the Perilous Adventures of Rev. James W. Parker . . . to which is appended a Narrative of the capture and subsequent sufferings of Mrs. Rachel Plummer. . . .* (Louisville, Ky.: privately printed, 1844; reprint ed., Palestine, Tex.: privately printed, 1926).

Replica of Fort Parker, near Groesbeck. (*Courtesy Joseph E. Taulman Collection, Barker Texas History Center, University of Texas at Austin*)

their farms in the neighborhood, and there were only six men in it, viz: my grandfather, Elder John Parker, my two uncles, Benjamin and Silas Parker, Samuel Frost and his son Robert, and Frost's son-in-law, G. E. Dwight. All appeared in a state of confusion, for the Indians (numbering something not far from eight hundred) had raised a white flag.

On the first sight of the Indians, my sister (Mrs. Nixon) started to alarm my father and his company at the farm, whilst the Indians were yet more than a quarter of a mile from the fort, and I saw her no more. I was in the act of starting to the farm, but I knew I was not able to take my little son, (James Pratt Plummer). The women were all soon gone from the fort, whither I did not know; but I expected towards the farm. My old grandfather and grandmother, and several others, started through the farm, which was immediately joining the fort. Dwight started with his family and Mrs. Frost and her little children. As he started, Uncle Silas said, "Good Lord, Dwight, you are not going to run?" He said, "No, I am only going to try to hide the women and children in the woods." Uncle said, "Stand and fight like a man, and if we have to die we will sell our lives as dearly as we can."

The Indians halted; and two Indians came up to the fort to inform the inmates that they were friendly, and had come for the purpose of making a treaty with the Americans. This instantly threw the people off their guard, and Uncle Benjamin went to the Indians, who had now got within a few hundred yards of the fort. In a few minutes he returned, and told Frost and his son and Uncle Silas that he believed the Indians intended to fight, and told them to put everything in the best order for defense. He said he would go back to the Indians and see if the fight could be avoided. Uncle Silas told him not to go, but to try to defend the place as well as they could; but he started off again to the Indians, and appeared to pay but little attention to what Silas said. Uncle Silas said, "I know they will kill Benjamin"; and said to me, "Do you stand there and watch the Indians' motion until I run into my house"—I think he said for his shot pouch. I suppose he had got a wrong shot pouch as he had four or five rifles. When Uncle Benjamin reached the body I was now satisfied they intended killing him. I took up my little James Pratt, and thought I would try to make my escape. As I ran across the fort, I met Silas returning to the place where he left me. He asked me if they had killed Benjamin. I told him, "No; but they have surrounded him." He said, "I know they will kill him, but I will be good for one of them at least." These were the last words I heard him utter.

I ran out of the fort, and passing the corner I saw the Indians drive their spears into Benjamin. The work of death had already commenced. I shall not attempt to describe their terrific yells, their united voices that seemed to reach the very skies whilst they were dealing death to the inmates of the fort. It can scarcely be comprehended in the wide field of imagination. I know it is utterly impossible for me to give every particular in detail, for I was much alarmed.

I tried to make my escape, but alas, alas, it was too late, as a party of the Indians had got ahead of me. Oh! how vain were my feeble efforts to try to run to save myself and little James Pratt. A large sulky looking Indian picked up a hoe and knocked me down. I well recollect of their taking my child out of my arms, but whether they hit me any more I do not know, for I swooned away. The first I recollect, they were dragging me along by the hair. I made several unsuccessful attempts to raise to my feet before I could do it. As they took me past the fort, I heard an awful screaming near the place where they had first seized me. I heard some shots. I then heard Uncle Silas shout a triumphant huzza! I did, for one moment, hope the men had gathered from the neighboring farms, and might release me.

I was soon dragged to the main body of the Indians, where they had killed Uncle Benjamin. His face was much mutilated, and many arrows were sticking in his body. As the savages passed by, they thrust their spears through him. I was covered with blood, for my wound was bleeding freely. I looked for my child but could not see him, and was convinced they had killed him, and every moment expected to share the same fate myself. At length I saw him. An Indian had him on his horse; he was calling mother, oh, mother! He was just able to lisp the name of mother, being only about 18 months old. There were two Comanche women with them (their battles always brought on by a woman), one of whom came to me and struck me several times with a whip. I suppose it was to make me quit crying.

I now expected my father and husband, and all the rest of the men were killed. I soon saw a party of the Indians bringing my Aunt Elizabeth Kellogg and Uncle Silas' two oldest children, Cynthia Ann, and John, also some bloody scalps; among them I could distinguish that of my grandfather by the grey hairs, but could not discriminate the balance.

Most of the Indians were engaged in plundering the fort. They cut open our bed ticks and threw the feathers in the air, which was literally thick with them. They brought out a great number of my father's books and medicines. Some of the books were torn up, most of the bottles of medicine were broken; though they took on some for several days.

I had a few minutes to reflect, for they soon started back the same way they came up. As I was leaving, I looked back at the place where I was one hour before, happy and free, and now in the hands of a ruthless, savage enemy.

They killed a great many of our cattle as they went along. They soon convinced me that I had no time to reflect upon the past, for they commenced whipping and beating me with clubs, etc., so that my flesh was never well from bruises and wounds during my captivity. To undertake to narrate their barbarous treatment would only add to my present distress, for it is with feelings of the deepest mortification that I think of it, much less to speak or write of it; for while I record this painful part of my narrative; I can almost feel the same heart-rending pains of body and mind that I then endured, my very soul becomes sick at the dreadful thought.

About midnight they stopped. They now tied a plaited thong around my arms, and drew my hands behind me. They tied them so tight that the scars can be easily seen to this day. They then tied a similar thong around my ankles, and drew my feet and hands together. They now turned me on my face and I was unable to turn over, when they commenced beating me over the head with their bows, and it was with great difficulty I could keep from smothering in my blood; for the wound they gave me with the hoe, and many others were bleeding freely.

I suppose it was to add to my misery that they brought my little James Pratt so near me that I could hear him cry. He would call for mother; and often his voice was weakened by the blows they would give him. I could hear the blows. I could hear his cries; but oh, alas, could offer him no relief. The rest of the prisoners were brought near me, but we were not allowed to speak one word together. My aunt called me once, and I answered her; but indeed, I thought she would never call or I answer again, for they jumped with their feet upon us, which nearly took our lives. Often did the children cry, but were soon hushed by such blows that I had no idea they could survive. They commenced screaming and dancing around the scalps, kicking and stamping the prisoners.

I now ask you, my Christian reader, to pause. You who are living secure from danger—you who have read the sacred scriptures of truth—who have been raised in a land boasting of Christian philanthropy—I say, I now ask you to form some idea of what my feelings were. Such dreadful savage yelling! Enough to terrify the bravest of hearts. Bleeding and weltering in my blood; and far worse, to think of my little darling Pratt! Will this scene ever be effaced from my memory? Not until my spirit is called to leave this tenement of clay; and may God grant me a heart to pray for them, for "they know not what they do."

Next morning, they started in a northern direction. They tied me every night, as before stated, for five nights. During the first five days, I never ate one mouthful of food, and had but a very scanty allowance of water. . . .

After we reached the Grand Prairie, we turned more to the east; that is, the party I belonged to. Aunt Elizabeth fell to the Kitchawas, and my nephew and niece to another portion of the Comanches.

I must again call my reader to bear with me in rehearsing the continued barbarous treatment of the Indians. My child kept crying, and almost continually calling for "Mother," though I was not allowed even to speak to it. At the time they took off my fetters, they brought my child to me, supposing that I gave suck. As soon as it saw me, it, trembling with weakness, hastened to my embraces. Oh, with what feelings of love and sorrow did I embrace the mutilated body of my darling little James Pratt. I now felt that my case was much bettered, as I thought they would let me have my child; but oh, mistaken, indeed, was I; for as soon as they found that I had weaned him, they, in spite of all my efforts, tore him from my embrace. He reached out his hands towards me, which were covered with blood, and cried, "Mother, Mother, oh, Mother!" I looked after him as he was borne away from me, and I sobbed aloud. This was the last I ever heard of my little Pratt. Where he is, I do not know.

Progressing farther and farther from my home, we crossed Big Red River, the head of Arkansas, and then turned more to the northwest. We now lost sight of timber entirely.

For several hundred miles after we had left the Cross Timber country, and on the Red River, Arkansas, etc., there is a fine country. The timber is scarce and scrubby. Some streams as salt as brine; and others, fine water. The land, in part, is very rich, and game plenty.

We would travel for weeks and not see a riding switch. Buffalo dung is all the fuel. This is gathered into a round pile; and when set on fire, it does very well to cook by, and will keep a fire for several days.

In July, and in part of August, we were on the Snow Mountains. There it is perpetual snow; and I suffered more from cold than I ever suffered in my life before. It was very seldom I had any thing to put on my feet, but very little covering for my body. I had to mind the horses every night, and had a certain number of buffalo skins to dress every moon. This kept me employed all the time in day light; and often would I have to take my buffalo skin with me, to finish it whilst I was minding the horses. My feet would be often frozen, even while I would be dressing skins, and I dared not complain; for my situation still grew more and more difficult.

In October, I gave birth to my second son. As to the months, etc., it was guess work with me, for I had no means of keeping the time. It was an interesting and beautiful babe. I had, as you may suppose, but a very poor chance to comfort myself with anything suitable to my situation, or that of my little infant. The Indians were not as hostile now as I had feared they would be. I was still fearful they would kill my child; and having now been with them some six months, I had learned their language. I would often expostulate with my mistress to advise me what to do to save my child; but all in vain. My child was some six or seven weeks old, when I suppose my master thought it too much trouble, as I was not able to go through as much labor as before. One cold morning, five or six large Indians came where I was suckling my infant. As soon as they came in I felt my heart sick; my fears agitated my whole frame to a complete state of convulsion; my body shook with fear indeed. Nor were my fears ill-grounded. One of them caught hold of the child by the throat; and with his whole strength, and like an enraged lion actuated by its devouring nature, held on like the hungry vulture, until my child was to all appearance entirely dead. I exerted my whole feeble strength to relieve it; but the other Indians held me. They, by force, took it from me and threw it up in the air, and let it fall on the frozen ground, until it was apparently dead.

They gave it back to me. The fountain of tears that had hitherto given vent to my grief, was now dried up. While I gazed upon the bruised cheeks of my darling infant, I discovered some symptoms of returning life. Oh, how vain was my hope that they would let me have it if I could revive it. I washed the blood from its face; and after some time, it began to breathe again; but a more heart-rending scene ensued. As soon as they found it had recovered a little, they again tore it from my embrace and knocked me down. They tied a plaited rope round the child's neck and drew its naked body into the large hedges of prickly pears, which were from eight to twelve feet high. They would then pull it through the pears. This they repeated several times. One of them then got on a horse, and tying the rope to his saddle, rode round a circuit of a few hundred yards, until my little innocent one was not only dead, but literally torn to pieces. I stood horror struck. One of them then took it up by the leg, brought it to me, and threw it into my lap. But in praise to the Indians, I must say, that they gave me time to dig a hole in the earth and bury it. After having performed this last service to the lifeless remains of my dear babe, I sat down and gazed with joy on the resting place of my now happy infant; and I could, with old David, say "You cannot come to me, but I must go to you;" and then, and even now, whilst I record the awful tragedy, I rejoice that it passed from the sufferings and sorrows of this world. I shall hear its deathly cries no more; and fully and confidently believing, and solely relying on the imputed righteousness of God in Christ Jesus, I feel that my happy babe is now with its kindred spirits in that eternal world of joys. Oh! will my dear Savior, by his grace, keep me through life's short journey, and bring me to dwell with my happy children in the sweet realms of endless bliss, where I shall meet the whole family of Heaven—those whose names are recorded in the Lamb's Book of Life.

I would have been glad to have had the pleasure of laying my little James Pratt with this my happy infant. I do really believe I could have buried him without shedding a tear; for, indeed, they had ceased to flow in relief of my grief. My heaving bosom could do no more than breathe deep sighs. Parents, you little know what you can bear. Surely, surely, my poor heart must break. . . .

On one occasion, my young mistress and myself were out a short distance from town. She ordered me to go back to the town and get a kind of instrument with which they dig roots. Having lived as long, and indeed longer than life was desirable, I determined to aggravate them to kill me.

I told her I would not go back. She, in an enraged tone, bade me go. I told her I would not. She then with savage screams ran at me. I knocked, or, rather pushed her down. She, fighting and screaming like a desperado, tried to get up; but I kept her down; and in the fight I got hold of a large buffalo bone. I beat her over the head with it, although expecting at every moment to feel a spear reach my heart from one of the Indians; but I lost no time. I was determined if they killed me, to make a cripple of her. Such yells as the Indians made around us— being nearly all collected—a Christian mind cannot conceive. No one touched me. I had her past hurting me, and indeed, nearly past breathing, when she cried out for mercy. I let go my hold of her, and could but be amazed that not one of them attempted to arrest or kill me, or do the least thing for her. She was bleeding freely; for I had cut her head in several places to the skull. I raised her up and carried her to the camp.

A new adventure this. I was yet undetermined what would grow out of it. All the Indians seemed as unconcerned as if nothing had taken place. I washed her face and gave her water. She appeared remarkably friendly. One of the big chiefs came to me, and appeared to watch my movements with a great deal of attention. At length he observed—

"You are brave to fight—good to a fallen enemy—you are directed by the Great Spirit. Indians do not have pity on a fallen enemy. By our law you are clear. It is contrary to our law to show you foul play. She began with you, and you had a right to kill her. Your noble spirit forbid you. When Indians fight, the conquerer gives or takes the life of his antagonist—and they seldom spare them."

This was like a balm to my soul. But my old mistress was very mad. She ordered me to go and get a large bundle of straw. I soon learned it was to burn me to death. I did not fear that death; for I had prepared a knife, with which I intended to defeat her object in putting me to death by burning, having determined to take my own life. She ordered me to cross my hands. I told her I would not do it. She asked me if I was willing for her to burn me to death without being tied. I told her that she should not tie me. She caught up a small bundle of straw, and setting it on fire, threw it on me. I was as good as my word. I pushed her into the fire, and as she raised, I knocked her down into the fire again, and kept her there until she was as badly burned as I was. She got hold of a club and hit me a time or two. I took it from her, and knocked her down with it. So we had a regular fight. I handled her with more ease than I did the young woman. During the fight, we had broken down one side of the house, and had got fully out into the street. After I had fully overcome her, I discovered the same indifference on the part of the Indians as in the other fight. The whole of them were around us, screaming as before, and no one touched us. I, as in the former case, immediately administered to her. All was silent again, except now and then, a grunt from the old woman. The young woman refused to help me into the house with her. I got her in, and then fixed up the side of the house that we had broken.

Next morning, twelve of the chiefs assembled at the Council House. We were called for, and we attended; and with all the solemnity of a church service, went into the trial. The old lady told the story without the least embellishment. I was asked if these things were so. I answered, "Yes." The young woman was asked, "Are these things true?" She said they were. We were asked if we had anything to say. Both of the others said "No." I said I had. I told the Court that they had mistreated me—they had not taken me honorably; that they had used the white flag to deceive us, by which they had killed my friends—that I had been faithful, and had served them from fear of death, and that I would rather die than be treated as I had been. I said that the Great Spirit would reward them for their treachery and their abuse to me. The sentence was, that I should get a new pole for the one that we had broken in the fight. I agreed to it, provided the young woman helped me. This was made a part of the decree, and all was peace again.

This answered me a valuable purpose afterwards, in some other instances. I took my own part, and fared much the better by it. . . .

One evening as I was at my work (being north of the Rocky Mountains), I discovered some Mexican traders. Hope instantly mounted the throne from whence it had long been banished. My tottering frame received fresh life and courage, as I saw them approaching the habitation of sorrow and grief where I dwelt. They asked for my master, and we were directly with him. They asked if he would sell me. No music, no sounds that ever reached my anxious ear, was half so sweet as *"ce senure"* (yes, sir). The trader made an offer for me. My owner refused. He offered more, but my owner still refused. Utter confusion hovers around my mind while I record this part of my history; and I can only ask my reader, if he can, to fancy himself in my situation; for language will fail to describe the anxious thoughts that revolved in my throbbing breast when I heard the trader say he could give no more. Oh! had I the treasures of the universe, how freely I would have given it; yea, and then consented to have been a servant to my countrymen. Would that my father could speak to him; but my father is no more. Or one of my dear uncles; yes, they would say "stop not for price." Oh! my good Lord, intercede for me. My eyes, despite my efforts, are swimming in tears at the very thought. I only have to appeal to the treasure of your hearts, my readers, to conceive the state of my desponding mind at this crisis. At length, however, the trader made another offer for me, which my owner agreed to take. My whole feeble frame was now convulsed in an ecstasy of joy, as he delivered the first article as an earnest of the trade. MEMORABLE DAY!

Col. Nathaniel Parker, of Charleston, Illinois, burst into my mind; and although I knew he was about that time in the Illinois Senate, I knew he would reach his suffering niece, if he could only hear of her. Yes, I knew he would hasten to my relief, even at the sacrifice of a seat in that honorable body, if necessary.

Thousands of thoughts revolved through my mind as the trader was paying for me. My joy was full. Oh! shall I ever forget the time when my new master told me to go with him to his tent? As I turned from my prison, in my very soul I tried to return thanks to my God who always hears the cries of his saints:

> My God was with me in distress,
> My God was always there
> Oh! may I to my God address
> Thankful and devoted prayer.

I was soon informed by my new master that he was going to take me to Santa Fe. That night, sleep departed from my eyes. In my fancy I surveyed the steps of my childhood, in company with my dear relations. It would, I suppose, be needless for me to say that I watched with eagerness the day to spring, and that the night was long filled with gratitude to the Divine Conservator of the divine law of heaven and earth.

In the morning quite early, all things being ready, we started. We traveled very hard for seventeen days, when we reached Santa Fe. Then, my reader, I beheld some of my countrymen, and I leave you to conjecture the contrast in my feelings when I found myself surrounded by sympathizing Americans, clad in decent attire. I was soon conducted to Col. William Donoho's residence. I found that it was him who had heard of the situation of myself and others, and being an American indeed, his manly and magnanimous bosom, heaved with sympathy characteristic of a Christian, had devised the plan for our release. I have no language to express my gratitude to Mrs. Donoho. I found in her a mother, to direct me in that strange land, a sister to console with me in my misfortune, and offer new scenes of amusement to me to revive my mind. A friend? Yes, the best of friends; one who had been blessed with plenty, and was anxious to make me comfortable; and one who was continually pouring the sweet oil of consolation into my wounded and trembling soul, and was always comforting and admonishing me not to despond, and assured me that everything should be done to facilitate my return to my relatives; and though I am now separated far from her, I still owe her a debt of gratitude I shall never be able to repay but with my earnest prayers for the blessing of God to attend her through life.

The people of Santa Fe, by subscription, made up $150 to assist me to my friends. This was put into the hands of Rev. C——, who kept it and never let me have it; and but for the kindness of Mr. and Mrs. Donoho, I could not have got along. Soon after I arrived in Santa Fe, a disturbance took place among the Mexicans. They killed several of their leading men. Mr. Donoho considered it unsafe for his family, and started with them to Missouri, and made me welcome as one of his family. The road led through a vast region of prairie, which is nearly one thousand miles across. This, to many, would have been a considerable undertaking, as it was all the way through an Indian country. But we arrived safely at Independence, in Missouri, where I received many signal favors from many of the inhabitants, for which I shall ever feel grateful. I stayed at Mr. Donoho's but I was impatient to learn something of my relatives.

My anxiety grew so great that I was often tempted to start on foot. I tried to pray, mingling my tears and prayers to Almighty God to intercede for me, and in his providence to devise some means by which I might get home to my friends. Despite of all the kind entreaties of that benevolent woman, Mrs. Donoho, I refused to be comforted; and who, I ask, under these circumstances, could have been reconciled?

One evening I had been in my room trying to pray, and on stepping to the door, I saw my brother-in-law, Mr. Nixon. I tried to run to him, but was not able. I was so much overjoyed I scarcely knew what to say or how to act. I asked, "Are my husband and father alive?" He answered affirmatively. "Are mother and the children alive?" He said they were. Every moment seemed an hour. It was very cold weather, being now in dead of winter.

Mr. Donoho furnished me a horse, and in a few days we started, Mr. Donoho accompanying us. We had a long and cold journey of more than one thousand miles, the way we were compelled to travel, and that principally through a frontier country. But having been accustomed to hardships, together with my great anxiety, I thought I could stand anything, and the nearer I approached my people, the greater my anxiety grew. Finally on the evening of the 19th day of February, 1838, I arrived at my father's house in Montgomery County, Texas. Here united tears of joy flowed from the eyes of father, mother, brothers and sisters; while many strangers, unkown to me, (neighbors to my father) cordially united in this joyful interview.

I am now not only freed from my Indian captivity, enjoying the exquisite pleasure that my soul has long panted for.

> Oh! God of Love, with pitying eye
>   Look on a wretch like me;
> That I may on thy name rely,
>   Oh, Lord! be pleased to see.
>
> How oft have sighs unuttered flowed
>   From my poor wounded heart,
> Yet thou my wishes did reward,
>   And sooth'd the painful smart.

*   *   *

In her preface to "The Rachel Plummer Narrative," Rachel wrote: "With these remarks, I submit the following pages to the perusal of a generous public, feeling assured that before they are published, the hand that penned them will be cold in death." She was right. On February 19, 1839, one year after her release from captivity, Rachel Plummer died.

The other four members of the Parker clan who had been abducted all eventually returned to civilization. Elizabeth Kellogg was ransomed six months after her capture. James Pratt Plummer was rescued six years later. John Parker refused to return to civilization until he contracted smallpox and was abandoned by the Indians. He then became a rancher in Mexico and died in 1915. Cynthia Ann Parker's story was as tragic as that of Rachel. She became the wife of one Indian chief and the mother of another. She was captured and returned to her family in 1860, but she never adjusted to civilized life and died in 1864, shortly after the death of her daughter, Prairie Flower.

Mary Ann Adams Maverick

"What a day of horrors! And the night was as bad which
followed."

"She is a noble woman, wife, mother and patriot—a woman
of great thought and great heart—yet the most modest and unpretentious of women. She has fine administrative abilities, and in all
respects is justly entitled to be classed as a model woman. Texas is
proud of her." Thus was Mary Ann Adams Maverick (1818–98)
described by one of her contemporaries.

Mary Maverick's husband was Samuel Augustus Maverick, a
lawyer and a member of a prominent South Carolina family. Samuel, who migrated to Texas in 1835, joined the Texas volunteer
army, served as a guide during the siege of Bexar, and later signed
the Texas Declaration of Independence. After the victory at San
Jacinto, he went to Tuscaloosa, Alabama, where he met Mary Ann
Adams. This meeting is described in *Samuel A. Maverick* by Irwin
and Kathryn Sexton. "Because of a handkerchief dropped on a
muddy road, Maverick did not return to Texas as quickly as he had
planned. While visiting his sister in Alabama, he rode out one day
on horseback. Passing on the other side of a mudhole was a pretty
young woman who dropped her handkerchief. Sam dismounted
and picked it up for Mary Ann Adams. After this meeting he
courted her for four months. They were married in August, 1836."

Before her marriage, Mary, who was the daughter of Agatha
Strother (Lewis) and William Lewis Adams, had lived on a plantation with her widowed mother. Mary was eighteen and Samuel
was thirty-three when they married.

The couple visited relatives in Alabama and South Carolina
until December, 1837. By the time they set out for their new
home in San Antonio, they had with them their infant son, Sam.
In 1838, San Antonio was still a dangerous place to live. For almost one hundred years Comanches and Apaches had raided the
Mexican settlement, and they had no intention of stopping their
forays just because San Antonio had become a part of the Republic
of Texas.

From Mary A. Maverick, *Memoirs of Mary A. Maverick*, ed. Rena Maverick
Green (San Antonio: privately printed, 1921).

Mary Maverick (*left*); Susan Hays, wife of Texas Ranger Jack Hays; and another friend. (*Courtesy Barker Texas History Center, University of Texas at Austin*)

Thus, the tall, blonde Mary and her distinguished husband settled into a veritable hornet's nest. Mary's diary describing her life in Texas was edited for publication by her granddaughter Rena Maverick Green. The excerpt included here begins soon after the Mavericks' arrival in San Antonio.

*   *   *

Early in February, 1839, we had a heavy snow storm, the snow drifted in some places to a depth of two feet, and on the north side of our house it lasted five or six days. Anton Lockmar rigged up a sleigh and took some girls riding up and down Soledad Street. Early in February, we moved in to our own house, at the northeast corner of Commerce and Soledad Streets, being also the northeast corner of the Main Plaza, (Plaza Mayor). This house remained our homestead until July '49, over ten years, although five of the ten years,—from '42 to '47, we wandered about as refugees. It was known as the Barrera place, when Mr. Maverick purchased it, and the deed dated January 19th, 1839.

The main house was of stone, and had three rooms, one fronting south on Main Street and west on Soledad Street and the other two fronting west on Soledad Street—also a shed in the yard along the east wall of the house towards the north end. This shed we closed in with an adobe wall and divided into a kitchen and servant's room. We also built an adobe servant's room on Soledad Street, leaving a gateway between it and the main house, and we built a stable near the river.

We built a strong but homely picket fence around the garden to the north and fenced the garden off from the yard. In the garden were sixteen large fig trees and many rows of old pomegranates. In the yard were several China trees, and on the river bank just below our line in the De la Zerda premises was a grand old cypress, which we could touch through our fence, and its roots made ridges in our yard. The magnificent old tree stands there today. It made a great shade and we erected our bath house and wash place under its spreading branches.

Our neighbors on the east, Main or Commerce Street, were the De la Zerdas. In 1840, their place was leased to a Greek, Roque Catahdie, who kept a shop on the street and lived in the back rooms. He married a pretty, bright-eyed Mexican girl of fourteen years, dressed her in jewelry and fine clothes and bought her a dilapidated piano—he was jealous and wished her to amuse herself at home. The piano had the desired effect, and she enjoyed it like a child with a new trinket. The fame of her piano went through the town, and, after tea, crowds would come to witness her performance. One night Mrs. Elliot and I took a peep and we found a large crowd inside laughing and applauding, and other envious ones gazing in from the street.

Our neighbor on the north side, Soledad Street, was Dona Juana Varcinez, and I must not omit her son Leonicio. She had cows and sold me the strippings of the milk at twenty-five cents per gallon, and we made our butter from this. Mrs. McMullen was the only person then who made butter for sale, and her butter was not good, although she received half a dollar per pound for it. Old Juana was a kind old soul— had the earliest pumpkins, a great delicacy, at twenty-five cents and spring chickens at twelve and a half cents. She opened up the spring gardening by scratching with a dull hoe, some holes in which she planted pumpkin seed—then later she planted her corn, red pepper, garlic, onions, etc. She was continually calling to Leonicio to drive the chickens out of the garden, or to bring in the dogs from the street. She told me this answered two purposes—it kept Leonicio at home out of harm's way, and gave him something to do. She had lots of dogs—one fat, lazy pelon (hairless dog) slept with the old lady to keep her feet warm. When we returned from the coast in '47, Sam S. Smith had purchased the place from her and he was living there. He was a good and kind neighbor.

We moved into our home in good time, for here on Sunday morning, March 23rd, 1839, was born our second child, Lewis Antonio. All my friends have always told me, and, until quite recently I was persuaded Lewis was the first child of pure American stock born in San Antonio. But now I understand a Mr. Brown with his wife came here in 1828 for two years from East Texas, and during that time a son was born to them in San Antonio. Mr. Brown, the father, died about the same time of consumption, and his wife moved away further East. The son named John Brown, is now said to be a citizen of Waco, Texas.

During the summer, Sammy had difficulty teething. Dr. Weideman, a Russian scholar and naturalist, and an excellent physician and surgeon, took a great liking to Sammy and prescribed for him with success. This summer, William B. Jacques brought his wife and two little girls, and settled on Commerce Street. In the latter part of August, Mr. William Elliott brought his wife and two children, Mary and

Billy, to San Antonio. They bought a house on the west side of Soledad Street, opposite the north end of our garden, and we were a great many years neighbors and always friends. This year our negro men plowed and planted one labor above the Alamo and were attacked by Indians. Griffen and Wiley ran into the river and saved themselves. The Indians cut the traces and took off the work animals and we did not farm there again. Mr. Thomas Higginbotham, a carpenter, with his wife, came to San Antonio and took the house opposite us on the corner of Commerce Street and Main Plaza. His brother and sister settled in the country, on the river below San Jose Mission. This year the town of Seguin on the Guadalupe thirty-five miles east of San Antonio, was founded.

In November, 1839, a party of ladies and gentlemen from Houston came to visit San Antonio—they rode on horseback. The ladies were Miss Trask of Boston, Mass., and Miss Evans, daughter of Judge Evans of Texas. The gentlemen were Judge Evans and Colonel J. W. Dancey, Secretary of War, Republic of Texas. They were, ladies and all, armed with pistols and bowie knives. I rode with this party and some others around the head of the San Antonio River. We galloped up the west side, and paused at and above the head of the river long enough to view and admire the lovely valley of the San Antonio. The leaves had mostly fallen from the trees, and left the view open to the missions below. The day was clear, cool and bright, and we saw three of the missions, including San Juan Capistrano seven miles below town. We galloped home, down the east side, and doubted not that Indians watched us from the heavy timber of the river bottom. The gentlemen of the party numbered six, and we were all mounted on fine animals. . . .

On Tuesday, 19th of March, 1840, "dia de San Jose" sixty-five Comanches came into town to make a treaty of peace. They brought with them, and reluctantly gave up, Matilda Lockhart, whom they had captured with her younger sister in December 1838, after killing two other children of her family. The Indian chiefs and men met in council at the Court House, with our city and military authorities. The calaboose or jail then occupied the corner formed by the east line of Main Plaza and the north line of Calabosa (now Market) Street, and the Court House was north of and adjoining the jail. The Court House yard, back of the Court House, was what is now the city market on Market Street. The

Court House and jail were of stone, one story, flat roofed, and floored with dirt. Captain Tom Howard's Company was at first in the Court House yard, where the Indian women and boys came and remained during the pow-wow. The young Indians amused themselves shooting arrows at pieces of money put up by some Americans; and Mrs. Higginbotham and myself amused ourselves looking through the picket fence at them.

This was the third time these Indians had come for a talk, pretending to seek peace, and trying to get ransom money for their American and Mexican captives. Their proposition now was that they should be paid a great price for Matilda Lockhart, and a Mexican they had just given up, and that traders be sent with paint, powder, flannel, blankets and such other articles as they should name, to ransom the other captives. This course had once before been asked and carried out, but the smallpox breaking out, the Indians killed the traders and kept the goods—believing the traders had made the smallpox to kill them. Now the Americans, mindful of the treachery of the Comanches, answered them as follows: "We will according to a former agreement, keep four or five of your chiefs, whilst the others of your people go to your nation and bring all the captives, and then we will pay all you ask for them. Meanwhile, these chiefs we hold we will treat as brothers and 'not one hair of their heads shall be injured.' This we have determined, and, if you try to fight, our soldiers will shoot you down."

This being interpreted, the Comanches instantly, with one accord raised a terrific war-whoop, drew their arrows, and commenced firing with deadly effect, at the same time making efforts to break out of the Council Hall. The order "fire" was given by Captain Howard, and the soldiers fired into the midst of the crowd, the first volley killing several Indians and two of our own people. All soon rushed out to the public square, the civilians to procure arms, the Indians to flee, and the soldiers in pursuit. The Indians generally made for the river—they ran up Soledad, east on Commerce Street and for the bend, now known as Bowen's, southeast, below the square. Citizens and soldiers pursued and overtook them at all points, shot some swimming in the river, had desperate fights in the streets—and hand to hand encounters after firearms had been exhausted. Some Indians took refuge in stone houses and fastened the doors. Not one of the sixty-five Indians escaped—thirty-three were killed and thirty-two were taken prisoner. Six Ameri-

cans and one Mexican were killed and ten Americans wounded. Our
killed were Julian Hood, the sheriff, Judge Thompson, advocate from
South Carolina, G. W. Cayce from the Brazos, one officer and two
soldiers whose names I did not learn, nor that of the Mexican. The
wounded were Lieutenant Thompson, brother of the Judge, Captain
Tom Gonzales, Judge Robinson, Mr. Morgan, deputy sheriff, Mr. Higginbotham and two soldiers. Others were slightly wounded.

When the deafening war-whoop sounded in the courtroom, it was
so loud, so shrill and so inexpressibly horrible and suddenly raised,
that we women looking through the fence at the women's and boy's
marksmanship for a moment could not comprehend its purport. The
Indians however knew the first note and instantly shot their arrows
into the bodies of Judge Thompson and the other gentlemen near by,
instantly killing Judge Thompson. We fled into Mrs. Higginbotham's
house and I, across the street to my Commerce Street door. Two Indians ran past me on the street and one reached my door as I got in. He
turned to raise his hand to push it just as I beat down the heavy bar;
then he ran on. I ran in the north room and saw my husband and
brother Andrew sitting calmly at a table inspecting some plats of sur-
veys—they had heard nothing. I soon gave them the alarm, and hurried on to look for my boys. Mr. Maverick and Andrew seized their
arms, always ready—Mr. Maverick rushed into the street, and Andrew into the backyard where I was shouting at the top of my voice
"Here are Indians! Here are Indians!" Three Indians had gotten in
through the gate on Soledad Street and were making direct for the
river! One had paused near Jinny Anderson, our cook, who stood
bravely in front of the children, mine and hers, with a great rock lifted
in both hands above her head, and I heard her cry out to the Indian,
"If you don't go 'way from here I'll mash your head with this rock!" The
Indian seemed regretful that he hadn't time to dispatch Jinny and her
brood, but his time was short, and pausing but a moment, he dashed
down the bank into the river and struck out for the opposite shore.

As the Indian hurried down the bank and into the river Andrew
shot and killed him, and shot another as he gained and rose up on the
opposite bank,—then he ran off up Soledad Street looking for more
Indians.

I housed my little ones, and then looked out of the Soledad Street
door. Near by was stretched an Indian, wounded and dying. A large

man, journey-apprentice to Mr. Higginbotham, came up just then and aimed a pistol at the Indian's head. I called out: "Oh, don't he is dying," and the big American laughed and said: "To please you, I won't, but it would put him out of his misery." Then I saw two others lying dead near by.

Captain Lysander Wells, about this time, passed by riding north on Soledad Street. He was elegantly dressed and mounted on a gaily caparisoned Mexican horse with silver mounted saddle and bridle— which outfit he had secured to take back to his native state, on a visit to his mother. As he reached the Verimendi House, an Indian who had escaped detection, sprang up behind him, clasped Wells' arms in his and tried to catch hold of the bridle reins. Wells was fearless and active. They struggled for some time, bent back and forward, swayed from side to side, till at last Wells held the Indian's wrists with his left hand, drew his pistol from the holster, partly turned, and fired into the Indian's body—a moment more and the Indian rolled off and dropped dead to the ground. Wells then put spurs to his horse which had stood almost still during the struggle, dashed up the street and did good service in the pursuit. I had become so fascinated by this struggle that I had gone into the street almost breathless, and wholly unconscious of where I was, till recalled by the voice of Lieutenant Chavallier who said: "Are you crazy? Go in or you will be killed." I went in but without feeling any fear, though the street was almost deserted and my husband and brother both gone in the fight. I then looked out on Commerce Street and saw four or five dead Indians. I was just twenty-two then, and was endowed with a fair share of curiosity.

Not till dark did our men get back, and I was grateful to God, indeed, to see my husband and brother back alive and not wounded.

Captain Mat Caldwell, or "Old Paint," as he was familiarly called, our guest from Gonzales, was an old and famous Indian fighter. He had gone from our house to the Council Hall unarmed. But when the fight began, he wrenched a gun from an Indian and killed him with it, and beat another to death with the butt end of the gun. He was shot through the right leg, wounded as he thought by the first volley of the soldiers. After breaking the gun, he then fought with rocks, with his back to the Court House wall.

Young G. W. Cayce had called on us that morning, bringing an introductory letter from his father to Mr. Maverick, and placing some papers in his charge. He was a very pleasant and handsome young man and it was reported, came to marry Gertrude Navarro, Mrs. Dr. Allsbury's sister. He left our house when I did, I going to Mrs. Higginbotham's and he to the Council Hall. He stood in the front door of the Court House and was instantly killed at the beginning of the fight, and fell by the side of Captain Caldwell. The brother of this young man afterwards told me he had left home with premonition of his death being very near. Captain Caldwell was assisted back to our house and Dr. Weideman came and cut off his boot and found the bullet had gone entirely through the leg, and lodged in the boot, where it was discovered. The wound, although not dangerous, was very painful, but the doughty captain recovered rapidly and in a few days walked about with the aid of a stick.

After the captain had been cared for, I ran across to Mrs. Higginbotham's. Mr. Higginbotham, who was as peaceful as a Quaker to all appearances, had been in the fight and received a slight wound. They could not go into their back yard, because two Indians had taken refuge in their kitchen, and refused to come out or surrender as prisoners when the interpreter had summoned them. A number of young men took counsel together that night, and agreed upon a plan. Anton Lockmar and another got on the roof, and, about two hours after midnight dropped a candlewick ball soaked in turpentine, and blazing, through a hole in the roof upon one Indian's head and so hurt him and frightened them both that they opened the door and rushed out—to their death. An axe split open the head of one of the Indians before he was well out of the door, and the other was killed before he had gone many steps— thus the last of the sixty-five were taken. The Indian women dressed and fought like the men, and could not be told apart. As I have said thirty-three were killed and thirty-two were taken prisoner. Many of them were repeatedly summoned to surrender, but numbers refused and were killed. All had a chance to surrender, and every one who offered or agreed to give up was taken prisoner and protected.

What a day of horrors! And the night was as bad which followed.

Lieutenant Thompson, who had been shot through the lungs, was taken to Madam Santita's house, on Soledad Street, just opposite us, and that night he vomited blood and cried and groaned all night—I shall never forget his gasping for breath and his agonizing cries. Dr. Weideman sat by and watched him, or only left to see the other sufferers, nearby; no one thought he would live till day, but he did, and got to be well and strong again, and in a few weeks walked out.

The captive Indians were all put in the calaboose for a few days and while they were there our forces entered into a twelve days truce with them—the captives acting for their Nation. And, in accordance with the stipulations of the treaty, one of the captives, an Indian woman, widow of a chief, was released on the 20th, the day after the fight. She was given a horse and provisions and sent to her Nation to tell her people of the fight and its result. She was charged to tell them, in accordance with the truce, to bring in all their captives, known to be fifteen Americans and several Mexicans, and exchange them for the thirty-two Indians held. She seemed eager to effect this, and promised to do her best. She said she would travel day and night, and could go and return within five days. The other prisoners thought she could in five days return with the captives from the tribe. The Americans said "Very well we give twelve days truce and if you do not get back by Thursday night of the 29th, these prisoners shall be killed, for we know you have killed our captive friends and relatives."

In April, as I shall mention again, we were informed by a boy, named B. L. Webster, that when the squaw reached her tribe and told of the disaster, all the Comanches howled, and cut themselves with knives, and killed horses, for several days. And they took all the American captives, thirteen in number, and roasted and butchered them to death with horrible cruelties; that he and a little girl named Putman, five years old, had been spared because they had previously been adopted into the tribe. Our people did not, however, retaliate upon the captives in our hands. The captive Indians were all put into the calaboose, corner of Market Street and the public square adjoining the courthouse, where all the people in San Antonio went to see them. The Indians expected to be killed, and they did not understand nor trust the kindness which was shown them and the great pity manifested toward them. They were first removed to San Jose Mission, where a company of soldiers was stationed, and afterwards taken to Camp "Cook," named after W. G. Cook, at the head of the river, and strictly guarded for a time. But afterwards the strictness was relaxed, and they gradually all, except for a few, who were exchanged, escaped and returned to their tribe. They were kindly treated and two or three of them were taken into families as domestics, and were taught some little, but they too, at last, silently stole away to their ancient freedom. . . .

We now began to have a society and great sociability amongst ourselves, the Americans. During the summer 1841, Mr. Wilson Riddle brought out his bride, and Mr. Moore his family. These gentlemen were both merchants on Commerce Street. Mr. Campbell married a second wife with whom and her sister, Miss O'Neill, he returned to San Antonio. Mr. Davis opened a store on Commerce Street. Mr. John Twobig started a small grocery store on corner of Commerce Street and Plaza Mayor.

Mrs. Jacques had a boarding house at [the] southwest corner of Commerce and Yturri—she had a whole block from Yturri and boarded all the nice young Americans, and was very hospitable and pleasant. She was a good nurse and extremely kind to any sick or wounded, and consequently a great favorite with the gentlemen. On Easter Sunday of this year, she invited all the American families, and many young gentlemen to dine with her. She served dinner at the long room, (sagnan). Her dinner was simply elegant, the company large and lively and we all enjoyed the day very much. In the afternoon we promenaded up Soledad Street in a gay and happy throng.

Easter Monday, April 12th, 1841, Agatha, our first daughter was born and named for my mother. She was a very beautiful and good baby.

My mother talked of coming out to visit us. Her idea was that she would come to some port on the coast, and we would go down at the appointed time and meet her there. But I had too many babies to make such a journey, and the risk from Indians was too great, and we did not encourage the plan. Her letters were one month to six weeks old when we received them.

President Lamar with a very considerable suite visited San Antonio in June. A grand ball was given him in Mrs. Yturri's long room— (all considerable houses had a long room for receptions). The room was decorated with flags and evergreens; flowers were not much cultivated then. At the ball, General Lamar wore very wide white pants which at the same time were short enough to show the tops of his shoes. General Lamar and Mrs. Juan N. Seguin, wife of the Mayor, opened the ball with a waltz. Mrs. Seguin was so fat that the General had great difficulty in getting a firm hold on her waist, and they cut such a figure that we were forced to smile. The General was a poet, a polite and brave gentleman and first rate conversationalist—but he did not dance well.

At the ball, Hays, Chevalier, and John Howard had but one dress coat between them, and they agreed to use the coat and dance in turn. The two not dancing would stand at the hall door watching the happy one who was enjoying his turn—and they reminded him when it was time for him to step out of that coat. Great fun it was watching them and listening to their wit and mischief as they made faces and shook their fists at the dancing one.

John D. Morris, the Adonis of the company, escorted Miss Arceneiga who on that warm evening wore a maroon cashmere with black plumes in her hair, and her haughty airs did not gain her any friends. Mrs. Yturri had a new silk, fitting her so tightly that she had to wear corsets for the first time in her life. She was very pretty, waltzed beautifully and was much sought after as a partner. She was several times compelled to escape to her bedroom to take off the corset and "catch her breath" as she said to me who happened to be there with my baby.

By the way, speaking of Mrs. Yturri, I am reminded of a party I gave several months before this. It blew a freezing norther that day and we had the excellent luck of making some ice cream, which was a grateful surprise to our guests. In fact those of the Mexicans present, who had never travelled, tasted ice cream that evening for the first time in their lives, and they all admired and liked it. But Mrs. Yturri ate so much of it, tho' advised not to, that she was taken with cramps. Mrs. Jacques and I took her to my room and gave her brandy, but in vain, and she had to be carried home. At that party some natives remained so late in the morning that we had to ask them to go. One man of reputable standing carried off a roast chicken in his pocket, another a carving knife, and several others took off all the cake they could well conceal, which greatly disgusted Jinny Anderson, the cook. Griffin followed the man with the carving knife and took it away from him.

During this summer, the American ladies led a lazy life of ease. We had plenty of books, including novels, we were all young, healthy and happy and were content with each others' society. We fell into the fashion of the climate, dined at twelve, then followed a siesta, (nap) until three, when we took a cup of coffee and a bath.

Bathing in the river at our place had become rather public, now that merchants were establishing themselves on Commerce Street, so we ladies got permission of old Madame Tevino, mother of Mrs. Lockmar, to put up a bath house on her premises, some distance up the river on Soledad Street, afterwards the property and homestead of the Jacques family. Here between two trees in a beautiful shade, we went in a crowd each afternoon at about four o'clock and took the children and nurses and a nice lunch which we enjoyed after the bath. There we had a grand good time, swimming and laughing, and making all the noise we pleased. The children were bathed and after all were dressed, we spread our lunch and enjoyed it immensely. The ladies took turns in preparing the lunch and my aunt Mrs. Bradley took the lead in nice things. Then we had a grand and glorious gossip, for we were all dear friends and each one told the news from our far away homes in the "States," nor did we omit to review the happenings in San Antonio. We joked and laughed away the time, for we were free from care and happy. In those days there were no envyings, no backbiting.

*   *   *

The happy summer of 1841 was merely a lull. The next year persistent rumors of a new invasion by Mexico caused the Mavericks and many other families to flee San Antonio. The Mavericks moved in with friends in La Grange, Texas. In August, 1842, Samuel returned to San Antonio for the fall session of court, and Mary states: "Alas! too surely and swiftly came a terrible sorrow."

San Antonio was captured by a large Mexican force, and Samuel was among those captured and marched to a prison in Mexico. After seven months he was released, and he returned to his family in May, 1843. The family moved to Decrow's Point on Matagorda Peninsula, where they resided for three years before returning to San Antonio.

In a chapter entitled "The Angel of Death," Mary describes the sorrowful time between April, 1848, and April, 1849, when two of the Mavericks' daughters died from disease. Two other children died soon after birth, and one of their sons died in his twenties. In 1870 Mary's beloved husband died. Among his possessions Mary was surprised to find a piece of the green dress which she had worn when they had first met.

In spite of war, sickness, and death, Mary Ann Adams Maverick was undefeated. The last paragraph in her *Memoirs* shows her indomitable spirit: "Since the death of my beloved husband, not a death has occurred in our family. My five remaining children have married happily, and I am now the mother of ten children again. If Mr. Maverick were here to look in upon us today, he would be gratified at the good will, the good health and the good fortune which have come and remained with us during the ten years past. I am thankful that God has spared me this long, to see my descendants all happy and prosperous—and I hope it will be many years before the pleasant scene I am contemplating shall be marred by misfortune or the hand of death."

III. Texas Tears, 1846—69

The period from 1846 to 1869 was a time of both happiness and sorrow for Texas women. They rejoiced when Texas became a state in 1845, but their joy was short-lived as they watched their sons, husbands, brothers, and sweethearts ride away into the battlefields of the Civil War.

Those left behind faced many problems. In some areas the frontier was pushed back a hundred miles as the Indians began to reappear, robbing and killing wherever they could. Also, vigilante groups roamed through the Hill Country, hounding and murdering German immigrants who refused to enlist.

Many of those at home suffered from lack of food, clothing, and medical supplies. One anonymous Texas woman who lived through the war describes how the women managed to survive: "The old fashioned spinning wheel, loom, and knitting needles were brought into requisition by our noble women, who worked busily through the days of the storm that was the war, and far into the night, to supply the soldiers at the front and the dependent members of the family at home with needed clothing . . . the greater part of what was needed was obtained by our own invention. For medicines, in many instances, we used barks, roots, and herbs, as the Indians do. For soda, we burned corncobs and used the ashes. For coffee, there were various substitutes, such as parched sweet potatoes, rye and okra-beans. Dry goods were not to be had, except in very small quantities, and at fabulous prices. Calico of the best quality cost fifty dollars a yard, Confederate money."

During the war Rebecca Bass Adams was left in charge of not only her family but also a plantation and fifty slaves. Her letters to her husband reveal her efforts to care for all of those people and the feelings of desperation which she at times experienced.

Although Texas was not laid to waste, as were other parts of the South, the war did cause great changes in the state. For one thing, the slaves were freed. Amelia Barr vividly describes the reaction of her servant when she learned that she was free. Too, the Texans were faced with the injustices of Reconstruction. Eudora Moore describes the indignities that she and her family suffered after the war.

Some Texas women were faced with the most terrible scourge of all, epidemic disease. Mathilda Wagner describes a cholera epidemic in San Antonio. Amelia Barr survived the yellow fever epidemic of 1867 in which her husband and two sons died horrible deaths. A son born to Amelia shortly after the epidemic also died.

Through deprivation, war, sickness, and death Mathilda Wagner, Silvia King, Rebecca Bass, Eudora Moore, and Amelia Barr cared for their families, taught the younger generation—and survived.

Mathilda Doebbler Gruen Wagner

"It was not long before I too was sent away."

"Unto all my children I want to say that I love each and every one the same. Each one's happiness has been my happiness. Each one's sorrow and burden I have felt, ever the same. Not one is dearer than the others and I say with all my heart, stay close together always and love each other, for after all, in looking back over a long, long lifetime I know that is the greatest thing in life." Thus ends the life story of Mathilda Doebbler Gruen Wagner, which was edited by her granddaughter Winifred Cade and published under the title *I Think Back*. It was reprinted in *The Golden Free Land* by Crystal Ragsdale. Mathilda's memoirs were a wonderful gift to give to her children and to others interested in life in early Texas. Mathilda's thoughts were always with her children, to whom she had devoted her life. Their happy childhoods with a loving mother contrasted sharply with Mathilda's youth.

Mathilda begins her memoirs with a description of the situation in the German states in 1848 which caused so many German people to emigrate. Mathilda's father was involved in one of the German revolutionary movements and had to flee the country, leaving a wife and four children. Since many Germans had already settled in Texas, he decided to go to Texas. After working for several years as a stonemason, he was granted a homestead near Fredericksburg. He sent for his wife and their children. Soon after their arrival, the first of many disasters struck.

*　　*　　*

Just a few weeks after my mother got here with the four children, my little brother, Louie, drowned in the mill dam stream. The old mill dam was there many, many years, but it is gone now.

My father built a two-room house on the farm. It had a room in

Reprinted with permission of Winifred S. Cade and Crystal S. Ragsdale, from Winifred Cade, ed., *I Think Back: Being the Memoirs of Grandma Gruen* (San Antonio: privately printed, 1937). Reprinted in Crystal Sasse Ragsdale, ed., *The Golden Free Land* (Austin: Landmark Press, 1976).

which the family slept and the kitchen in which the family ate and cooked. The majority of the houses, even in towns, had this arrangement. My mother, however, spent little time on the farm, but lived most of the time in Fredericksburg. She worked and sewed there. She made beautiful caps and was a neat, fine housekeeper. She did everything well. When I grew up the people who knew her told me that she was a wonderful woman. My mother must have come over to America sometime in 1854. My sister, Laura, was born in Fredericksburg in 1855, and I was born in the same house on August 29, 1856. While I was still a little girl, little Amelia, the last baby, was born. Not long after her birth our mother died. She had had a bad spell of nose-bleed and after it was over she lay down to rest. It was thought a fly infected her irritated nostril and she died a terrible death a little later. She suffered a great deal with an infection of her nose and what would now be called sinus. I do not remember her much. I was very small.

My little sister, Amelia, was adopted, that is, she was taken into the home of a family named Goff, because, of course, my father couldn't take care of all of us. I was just a little girl then and Laura was small, too. When little Amelia was about a year old she climbed upon the kitchen table. In those days there were no screens and flies were very bad. The Goffs had some fly poison mixed with sugar on the kitchen table. The little Amelia, after she had climbed upon the table, ate some of the poison before she was discovered. She died in a short while, in convulsions. When I think back, I remember that the little pine coffin, which the family made themselves, was placed on the wagon used for hauling stones, a wagon built low and with no sides, drawn by oxen. I was put upon it too, as I was so little I couldn't walk much. There was no other wagon or vehicle to use, either for the coffin or for the people. Back of the wagon all the friends of the family walked with my father and the other children. The wagon moved very slowly and everyone walked the distance to the cemetery. The old graveyard is there yet. This is one of the earliest things I remember. My memory does not begin with happy things.

My mother was not old when she died. Her name was Mathilda, too; I was named after her. When she died, we were adopted by other people. The truth is the people merely took us to do all the work we could. There were no papers drawn. There was no orphanage in Fredericksburg, although there was one at New Braunfels at that time. It was established after a terrible epidemic had caused the death of hundreds of settlers. As the settlements were small that was a large percentage and many orphans were left without either parent. The epidemic was not as severe in Fredericksburg and the little orphans were spread out as we were, I suppose. Poor Laura was sent to Mason to work for someone. Clara and Nellie drifted off from one family to another and nobody knew for a long time where they were. I was taken by some people in Fredericksburg named Hertzberg.

At one place where Sister Nellie worked after our mother died her hand was crushed in the sugar press. The people in those days couldn't get a doctor for everything. Although there was a doctor in the little town his fees were high and medicine was hard to get. The settlers didn't pay much attention to such things like crushed fingers. Someone wrapped her hand, leaving all of the fingers together and they healed that way, together. They became little stumps that never grew, each finger joined together. When she grew up, even though she was very wealthy, nothing could be done about it. She always carried a handkerchief wrapped around it in a way that it would not be noticed. She never let anyone see it if she could keep from it.

I remember a few things in Fredericksburg before my mother died, but very few. There was an old church in which I and all of the children, except Otto, were christened. It was the first church in Fredericksburg and was like an old coffee mill. It was torn down just before 1896 but a new church never looked right and Fredericksburg built the old one up again. I don't know if it was built in exactly the same place, for the old one was right in the middle of the street. It had just one wall and was made of wood. When I was very little we had to go to church every Sunday. Almost everyone who was well went Sunday morning, young and old. People were more religious then than now. After I married and as long as Grandpa Gruen lived, we went to church every Sunday. Grandpa Gruen thought it was terrible if people did not go to church if they were well enough to get there. . . .

The Indians often came to Fredericksburg to trade their beads and pecans they gathered, or whatever they had made for things the settlers had. They would sometimes trade a big sack of pecans for a handful of salt or tobacco. As the church was just next to the market square they were often around it. I remember we often picked up many beads around the church and made rings and necklaces for ourselves out of them. The beads were very beautiful. They were bright and gay. How the Indians made them I do not know.

Looking for beads around the old church, I found the earring of the sister of the man who later became my daughter's husband. It was a very nice gold earring. Someone knew that she had lost it and when I found it they told me who it probably belonged to. It was Clara Siemering's. I was happy that I found it and took it to her. She said, "Oh, you sweet little girl," and kissed me.

The Indians were friendly and helpful until the settlers started driving them out as though they were cattle. Then they became mean and would steal and sometimes kill. I remember one old man was going after the oxen, which were staked out to feed. All he had was his lunch tied on a stick. The Indians fell upon him and he thought he was at the end of his days, but they took only his lunch and didn't harm him. Often, though, they did terrible things. One time two young girls going to school were attacked by the Indians. The Indians scalped them and cut off their breasts. The whole town was aroused against the Indians then.

My father must have married again soon after my mother died, for I was still quite small. After his marriage he gathered all of his children together again, except Clara and Nellie, who were away some place working for people. My step-mother was very mean. She had two children by a former marriage when she married my father. She was mean to them, too, although at times she could be nice to her own children. I had to work hard, even though I was so little. Very little schooling we had, very little. My father's farm was near the little settlement of Grape Creek and there was no school there. School was sometimes held in the church in Fredericksburg but we didn't get to go there, for it was too far as we traveled in those days.

When I was still a little girl, after my father married again, my father called me one day. As I ran to him he said, "Get me a cool drink of water." We had a spring at the back of the house, at the foot of a hill. The water was always nice and cool. In a field across the creek a horse was tied out on the hill. When I went to the spring to get the water, I saw an Indian trying to steal the horse. The horse was rearing up on his hind legs trying to fight off the Indian. I screamed, "The Indians! The Indians!"

The houses in those early days were all built on the corners of the farms, where a number of farms came together. This was done so that the houses wouldn't be so far apart and so that each neighbor could hear signals from the others and in this way have a little protection from the Indians. Every house had a horn made from a cow's horn, and when the other settlers heard it blow, they knew there were Indians around. My father blew the horn and the neighbors came running with their guns. At that time Father was established and doing well. He had a team of mules and a driver, which he sent out on trips, hauling things here and there, sometimes a great distance, as distance was figured then. It was on the order of a freight line. At this time when I saw the Indian, the mules were out in the front of the house eating grass. The Indians were getting up a raid to steal all the horses and mules, but when the alarm was given the horses and other stock were rounded up everywhere around us and nothing was stolen. This was right around the time of the Civil War.

I remember how the people who sympathized with the North during the Civil War had to hide out and sleep in the bushes at night to prevent being killed. There were those who were bitter against Northern sympathizers. There were a large majority of Germans around Fredericksburg who felt the cause of the North was the right cause. A band of men, mostly hard, bad characters, called guerillas, murdered many people. One man who was murdered I knew well. He had a sick wife, who was going to be down soon with a baby. Each morning he would come out of hiding to get water from the spring for his wife and try to help her. The guerillas, or a group of men just as bad, learned of this and one morning they killed him just as he stooped at the spring to bring the water to his wife. It was just before their baby was born. It was a terrible time. My Uncle William believed the North was right in their stand and he wrote about it. Because of his feeling and his work, he was arrested and put in jail in San Antonio. When they took him off, his wife didn't know if she would ever see him again, but he escaped some way or another and went to Mexico. His wife, while he was gone, had to take care of all the children and herself alone. Laura remembers the time Mr. Louis Schuetze was killed. He was the school teacher. Sometimes he was the preacher, too. He was very prominent and influential. Just as Laura was leaving for school one morning news came that Mr. Schuetze had been murdered by the guerillas during the night. They had entered his house and taken him away. He was found that morning, murdered.

The people on these frontiers had no conveniences. Not even their houses were decent. The men had to make their own shingles. Around Comfort there were many nice trees that made fine shingles. I believe they were called cypress, *Presser* in German. The men cut the trees up in logs the length they wanted the shingles to be and then split them by hand. It took many days to make enough shingles for a house but the men made them good. The wood from these trees split easily and the shingles lasted much longer than they do now. The windows had no glass; there was no glass for such things on the frontier. They were made like doors, that is, the part that closed over them was like a door, made of lumber and swung on hinges. In good weather we opened them all. In cold or rainy weather it was of course dark in our rooms, for everything had to be closed.

The house my father made for us first had only two rooms, the kitchen and the room where we slept. There was no stove in the kitchen, only the chimney. We made bread and everything in the chimney fire. We used a Dutch oven to bake in and put it on the coals, with coals stacked on the top of it. The coffee pot was large and made of iron. Coffee was made for breakfast, dinner and supper and in between. We had to grind our own coffee, after we parched it ourselves. It came green. We always had plenty of meat, for there were many wild hogs, deer and wild turkeys. The hogs got fat on acorns, for there were many oak trees around there. Gradually, the settlers got tame hogs. We always had corn bread, for there wasn't much wheat flour. It was too hard to go as far as the people had to go to get it, and when it was brought in it was very expensive. Before large fields could be planted the trees and bushes had to be grubbed out. When the farmers had cleared a space, they used oxen to pull the plows. After the people had enough land in cultivation they planted wheat and had more wheat flour. The mill took so much flour, either wheat or corn, for grinding the grain. I remember the people usually had the flour put in a sheet before it was put in the barrels so that none would sift through the cracks, it was that precious. Flour sacks weren't used then, for it was hard to get enough cloth for clothes. When we traveled in those days oxen pulled the wagon. They went so slowly that my stepmother sat beside my father and knitted as we took the grain to Fredericksburg. The trip to the mill was quite an event. Because of our mode of travel, it was necessary to stay over night in Fredericksburg. The trip to the mill was a two-day job, although now the ones living on the old home place can make the trip in an hour easily. We stayed at Uncle William's house when we went to Fredericksburg and these layovers were always red letter days, for we always had a nice time there.

Father didn't have many acres that could be planted when I was real small. My father did every bit of the work of grubbing out the brush and trees, plowing the land with oxen and planting seed by hand, as well as cultivating afterwards. It was very hard work to get the land ready for the plow and in good condition, for it had never been worked before, but every year a little more land was added to the fields. We had nice gardens, however, and my father worked out a way of irrigating his. It was always close to the house and was usually taken care of by the women alone.

Getting supplies was always quite a problem, especially during the Civil War. Then we couldn't get coffee at all, and coffee was a big item in the German households. We felt terrible without it. We parched rye and wheat and used that. Some people used parched corn but it didn't taste like coffee. We made all of our own soap out of the fat of the wild hogs. We rendered the fat first for our lard and what was unfit for use as lard was made into soap. Father made an ash bin, funnel-shaped very much like a gigantic ice cream cone with a little hole at the bottom. It was hung outside and each morning when the ashes were cleaned out of the fireplace they were placed in this ash bin. There was an arrangement whereby water dripped into the top of the bin, slowly, drop by drop. As it seeped through the ashes it caused a reaction upon it, and, as the water and ashes came through the hole at the bottom of the bin, it was lye. We tested its strength by placing an egg upon the lye. If the egg floated it was strong enough, but if the egg sank we waited a while longer before using it for soap.

People who have never gone through it can't realize how these people who started the little Texas towns and made them grow had to starve and do.

We made clothes out of the kind of cloth that overalls are made of now. There were two widths in the skirt, a little waist and sleeves, that was all, and that was our dress. We had few dresses, maybe a calico dress for nice, but never more than one nice dress and one or two of the heavy dresses. Stockings were made from thread spun on wheels brought from Germany and knitted by us into stockings to fit. After I was married a good while we could buy thread. We did not know what it was to have shoes. All summer we went barefooted, part of the winter, too, especially if it was warm, as we had to save the shoes we had. I imagine we often wore shoes too small for us. Even the grown people went barefooted a great deal. Some of the settlers brought shoes with them. The people soled their own shoes. The raw hide was shipped from way off. In many homes the leather was cured by the settlers themselves. Every house had some tool or something to work on their own shoes. There were shoemakers in Fredericksburg but the shoes were very expensive.

The first doll I ever had my father cut out of wood. The arms were put on with wire. The hands were just little fists. There were no dolls to be bought in the country. We were very pleased with our wooden dolls and thought they were lovely. We also dressed corn cobs or wrapped a rag around them and played that they were dolls.

I was never happy as a small child. My stepmother saw to that. It is sad how all the little children who lost their mothers were scattered about; I guess ours wasn't the only family of children sent around as we were. Everyone had all the work they could do, and they didn't feel like taking on the burden of their brothers' and sisters' children. Maybe it was best that I had a stepmother, for I still lived with my real father, but my stepmother was never kind . . . she would sometimes knock the heads of her own children against the house.

In addition to my brothers and sister and the two children of my stepmother, there was, of course, a baby now and then. As the additional children came I helped care for them. I always had to take care of Alfred. He was my particular charge. I remember once when we were making sugar at Uncle Ferdinand's sugar press. I had to help cut the cane and carry it to the press and even though I had to do this I had to watch Alfred, too. For a long time he wouldn't walk, although he was two years old. He said he had a bone in his leg, but he was really too lazy to walk. This time he was running around, however. I was cutting cane, cutting it off with a butcher knife. As I swung the knife to cut a stalk of cane I didn't take the hand holding the cane away quickly enough and I cut my finger very deep. Every time I took a bundle of sugar cane to carry it to the press the blood would start again and it would hurt. Little Alfred was running around and ran over some of the coals from the fire under the molasses boiler. His feet were burned. There were lots of others standing around the press and the fire where the molasses was cooking but I was supposed to watch Alfred, cut the cane and carry it to the press, and get along as well as I could with my cut and hurting finger. When Alfred burned his feet my stepmother got awfully angry. I was coming to the press with an armful of cane when she picked up a stave and hit me with it. I remember the pain yet. She said I did not take care of Alfred. She would not give me anything to eat at the next meal. She was so mean and ugly.

One winter day, around noon, I was sent to the smoke house to cut a sausage off for dinner. The sausages were all tied together, one after the other. I had Alfred with me, of course. When I put him down on the floor and turned the other way to cut off the sausage, Alfred crawled to the door. The door was very heavy. Doors then weren't made out of thin, finished boards. They were sometimes made out of tree trunks, split in half. Alfred put his hands in the door as it slammed to. The hand was hurt and he cried terribly. My stepmother was very angry again. She made me go out in the fields and wouldn't give me a bite to eat. I was hungry and found a potato which had been left behind in the harvest. I dug it up with my bare hands, washed it in the stream and ate it. I also found something else which I ate, but it wasn't anything good. That was all I had until night. That night when I came home, for I was afraid not to come home, my father saw that I had been crying. "What's the matter with you?" he asked. I told him and said that I hadn't anything to eat all day but the raw potato I had dug up in the fields. He asked, "Do you know where the eggs are? Well, go get them." I knew where a nest was so I ran out and found some eggs. My father put them in a pan and was cooking them over the chimney fire when my stepmother came in. She took the pan, eggs and all, and threw it out the door. She said I could not have anything to eat. My father was quite angry, but he couldn't manage that woman.

He said to me, "Well, I have got to eat and you have to eat, too," so he took me, and we went to the old man Grutcher. He was a musician. "Can we get a little bite to eat here?" my father asked, and told Mr. Grutcher how my stepmother treated me. He fixed us a nice supper. After we were through, he said, "You can sleep here," but my father answered, "No. We are going home. If she throws us out we will come back." She must have felt better or something, for she didn't throw us out when we got home.

Sometime we had company, but we children never got any of the supper for the company. Laura and I might have a little rice or mush made out of bran or something like that. Sometime we didn't have anything, at least not enough.

One time we had company Laura and I were sent to bed. Laura said, "If they go to sleep we will get up and get us something to eat." Next morning when we awakened, I said, "What did we get to eat?" Then we remembered. We didn't get anything, for we had fallen asleep.

The company we had had that night were some people from Mason, Texas, who had come to see about taking Laura to live with them and work for them. The next day they took poor Laura away. She never came back home, but lived and married in Mason and is now one of its older citizens. Her husband was very good to her and they lived happily. He did well and they acquired property and a big family. Their home was very nice.

It was not long before, I, too, was sent away. . . .

Arrangements were made for me to stay with a family by the name of Longraper in San Antonio. My father sent me on the stage all alone. I was just about nine years old, maybe only eight. I cried all the way to San Antonio. Of course, my stepmother was mean and ugly, but I didn't know where in the world I was going. I felt very lost and alone. Longraper worked in a hardware store on Main Avenue. Their house was on South Street. It had only two rooms. There was no floor, just the dirt of the earth, packed by much walking upon it. A double chimney was used in cooking and for warmth. In the kitchen they also had an iron grate, with three feet, something like women use now for the wash boiler. It was used for cooking at times and held two or three pots. Wood was used for fuel and the fire was built on the floor. The house itself was made of adobe and rock. There are still many houses of this type on North and South streets. Probably the one in which the Longrapers lived is there yet. The Longrapers had a cow which gave a lot of milk, but I don't remember if they made any butter. They probably did and sold it all, for butter was very high. I don't think I had any to eat. All the time I had to work. I helped with the housework and did

Main Plaza, San Antonio, 1870's. While yet a child, Mathilda Doebbler was sent to San Antonio to live with and work for a family there. (*Courtesy San Antonio Conservation Society Foundation, Raba Collection*)

errands for everybody. I made many a trip from South Street to Main Avenue. I did whatever I could. She was never nice and kind to me, Mrs. Longraper. I never had a home since the time my mother died, not one worthy of the name Home, but nevertheless I got homesick for even the kind I had known.

I was sent to school by the Longrapers. The school was located where the Arsenal is now. A German man had a store underneath and a school upstairs. There was only one bridge across the river on Commerce Street at this time. It was set on barrels with boards nailed across. I always hated to cross this bridge. I crawled across it in rainy weather, holding on tight on each side. At other times I always stayed right in the middle. The boards were about four feet wide. Wagons and horses crossed the river at shallow fords. One morning while I was on my way to school I met two little Mexican children near this bridge. A fish had gotten caught in a place where water was seeping from an irrigation ditch back into the river. There were irrigation ditches all over the town. The Mexican children were trying to catch the fish with their hands, but it always slipped through their fingers. I caught it by its tail and gave it to them. They were quite pleased, and I was glad that I could do something to make someone happy. I went on to school.

The old German schoolmaster was rather mean and strict. He would often spank the children. Only German was taught at the school. We studied reading, writing, spelling and arithmetic. The fee for my schooling was a dollar a month. The schoolmaster had a large number of pupils. One was a little orphan girl who worked for the teacher's wife. She wasn't very neat and didn't know how to take care of her clothes nor how to keep them dry when she washed clothes. Sometimes her dress was very dirty. She had even less clothes than I. Often she would have to leave the school room to go down to help the teacher's wife. We sat together, because we were both orphans. I tried hard to keep my clothes clean for I had only two dresses most of the time, the one which I wore to school and for nice and the one in which I worked. I always changed my dress as soon as I got home from school. Sometimes Mrs. Longraper was nice and would let me change my dress in the middle of the week. People for whom I did errands would sometime give me something, now and then a piece of material for a dress, so occasionally I had more than two dresses.

I made my communion in the old Rooster Church. It was St.

John's Lutheran but was called Rooster Church after a rooster was placed on the tower as a weather vane. The church was on the corner of Presa and Nueva, not far from the Longraper's home. I went to church every Sunday. Almost everybody went to church every Sunday then, that is, almost all of the people who lived around South Street. After I came home from church there wasn't much to do on Sunday, but I couldn't go out and play with the other children, as the children do now. When I got home, I had to do what work there was to be done and then just sit still.

The cholera hit San Antonio just a little while after I came here. The people died by the scores. The carts came to the doors early in the morning or late at night, sometimes with lanterns to light the way. The men in the carts would ask, "Any dead here?" Sometime, when a poor fellow was dying, they would sit by the wagon and wait so they might take his body away at once. The people wrapped their dead in sheets, often the sheet upon which they died. They were carted away in loaded carts and buried in long trenches. It was impossible to have separate graves or even coffins, for there were too many dying at the same time. The public officials had something poured around the house and did all they could think of that might stop the epidemic but very little was known about it.

One store owner on Alamo Street opened a whiskey barrel and put a tin cup on a string for anyone who wanted to drink. It was thought that maybe whiskey might prevent cholera. There was a bucket of water there, too, for the people who wanted to wash the cup to do so. This may not have helped prevent cholera; it may have helped to spread it, but no doubt it gave many a man a little more courage. Some people who saw they were taking the cholera died at once from fright. Victims took sick, vomited and started with diarrhea and in a few hours were dead. As soon as they were dead they were taken away, just hauled away. The graveyards filled in a hurry and many, many little orphans were made. There were few houses where death didn't come.

Commerce Street at this time was the only street that was built up. Market Street was also one of the main streets. There were a few houses on Alamo Street. On Commerce Street there were many little Mexican shacks which were built with a door and no windows. The Mexicans living in them had no furniture and in winter would squat around a fire on the floor, built as a camp fire is built. At night they would roll up in their blanket and sleep on the dirt floor. The inside of those huts were always dark, smoky and dirty.

While I stayed with the Longrapers I had to go to New Braunfels each summer to pick cotton. I had to bring every nickel I made home to Mrs. Longraper. The people for whom we were picking cotton fed us at noon, one thick piece of corn bread and a glass of buttermilk. We got twenty-five cents for one hundred pounds of cotton. Sometimes I didn't have a quilt to lie on at night, just the bare floor and a little pillow. The children have a heaven on earth now and they run the streets. When I was a child in New Braunfels, I do not know how many miles I had to walk to the fields each morning and back each night. I slept at the home of the brother of Mrs. Longraper.

When I was older, I was hired out to work for people. One of the first places I worked was for the mayor's wife. She was a very mean woman. She had all kinds of pots and pans hanging in rows in the kitchen, with lots of pewter things. Every Saturday I had to rub them first with wet ashes and then wash them off and rub them again with dry ashes. Then they were put in the sun for a while. Next I had to rub them again and if they didn't shine, I had to do it all over again. The woman had some mockingbirds in cages. The mockingbirds liked bores from the trees and when I had nothing else to do I had to split the bark from the trees and gather bores for the birds. The birds got much better care and attention than I did. If I didn't have anything else to do and the birds had all the bores they wanted, I had to wash the leaves of the oleander bushes. She had lots of them planted in pots standing around the yard. I had to wash them leaf by leaf.

I had typhoid fever at this place. My long, beautiful hair had to be cut off. I always had long, thick hair. Once someone who thought it was pretty gave me a hair ribbon, a red ribbon. I tied it in my hair. The mayor's wife, when she saw it, snatched it out and said I didn't have any business wearing anything like that, that it wasn't for poor people. One of the things I had to do while working at this place was to each night take a sack and a bucket of water to the mayor's room and leave it for him. Every night he took a sponge bath. There were no bath tubs. He stood on the sack, I suppose, so that it would catch the water. One night I forgot it and after I was asleep, the mayor's wife came and told me I had forgotten to bring it to his room. I trembled to hear her voice.

How far a few kind words would have gone. I didn't hear many of them. Not even the mayor was kind.

I couldn't spend a nickel of the money I earned for candy or something I would have liked, for I had to bring every cent to Mrs. Longraper. I couldn't play. I never had anything at Christmas time. If they gave me a little bag of candy or a handful of nuts that was all. I remember I was given a big red apple for Christmas one year, and I thought it so beautiful that I put it in my trunk with my clothes to make them smell good and now and then I would take it out and smell it, but I thought too much of it to eat it. When the lady who had given it to me asked once, "Did you eat your apple?" I told her I was saving it, but I went to see it and it had rotted.

I will never forget when I was a little girl and had such mean treatment. It wouldn't be allowed nowadays, treating children like I was treated. My family was a good family but my mother being dead my father didn't know how to manage. He was never overly good to my mother; she had to work very hard and had a hard life. His second wife bossed him and though he called her *"alt Pfeffer Schurze"* [old pepper apron] because her apron was always dirty, and sometimes *"alt Teufel"* [old devil], he was really afraid of her. She worked in the fields, too, and worked hard. All women did in those days. Probably my father sent his little children away so if they had to suffer he would not see it.

At any rate, my years in San Antonio were hard, lonesome years. It seems to me that I stayed there a long time, working and longing all the time. As I think back, there is one little incident which I remember very clearly. There was a spell of rainy weather. It had rained day after day until the river was up and all the irrigation ditches were running over. One night a group of people came to the mayor's house to say two little Mexican children were lost. A party was organized to search for them. The search went on all night and toward morning they were found in an irrigation ditch, one dead and the other hardly living. Whether or not it survived I cannot tell, but I wondered, no doubt, whether a search would have been made for me.

*   *   *

This tragic story of a motherless child has a happy ending. When Mathilda was fourteen, her father sent for her, and she returned to her family. She met Fredrick William Gruen, who was thirteen years older than she, and they were married in 1872, when she was only fifteen. She says of him, "Fredrick stuttered a little, and he wasn't very pretty; it wasn't love with me at first, but I will tell you the honest truth, I thought I'd have a home."

The Gruens fared well at first. Fredrick hauled freight from the coast, and after several years, they received 320 acres for their homestead. Mathilda was happy, but her life was very hard. She describes a typical day.

*   *   *

This was a little of my day. When you first get up in the morning, before daybreak, you start your fire in the wood stove or the chimney and put your coffee on. Then, just as it is getting light over the hills, you go after the calves. When you bring back the calves, you milk the cows; then bring the calves to their mother cows. Leaving them for a while, you fix breakfast, which is a big meal. After breakfast, at a time when people are getting up in the cities nowadays, you skim the milk and make the butter, feed the dogs, cats and the hogs, the clabber, and turn the calves into their pasture and the cows in theirs. When the butter is made and the dishes washed, the house spic and span, you go to help in the fields. The woman leaves the little baby at the edge of the field with a quilt put above it so the sun won't harm it. When the baby cries the woman leaves the hoe or plow or her work in the field and goes to tend it or nurse it. There was usually a little baby or several small children at a time. When the sun is in the middle of the sky it is time for dinner. The woman leaves for the house and prepares the food. After eating, the men might lay down for a little while to rest, but there is no rest for the women. There is always work to be done. In the afternoon there may be more work in the fields, or baking, candlemaking, soap-making, sewing, mending, any of the hundred pressing tasks, and then the calves must again be rounded up and brought home as the shadows fall, the cows milked, the chickens fed, always something, early and late.

*   *   *

The Gruens sold the farm and moved to Kerrville about 1890. They could find little work, so they took in boarders. Mathilda was pregnant, and all of the work fell on her because, as she says: "A German farmer is not one to help with the housework and the boarders required work that he felt was only woman's work."

Shortly after the Gruens moved to town, Fredrick accidentally killed himself when his gun went off shortly after a Fourth of July celebration. After struggling to make a living for many years in Kerrville, Mathilda took her six children who were still at home and moved to San Antonio. There she opened another boarding house, and her older children worked outside the home to help the family survive.

After a number of years, Mathilda married John Wagner and helped him rear his two boys. Mathilda had worked hard all her life. When she was eighty-one, she was still obsessed with working. She says, "Since I broke my hip I cannot get around so well but I can still piece quilts and I love to. When I am sick and lose a day or two I feel that I am way behind with my work and must make it up."

Mathilda Wagner had a miserable childhood, but she survived it to rear ten children. She worked hard all her life, but she was happy with her work and her children.

Silvia King

"De shoestring root am powerful strong."

During the years of 1936 through 1938 the Federal Writers' Project of the Works Projects Administration commissioned people in seventeen states to interview former slaves. Many of these interviews were printed in a nineteen-volume set of books entitled *The American Slave: A Composite Autobiography*. One of the former slaves who was interviewed was Silvia King. Her account of plantation life in Texas is one of the most detailed and interesting in the collection.

Silvia King was interviewed in Marlin, Texas. Although she did not know her age, she thought she was close to one hundred years old. The interviewer stated: "Silvia has the appearance of extreme age." Silvia begins her story in Africa, where she was abducted by slave traders, and ends her story in Marlin, Texas, in the mid-1930's, but the bulk of the narrative concerns plantation life in Texas, probably in the period between 1850 and 1870.

The WPA interviewers were instructed to record the interviews "as nearly word-for-word as is possible" and were given rudimentary instruction in recording dialect. The editor has reproduced the dialect exactly as it was printed in *The American Slave* in the interest of historical accuracy.

*   *   *

I know I was borned in Morocco, in Africa, and was married and had three chillen befo' I was stoled from my husband. I don't know who it was stole me, but dey took me to France, to a place called Bordeaux, and drugs me with some coffee, and when I knows anything 'bout it, I's in de bottom of a boat with a whole lot of other niggers. It seem like we was in dat boat forever, but we comes to land, and I's put

From George P. Rawick, ed., *The American Slave: A Composite Autobiography*, vol. IV (1941; reprint ed., Westport, Conn.: Greenwood Press, 1976).

on de block and sold. I finds out afterwards from my white folks it was in New Orleans where dat block was, but I didn't know it den.

We was all chained and dey strips all our clothes off and de folks what gwine buy us comes round and feels us all over. Iffen any de niggers don't want to take dere clothes off, de man gits a long, black whip and cuts dem up hard. I's sold to a planter what had a big plantation in Fayette County, right here in Texas, don't know no name 'cept Marse Jones.

Marse Jones, he am awful good, but de overseer was de meanest man I ever knowed, a white man name Smith, what boasts 'bout how many niggers he done kilt. When Marse Jones seed me on de block, he say, "Dat's a whale of a woman." I's scairt and can't say nothin', 'cause I can't speak English. He buys some more slaves and dey chains us together and marches us up near La Grange, in Texas. Marse Jones done gone ahead and de overseer marches us. Dat was a awful time, 'cause us am all chained up and whatever one does us all has to do. If one drinks out of de stream we all drinks, and when one gits tired or sick, de rest has to drag and carry him. When us git to Texas, Marse Jones raise de debbil with dat white man what had us on de march. He git de doctor man and tell de cook to feed us and lets us rest up.

After 'while, Marse Jones say to me, "Silvia, am you married?" I tells him I got a man and three chillen back in de old country, but he don't understand my talk and I has a man give to me. I don't bother with dat nigger's name much, he jes' Bob to me. But I fit [fought] him good and plenty till de overseer shakes a black-snake whip over me.

Marse Jones and Old Miss finds out 'bout my cookin' and takes me to de big house to cook for dem. De dishes and things was awful queer to me, to what I been brung up to use in France. I mostly cooks after dat, but I's de powerful big woman when I's young and when dey gits in a tight I helps out.

Fore long Marse Jones 'cides to move. He allus say he gwine git where he can't hear he neighbor's cowhorn, and he do. Dere ain't nothin' but woods and grass land, no houses, no roads, no bridges, no neighbors, nothin' but woods and wild animals. But he builds a mighty fine house with a stone chimney six foot square at de bottom. De sill was a foot square and de house am made of logs, but dey splits out two-inch plank and puts it outside de logs, from de ground clean up to de

This slave cabin, built in the 1850's, stands on the bank of the Brazos River near East Columbia, Texas. The chimney was a later addition. This cabin and several plantation houses in the area are owned and maintained by the First Capitol Historical Foundation.

eaves. Dere wasn't no nails, but dey whittles out pegs. Dere was a ell out de back and a well on de back porch by de kitchen door. It had a wheel and a rope. Dere was 'nother well by de barns and one or two round de quarters, but dey am fixed with a long, pole sweep. In de kitchen was de big fireplace and de big back logs am haul to de house. De oxen pull dem dat far and some men takes poles and rolls dem in de fireplace. Marse Jones never 'low dat fire go out from October to May, and in de fall Marse or one he sons light de fire with a flint rock and some powder.

De stores was a long way off and de white folks loans seed and things to each other. If we has de toothache, de blacksmith pulls it. My husband manages de ox teams. I cooks and works in Old Miss's garden and de orchard. It am big and fine and in fruit time all de women works from light to dark dryin' and 'servin' and de like.

Old Marse gwine feed you and see you quarters am dry and warm or know de reason why. Most ev'ry night he goes round de quarters to see if dere any sickness or trouble. Everybody work hard but have plenty to eat. Sometimes de preacher tell us how to git to hebben and see de ring lights dere.

De smokehouse am full of bacon sides and cure hams and barrels lard and 'lasses. When a nigger want to eat, he jes' ask and git he passel. Old Miss allus 'pend on me to spice de ham when it cure. I larnt dat back in de old country, in France.

Dere was spinnin' and weavin' cabins, long with a chimney in each end. Us women spins all de thread and weaves cloth for every-body, de white folks, too. I's de cook, but times I hit de spinnin' loom and wheel fairly good. Us bleach de cloth and dyes it with barks.

Dere allus de big woodpile in de yard, and de big, caboose kettle for renderin' hawg fat and beef tallow candles and makin' soap. Marse allus have de niggers take some apples and make cider, and he make beer, too. Most all us had cider and beer when we want it, but nobody git drunk. Marse sho' cut up if we do.

Old Miss have de floors sanded, dat where you sprinkles fine, white sand over de floor and sweeps it round in all kinds purty figgers. Us make a corn shuck broom.

Marse sho' a fool 'bout he hounds and have a mighty fine pack. De boys hunts wolves and painters [panthers] and wild game like dat. Dere was lots of wild turkey and droves of wild prairie chickens. Dere was rabbits and squirrels and Indian puddin', make of cornmeal. It am real tasty. I cooks goose and pork and mutton and bear meat and beef and deer meat, den makes de fritters and pies and dumplin's. Sho' wish us had dat food now.

On de cold winter night I's sot many a time spinnin' with two threads, one in each hand and one my feets on de wheel and de baby sleepin' on my lap. De boys and old men was allus whittlin' and it wasn't jes' foolishment. Dey whittle traps and wooden spoons and needles to make seine nets and checkers and sleds. We all sits workin' and singin' and smokin' pipes. I likes my pipe right now, and has two clay pipes and keeps dem under de pillow. I don't aim for dem pipes to git out of my sight. I been smokin' clost to a hunerd years now and it takes two cans tobaccy de week to keep me goin'.

Dere wasn't many doctors dem days, but allus de closet full of simples [home remedies] and most all de old women could git med'-cine out de woods. Ev'ry spring, Old Miss line up all de chillen and give dem a dose of garlic and rum.

De chillen all played together, black and white. De young ones purty handy trappin' quail and partridges and sech. Dey didn't shoot if dey could cotch it some other way, 'cause powder and lead am scarce. Dey cotch de deer by makin' de salt lick, and uses a spring pole to cotch pigeons and birds.

De black folks gits off down in de bottom and shouts and sings and prays. Dey gits in de ring dance. It am jes' a kind of shuffle, den it git faster and faster and dey gits warmed up and moans and shouts and claps and dances. Some gits 'xhausted and drops out and de ring gits closer. Sometimes dey sings and shouts all night, but come break of day, de nigger got to git to he cabin. Old Marse got to tell dem de tasks of de day.

Old black Tom have a li'l bottle and have spell roots and water in it and sulphur. He sho' could find out if a nigger gwine git whipped. He have a string tie round it and say, "By sum Peter, by sum Paul, by de Gawd dat make us all, jack don't you tell me no lie, if Marse gwine whip Mary, tell me." Sho's you born, if dat jack turn to de laft, de nigger git de whippin', but if Marse ain't makeup he mind to whip, dat jack stand and quiver.

You white folks jes' go through de woods and don't know nothin'. Iffen you digs out splinters from de north side a old pine tree what been struck by lightnin', and gits dem hot in a iron skillet and burns dem to ashes, den you puts dem in a brown paper sack. Iffen de officers gits you and you gwine have it 'fore de jedge, you gits de sack and goes outdoors at midnight and hold de bag of ashes in you hand and look up at de moon—but don't you open you mouth. Nex' mornin' git up early and go to de courthouse and sprinkle dem ashes in de doorway and dat law trouble, it gwine git tore up jes' like de lightnin' done tore up dat tree.

De shoestring root am powerful strong. Iffen you chews on it and spits a ring round de person what you wants somethin' from, you gwine git it. You can git more money or a job or most anythin' dat way. I had a black cat bone, too, but it got away from me.

I's got a big frame and used to weigh a [two] hunerd pounds but dey tells me I only weights a hunerd now. Dis Louis Southern I lives with, he's de youngest son of my grandson, who was de son of my youngest daughter. My marse, he knowed Gen. Houston and I seed him many a time. I lost what teeth I had a long time ago and in 1920 two more new teeth come through. Dem teeth sho' did worry me and I's glad when dey went, too.

Rebecca Ann Patillo Bass Adams

> "What shall I have done with the peach tree in the garden?"

Rebecca Ann Patillo Bass Adams started saving letters when she was a young girl in antebellum Georgia. Her girl friends would write to her about their parties and their beaux, and she would put the letters away in a trunk. After she married Robert Adams in 1845, he left her and their newborn baby with her parents while he attended medical school in Philadelphia. Rebecca saved the loving letters which he wrote, and they, too, went into the trunk. Rebecca's father bought Waldeck Plantation near Columbia, Texas, and the circle of correspondents expanded. Rebecca and Robert moved to East Texas, and more and more letters were written and deposited in a growing number of trunks.

The collection of letters was saved, and some of them were published in a book entitled *The Hicks-Adams-Bass-Floyd-Patillo and Collateral Lines, Together with Family Letters, 1840–1868.* These 260 letters from thirty correspondents give the reader a vivid picture of the life of a woman on a Southern plantation before and during the Civil War.

Born in 1826, Rebecca spent her childhood in the home of her wealthy parents Elizabeth (Saunders) and Hamblin Bass. After she married, however, her life was hard. She bore eleven children in eighteen years and moved from a comfortable home in Eatonton, Georgia, to a log house in East Texas. One of her children was born en route to Texas in mid-winter. Miraculously, only one of Rebecca's eleven children preceded her in death; but during her short life she lost her mother, her stepmother, her sister, and three brothers. She and her family were constantly beset by disease, and they often feared death. Many of the letters include references to sickness and death.

The letters included here were written by Rebecca during the Civil War. She was living on a plantation near Fairfield, Texas. Her husband and eldest son, Robert Hamblin Adams, called Bud-

From Gary Doyle Woods, *The Hicks-Adams-Bass-Floyd-Patillo and Collateral Lines, Together with Family Letters, 1840–1868* (Salado, Tex.: Anson Jones Press, 1963). Reprinted by permission of Anson Jones Press.

die or Bobbie, were serving in the Confederate Army, and she was left with the responsibility of caring for nine children, fifty slaves, and an extensive plantation. Her letters tell of sick children, the 9,219 pounds of pork put away, and the slave whom she lovingly cared for before he died. In the midst of all her care and responsibilities, Rebecca took the time to knit special gloves for her husband and son, using thread made from rabbit fur. The letters are filled with the minutiae of daily life and many questions to which Rebecca needed answers, but through them all runs the great love which she had for her husband, her children, and her servants.

*   *   *

From Rebecca Adams to Dr. Robert Adams

At home, October 21, 1863

My dear husband,

I received your letter last Sabbath morning written in camps near Harrisburg. It was brought out to me by Dr. T. B. Grayson who was on a visit to Jim, Susan's child. I have delayed answering your letter two days hoping there might be some favorable change in him but he continued to grow worse and died last night about 11 o'clock. It has been just two weeks since he was taken sick. I sent for old Dr. Grayson, he saw him twice every day, gave him calomel and ipecac. When the fever was lowest he gave quinine and ipecac, he pronounced it to be an obstinate case of bilious fever, said the medicine had no effect. When Dr. Grayson came home he brought his father out to see Jim, he recommended a blistering over the bowels and gave large doses of quinine, but he was too far gone for the blister to have the desired effect. His skin was never the least moist until the day before his death. Several days after he was taken sick I had him brought into the dining room where I could see him during the night and could give every dose of medicine myself. I have watched his case with the greatest anxiety, it being the only severe case of sickness we ever had during your absence from home. Old Dr. Grayson was very attentive to Jim, more so I think than if he had been his own servant. He said he felt a great responsibility resting on him and regretted very much to see him die. Susan said his last words were, Where is Master? The negroes all

thought if Master could only see him he would get well. In such cases
of sickness as his, I feel as if we were doing nothing for them unless
your prescriptions were being carried out. I have such entire confidence in your medical skill, believing that you are capable of doing
all that is in the power of man. Nearly all of the children have had
severe colds approaching the croup. Lizzie, Sallie Lou, Annie and
Georgia are better, well enough to be in school. Jennie and the baby
are sick, they had fever last night. Jennie has had fever all day, but I
hope it is nothing more than a cold. We have had such unpleasant
weather that it is almost sure to produce sickness. I thought of your
being exposed in all of this bad weather, hope that you might get in
some house for protection. I am glad to know that you are stationed so
near Pa's [Waldeck Plantation near Columbia, Texas] but your pleasant
visits down there would be greatly increased by his presence at home. I
do insist on your taking the very best care of yourself, recollect how
many anxious hearts you have left at home, anxious for your safe return. Jennie says, "Back home, Papa" and we all [wish you] back as
soon as you can come. I have written this letter hurriedly in order to
send it off tomorrow. Tell Bobbie I received his letter, will answer soon.
We send a great deal of love to yourself, Bobbie and George.

Your wife with much love,
R. Adams

I will write again by Dr. Grayson.

From Rebecca Adams, Fairfield, Texas, to Dr. Robert Adams

At home Monday morning
December 7th, 1863

My Dear Husband,

I received a long letter from you Saturday morning written from
Waldeck. I know your visit there this time would have been pleasant if
you had only been well enough to enjoy it. I was in hopes from what
you wrote in your last letter about your good health that you would not
be troubled with chills again. You can cure others, why not cure yourself. I hope you may succeed in breaking them up before you leave that
part of the country. How fortunate that you are camped so near Pa's. I
wish very much that you could remain there at least during the winter
months. How pleasant it would be if I and the children were there
to enjoy your many visits to that place but I know it is best for us

Waldeck Plantation, near Columbia, Texas, was the home of Rebecca Adams's father, Hamlin Bass. (*Courtesy Don E. Hutson and the Brazoria County Historical Museum*)

to remain at home and try to feel submissive to all privations caused by this cruel war. I think living at this place away from relations and friends has been a kind school for me. It has taught me to submit more willingly to inconveniences and privations of all kinds. A lesson which you know I very much needed. I feel that I am entirely a changed being in that respect. My daily prayer now is that you may be protected during this war and spared to return to your family. It is true I would like above all things to have you here at home with us, but I know it is a duty you owe your country. I submit.

You complain of not receiving letters from home. I acknowledge that I have not written as often as I should, but at the time you mentioned I was in bed suffering with severe pain in my face and head. Julia wrote to you that week. This is my fifth letter, but I know your great anxiety to hear from home often. I will try and do better in the future.

I regret very much not sending Jeff's letter to you by Pa. I hesitated some time about it but finally concluded that it would be best to keep it, hoping that you would be at home sometime soon. I will enclose the letter tomorrow and send it by mail. For fear that it may never reach you, I have taken the pains to copy it so if you don't get the original you can see the copy. Since I received your letter of the 17th Nov. I have been looking for you home. Do you think I have done wrong? Perhaps I have, but I am not expecting you now. You say in your last letter if the State is invaded you will be the last man in Texas to ask a furlough to come home. You are right. I shall not say anything more about your coming home but will be the gladder to see you when you do come. I know Pa will dislike to give up his well arranged home to the yankees. I hope he may not be compelled to leave it, but tell him if he is obliged to come, we will receive him with open arms, and do all we can to make him comfortable.

I frequently caution the negroes about saving the corn and not wasting it. They have used about a half a crib of corn. I sold thirteen bushels of corn, two dollars and a half per bushel. I have sold nothing else since you left home. George hauled ninety-nine loads of corn, putting nine in the government pen. They had twenty sacks of fodder; used all of one sack. Jack is using a good deal of corn to fatten the hogs in the pen, he put them up last week. You said nothing about fattening the hogs on the corn. Not knowing what you intended, I have waited this long expecting you would write. I walked down to see them a few days after he put them up, they are looking very well. I will have some killed the next change in weather. Jack has fifty-three in the pen, says he had three more to put in, leaving just seventy-five year and half old hogs for another year. I write you just as he tells me. Col. Moreland has bought a great many hogs expects to bacon them up for sale. He bought six pair of cards, will pay for them in bacon. I am needing some wool cards, but there is none in the country. The cotton cards that I have been using for wool are nearly ruined. The teeth are pulled nearly straight. The negro women are needing yarn sacks this winter. I have the wool but I don't want to ruin another pair of cotton cards. Mr. Caldwell has returned I hear, he has cards for sale with a good many other goods. Mrs. Garrett went in to see them, she says he has the highest price for everything. It is generally believed that he and Miss Sarah Moreland will marry soon. He brought a great many goods for that family. Amelia was here yesterday morning. It has been some time since Mary had done any weaving, she has a severe bone felon on her finger, but I think it now is getting well. Grayson cut it open twice. I have had Souvenia spinning for some time. Jane cooks in her place four days in the week, she spins faster than any of the others. George thinks he will get through sowing the grain tomorrow or the next day. Fed was badly hurt by one of the oxen. I thought one time it would kill him, but we nursed him well and he finally got over it. Old Black died last week. She was very poor, I think she died with old age. You say you will leave the employment of Mrs. Garrett entirely to me. I must say that I don't feel that I am a competent judge of such a matter, the proper education of our children is very important. It is true I have been with her and ought to know what she is competent to teach. I think she is a good teacher for children beginning. The other children have learned but little, Julia almost nothing. But one thing I do know they have learned no wicked sayings. I think it has been of great service to David to be entirely with his sisters. Julia's great anxiety to go to college has kept her from learning what she might have learned. I don't think Mrs. Garrett can teach her anything but Smith's Grammer. Mrs. Garrett is a *very plain* not neat but I think a well meaning woman. She would like to remain here if she could go to town every Saturday. If I don't hear from *you* before she closes her school I shall employ her another term but I had rather you would decide what is best to be done. I have been very busy lately knitting you some gloves, the thread was spun of mule eared rabbit furs with a little wool. I think the gloves will be warm, pleasant feeling to the skin. David and Old Allen caught the rabbits. Are you wearing your old gloves, or have you bought new ones? Are you or Robert needing anything in the way of clothing? You must let me know in time so I can have them ready. Jennie had another chill yesterday, her skin is yellow, I think her body is swollen. She has been calling for you at night in her sleep. Little Fannie has not looked well since Pa was here.

The children all send love to PaPa and Buddie. Mrs. G. sends respect. Write as often as you can and I hope you will not be sent from that section of the country. Your wife with much love,

R.A.

I think we will loose all our potatoes. I have had the hills taken down twice, but the top of the hills are smoking this morning like a chimney. Mr. Harris, Mr. Huckaby's brother-in-law, died last week.

Mr. Kendrick died the week before. Love to pa, brother and wife. The negroes send howdye to Master and Master Bobbie.

From Rebecca Adams, Fairfield, Texas, to Robert Adams

Friday Morning at Home
January 8th, 1864

My Dear Husband,

I received your letter of the 15th. Dec. last week. I would have answered before this but wanted to get through with the meat. The hogs are all killed and the meat safe in the smoke house, safe if cold weather will make it so, for I think we have had some of the coldest weather I ever felt in my life. The mercury is 18° this morning. We have had such a continued spell of cold weather that the tanks are all frozen over. I have————horses and cows watered at the well. On the twenty ninth of December the weather was very warm, mercury between 60° and 70°. A norther blew up after dark and we had a heavy snow during the night. The next morning, the last day of the year I had fourteen hogs killed. New Years day the mercury was as low as 7°, killed all of the hogs in the pen that morning, seventeen in number, making fifty six including the first killing. I had the meat salted over and spread in the smoke house, the next morning it was stiff frozen. By keeping a fire I managed to get it thawed by Monday evening so that it could be packed away. It is the first frozen meat we ever had, I hardly know what to do with it, but I knew enough not to pack it away while in a frozen state. The meat was very fat and nice looking, I do hope it will keep well. The thirty one hogs weighed 5,543 lbs. Including the 25 killed the 14th of Dec., we have now nine thousand two hundred and nineteen pounds of pork. Will there be enough or will we have some to spare. How much will go to the Government? Please answer that question when you write. I always thought it was a good deal of trouble to attend to the putting away of meat, but I acknowledge that I never knew anything about it until now. I had to attend to your part of the work and mine too. The weather has been so cold that the meat will certainly be good. I hope you may be at home to get your share of it. I have one hundred gallons of lard. There is only four sacks of salt left, two Liverpool sacks and two sacks from Pa's, did not take as much salt for the meat as I expected. . . .

Capt. Bradley will leave this evening. I have sent your valise to town this morning, he told me himself that he would take care of it and see that it was carried safe into camps. You must send down to his camp for it. He has the key to the valise. I send your coat, pants, vest, two shirts, cravat for you and Bobbie, a pair of scissors, two bars of soap, two pairs of gloves knit of rabbit fur, the gauntlets are all wool. The gloves with the black gauntlets are for Bobbie. I fixed up in a great hurry not knowing that he intended carrying a wagon until day before yesterday. I have also sent a box containing two hams, one cooked, one raw—two cakes, one sponge cake and one pound cake, small jar of peach preserves, some teacakes and biscuits. After hearing of your poor fare felt more anxious than ever to send you something from home. I hope I have sent something you will enjoy eating. I was anxious to send some flour but the wagon was crowded, our flour is poor, full of bran.

The excitement about the small pox still increases, about fourteen cases in town. They have a case at Dr. Moores. Dr. Grayson has promised to come down and vaccinate our family as soon as he can procure some vaccine matter. The children are well except for a very bad cough, almost like whooping cough. Little Jennie has another chill, has them every two weeks, she is very restless at night, talks during her sleep, often wakes up badly frightened. I keep her in the bed with me. Susan's baby had its hand burnt last week, nurse let it fall in the fire. It is a very bad looking place. I dressed it with flour and beef foot oil. I must close. The children sent a kiss to PaPa & Buddie. I will write you again the 15th. Your wife with much love,

R. Adams

What shall I have done with the peach tree in the garden?

From Rebecca Adams, Fairfield, Texas, to Dr. Robert Adams

Home, January 28th, 1864

My Dear Husband,

I wrote to you the 25th giving you the situation of the children as near as could and I promised to write again in a few days. I think today there has been a decided improvement in all except the babe. She continues about the same, the spells of coughing last longer, the cough is tighter and harder with her than with the other children, never throws off any thing without ipecac. Georgia is entirely free from fever today for the first time in six days. The children all cough a great deal with a loud distinct whoop, but the cough is looser. Georgia has taken two doses of calomel, I think it has been of great service to her. All of the children sleep in my room except David. He sleeps upstairs. Very often all coughing at the same time. You can easily imagine what kind of a noise we have at night for the children are very restless.

I have just received your letter of the 17th from Matagorda County. Your letters were always a great source of pleasure to me but that one is particularly so—I wrote to you the 18th, nineteenth anniversary of our marriage and thought perhaps the day would pass without ever thinking of it as you were surrounded by circumstances so entirely different from days past and gone. But I assure you that I was most agreeably surprised when I read your letter. What pleasant thoughts you had on that day of former times. How pleasing and gratifying it is for a wife to know that she has the love and confidence of her husband and occasionally to hear him express himself as you did in that letter. I do prize above all other blessings the *love* and *confidence* of my dear husband and if I know my heart it is to try and please him in all things. When I fail to do this it is not from an intention to do so. May the Lord bless and preserve you and may you be allowed to return in health and safety to your family is the daily prayer of your devoted wife.

Mrs. Garrett has not yet returned from Montgomery, I don't think she will before spring, if she ever does to remain any length of time. She expressed herself as being very much pleased here, said they were good children, easily managed and seemed to enjoy teaching them. But I think she dislikes very much to live in the country, says she never could content herself but a short time at any place. While here she went into town every Saturday morning. I think she has gone to Montgomery only for a change. She has promised to teach the children when she returns if they are not in school elsewhere, but they will have to remain at home as there are no schools in town on account of the smallpox. The smallpox is still spreading. They have five cases at Dr. Moores. I am almost afraid to send to the post office but I tell Rodrick to travel the new road in the woods, never to go by Dr. Moores. Dr. Grayson came down this morning, vaccinated all of the children, myself and all of the negroes that were at the house, says he will vaccinate the others sometime soon. Jennie was very opposed to his cutting her arm, told him, "she would tell PaPa, too now." But she finally acknowledged that it did not hurt much.

I have had a fence built across the lane gate, had the big gate to the house locked so as to prevent all passing through here to Rollers. There has been no deaths yet from smallpox. I have made a big trade this week entirely out of my line of business. I gave a refugee from Louisiana one hundred bushels of corn for three hundred pounds of sugar. I found my sugar was getting very low, little over half a barrel. Dr. Grayson made the same kind of trade for himself and attended to the weighing of my sugar and delivery of the corn. What do you think of the trade? I have been very economical with the sugar, had desert only three times since you left home, using sugar only for breakfast.

I gave twenty-one dollars for one coffee pot and four tin cups, gave ten dollars for a quire of paper, a sheet of which I am writing on now. Paid Mrs. Garrett one hundred dollars for the three months she lived here. Mr. Sheffield's son has paid the two hundred dollars note you left with me. Col. Moreland has never said anything about paying his note. I have seen him only a few times since you left but I am not needing any money. Mr. Caldwell has goods such as I would like to buy but his prices are too high, one hundred dollars for a calico dress, ———from five to seven dollars.

You never mentioned that you had received Jeff's letter. I sent you another letter from him about two weeks since, it was written the first of November. Mr. Carroll had the shoes made since Christmas, every pair is too large, but they are better than no shoes. Little Jennie and Georgia are very proud of theirs. The negroes are making out very well for shoes, some bought the leather, others tanned it themselves. I gave four of them soles for their shoes. They were almost entirely without clothes the first cool weather we had. I have woven two hundred fifty yards of cloth. Would have had more but for the bone felon on Mary's finger and the cold weather.

The children's next aprons and dresses must come out of the loom. I have enough calico to make them all one dress a piece that must be saved for Sunday wear. Their dresses ought to be woven before very long as their old ones are wearing out. I asked you in a former letter how long I should keep the spinners. We all send a great deal of love to you and Bobbie. Your loving wife,

R. A. Adams

At home, Feb. 16th, 1864

My Dear Husband,

What would I have given to have had you with us this week. I fear our little babe will never recover from this severe attack of whooping cough. During the last week she has suffered intensely—with high fever and seems hardly to have strength to stand the severe spells of coughing. I thought for several days she would have spasm. Today her fever is not so high as it has been, but she has not been entirely free from fever in nearly three weeks—last night she slept very well— today been asleep most of the time. I think it is from the effects of the brandy. Dr. Grayson recommended brandy every two hours. I have been giving it today. Her tongue and lips very red. Her gums not swollen. I think she is teething—she is very much reduced—hardly looks like the same child, keeps her little hands clasp together. During the fits of coughing presses them to her forehead. Dr. Grayson comes to see her every day, sometimes twice a day. She has taken three doses of calomel—will take another tonight. I succeeded in getting a few doses of oil for her, from Mrs. Moreland, which I gave the morning after giving the calomel. Sweet little creature, I do pray that she may be spared to us. The children all love her so much. She had a smile for every one that spoke to her. The other children are all getting better.

Georgia not so well as the others. She yet coughs very hard. Dr. Grayson tells me that he sent word by Dr. Moores to you to come home if you could, which I know you will do if such a thing be possible. I wish you were here tonight. I think you could relieve our dear little Fannie. Every child is wishing Pa-Pa was here. You must excuse this short letter. I have written only to let you know about the baby. Will write again in a few days. The children all send love to Pa-Pa and Buddie. Write often to your

Loving wife,

R. Adams

Tom has come home. He ran away. Came home last week.

*   *   *

The child lived, the war ended, and Rebecca's husband and son came home, but Rebecca Adams lived only three years longer. She died of tuberculosis in 1867 at the age of forty-one, and the letters of condolence are the last in the collection. Susan Adams Young, Rebecca's sister-in-law, describes Rebecca as "the best of wives . . . an excellent mother . . . and a dear sister." Mrs. Young goes on to say, "I knew Rebecca was a Christian years ago. It was this grace operating on a naturally kind heart that prompted so much self-denial and goodness."

Eudora Inez Moore

> "I saw him mount his horse, Grey Eagle, and ride away never to return."

As the waves wash onto the west side of Matagorda Bay, they endlessly cover and uncover several old cisterns, all that remain of once thriving Indianola. At the height of its prosperity in 1875, it had a population of six thousand. Two devastating hurricanes finally persuaded the inhabitants that the site was too vulnerable, and Indianola was deserted after a storm in 1886.

Eudora Inez Moore witnessed the rise and fall of Indianola. Her "Recollections of Indianola" were first published in the *Wharton Spectator* in 1934 and later included in a volume entitled *Indianola Scrap Book*.

Eudora's family moved to Indianola in 1849 when she was one year old. Her father, Robert B. Moore, was a building contractor. In the first part of her "Recollections," Eudora describes her childhood in the coastal town. This carefree childhood came to an abrupt end in 1861, when Texas seceded from the Union. In December, 1863, Indianola was captured and became one of the few towns in Texas to be occupied by Federal troops during the war. Although Eudora did not suffer from lack of food and clothing, as others did during the Civil War, she lost her brother Joe and many childhood friends.

Included here is Eudora Moore's account of life in Indianola during the war and the Reconstruction period when the town was again occupied by Federal troops. She also describes the yellow fever epidemic of 1867. Several quotations and many long lists of names of inhabitants of the town that she included have been omitted.

*   *   *

Texas seceded from the Union on the 4th day of March 1861. The U.S. troops on the frontier were ordered back North. A company came

From *Indianola Scrap Book* (Victoria, Tex.: Victoria Advocate Publishing Company, 1936; reprint ed., Port Lavaca, Tex.: Calhoun County Historical Survey Committee, 1974). Reprinted by permission of Victoria Advocate Publishing Company.

to Indianola to embark. They marched with lively steps to the tune of Yankee Doodle, down to the wharf, where they boarded a vessel and started on their way rejoicing. They had not proceeded far when they were overtaken by Col. Van Dorn of the Steamer *Rusk*, joined by volunteers, some of them from Indianola, captured and brought back to the city where they were paroled and allowed to proceed on their way. . . .

We soon began to feel the privations which war entailed upon us, but we met them with brave hearts for we were full of patriotism in those days. Mrs. D. C. Proctor and other ladies took the lead in carding cotton, spinning thread, knitting and making comforts for our soldier boys. Companies were being formed and men drilled in military tactics. . . .

The Indianola ladies made a flag for a company raised there. At its presentation by Miss Amelia Rouff, Mr. F. S. Stockdale who received the flag said, "I can wipe up with a cambric handkerchief every drop of blood that will be shed in this war." Some people were quite optimistic, but they little knew. . . .

Mrs. Anderson took much interest in getting up entertainments for the benefit of soldier boys, they were usually held in the court house. I remember taking part in one in which "The Confederate Constellation" represented one of the acts. Eleven young girls, each with a flag appropriate for her state and reciting a patriotic verse, participated in it. . . .

When Dudley Woodward or "Tip," as everybody called him, started to join his uncle's command, we girls went to see him off. He wore a handsome buck-skin suit and had a negro boy to attend him. He seemed quite a hero in our eyes, as in fact all the boys did who joined the army.

In the spring of 1862 a detachment of men was sent to guard Fort Esperanzo which commanded Pass Cavallo, the entrance to Matagorda Bay. That year yellow fever broke out among the men and Elija Stapp, son of Col. Darwin Stapp, took the fever and died. He was one of my early school mates and I mourned his death sincerely. His body was brought to Indianola and buried in the cemetery there. Jimmy Coates also took the fever and his mother went to Esperanzo to nurse him. He recovered but she succumbed to the fever. It soon spread to Indianola and a few died, a baby, Willie Gambol, and little Proctor Woodward

Eudora Moore in later years. (*Courtesy Martha L. Moore*)

fell victims to it. There had been an epidemic of fever there in 1853, my brother, Joe, took it while in town but would not come home on our account as it was considered very contagious. He was a thin, pale looking boy on his return.

The saying "Necessity is the mother of invention" was certainly exemplified in war times. Father bought a side of tanned leather for our shoe soles, the uppers were made of an old cloak of his, very heavy black material. Mother made a pair of pants out of a parlor table cover of wool, dyed it with the rind of pomegranates. Mr. Dan Sullivan, Sr., said he was going to have a pair made of the same kind of stuff, but just then his nephew sent him some material from the Rio Grande and the table cover was saved. I made hats for the boys out of shucks or palmetto and mother made them cloth caps for winter wear. After the Yankees left a great deal of cast off clothing was found. Mother boiled it in lye water, rinsed it thoroughly and dyed it with pomegranate rinds or pecan hulls and made it into clothes for the boys.

An iron mortar and pestle was used for pounding various things, as coarse salt, cloves, mustard, etc. Our bread was usually made of cornmeal as flour was scarce, but occasionally mother would make a batch of biscuits and we would count them to see how many there would be apiece. During the war we made tallow candles. Before that we used lamps with two tubes through which the wick passed at the tip and burned some kind of oil. It may have been the kind virgins used in Bible times for all I know.

In the spring and summer of 1863 a company of men under Capt. George was stationed at Indianola. They were a part of Hobby's regiment. The major was Ireland, afterwards governor of Texas. They were mostly from Seguin and vicinity. A number of the men boarded in private homes, some of them brought their families; Jep Dibrell, John George, three LeGette brothers, Joe Zorn, Goodrich and Douglas were a few names I remember. Parties were given and plays consisting of tableaux and charades for the benefit of sick soldiers. I recall one in which I represented Pocahontas saving the life of Capt. Smith. Miss Mattie LeGette took great interest in helping get up the entertainments, at a party she looked quite pretty in her white dress trimmed with cedar and the red buds of the oleander. Natural flowers were used a great deal for decorative purposes in those days. On the 17th of November, which was my 16th birthday, a few friends were invited to our home, for refreshments we had molasses cookies and candy, it was truly simple fare, but many a poor soldier would have considered it fine eating. . . .

Fort Esperanzo was evacuated the last of November, 1863, and the weather was very cold at the time, in a few days a Federal gunboat came up Matagorda Bay and demanded the surrender of Indianola, which was turned over to them peaceably by the mayor, Mr. Cleveland. No troops were stationed there at the time. They then went on to Port Lavaca and bombarded the town for some time. We could hear the cannonading very distinctly. They soon returned and a detachment occupied the town. On New Year's night of 1864 we were aroused from our slumbers by a dozen Yankees who demanded that they be allowed to enter the house, that they were about to freeze. They had been sent to guard a bridge over the bayou, when a fierce norther blew up bringing ice in its wake. My father opened the door for them and made a fire in the kitchen stove, suddenly they decided that they must search the house. I heard them coming up stairs and had the fright of my life. Father prevailed upon them not to enter my room (my door was locked) and they went on searching at other parts of the house. Not finding any confederates they settled down for the rest of the night. . . .

The regiment commanded by Dan Perry camped on my father's place. He gave his men orders not to molest anything on the premises and they obeyed his instructions. After a time some new men were added to the regiment and the first night after they came our chicken house was invaded and a dozen fowls stolen, with them was a waif they had picked up somewhere, and one day he and my brother, Dolph Moore, had a fight and he bit my brother badly on the ear. . . .

For some reason the transports which were to take the troops failed to come at the appointed time; they had already broken camp when a young captain was taken sick and asked permission to stay at our house, which was granted. He seemed very grateful for the privilege and took the names and commands of my two brothers in the army, assuring mother that if they ever fell into his hands as prisoners of war he would befriend them.

While the Yankees were at Indianola some youths rode up west of town, a regiment with cannon went out on the prairie to meet them and fired a number of shells but don't think any one was injured, though I heard a Yankee say "One saddle is emptied." The boys soon took their departure. This may have given rise to the statement about a battle having been fought in the streets of Indianola.

In the early part of the year 1864 all available troops were ordered into Louisiana. At Mansfield and Pleasant Hill many brave officers and men lost their lives. Col. Augustus Buchel of Indianola was mortally wounded while leading his regiment "The First Texas" in the charge at Mansfield and my brother, Joseph Moore, died soon after at Alexandria, La. . . .

When the main body of Federals under Gen. Warren arrived, they began digging rifle pits and building forts on the prairie back of town. All houses of Confederate soldiers were torn down to build barracks for the men. They would drive up herds of cattle and slaughter them, and by getting a permit from headquarters we could get some of our own beef to eat. It went mightily against the grain to do it, however.

The first Yankee that came to our house used very rough language to my mother and ordered her to get him something to eat, when told she had only corn meal and bacon, he said, "You need not trouble yourself, but I've got my eyes on you, old woman." A Yankee Chaplain was also rude to her but they were exceptions. It was rather hard on us to have to be cooped up in the house all the time. We couldn't even walk in the garden. One day I was in the back yard jumping over some boxes for exercise when I noticed a Yankee on the outside of our fence watching me. It is needless to say I quickly vanished indoors. . . .

After the Federals evacuated Indianola a vessel would occasionally come up the bay and land a few troops at Old Town, they would march down from there in order to capture any confederate that might be in town. Our house was searched twice by them. Once father was hidden in a loft over the gallery. He took a notion that they might carry him off. Well for him they did not find him for they would probably have made him a prisoner under the circumstances.

During the Federal occupation of the town we never learned a word from our soldier boys. Brother Will had been shot through the body at the battle of Murfreesboro, Tenn., in 1862, after many days of anxiety, a letter came from him stating that he was out of danger and would rejoin his regiment as soon as he was able to ride. He had three horses killed under him in different entanglements. Brother Joe made us his last visit in 1863. I saw him mount his horse, Grey Eagle, and ride away never to return. Oh, war, cruel, cruel war. . . .

In this writeup it is my desire to be as accurate as possible, but I do not seem to get my dates in chronological order, so I shall have to go back to the surrender of General Lee, April 9, 1865. The war between the North and South was over as far as the actual fighting was concerned. The soldiers began coming home, but some of them were a long time in arriving. Brother Will came in August, he spent some time in Georgia, then visited an aunt in Mobile, Alabama, before returning; Mr. Bill Kyle of the Terry Rangers came about the same time, also Hays Yarrington and John Coates of the same regiment. The Yankees were here before them. . . . They occupied all coast towns; the first Federal troops that made their appearance at the close of the war were white, they seemed angry at being sent South and were reckless as to their conduct. Often we could hear shots rattling through the tree tops around our house, a bullet made a round hole in our kitchen window; mother stooped to bring in some wood when a ball whistled over her head and lodged in a shed nearby, my little brother, Baxter, came very near being shot by them. They were quite troublesome about cistern water, several would come into the yard, put their canteens under the faucet, not caring how much they wasted.

Soon a company of negro soldiers was stationed near us. They seemed to be turned loose at first and went shouting around our places like a lot of demons; presently they began driving off our hogs, when father went out to protest and threatened to report them at headquarters, they picked up sticks and told him they would beat his brains out if he moved a step farther. I rushed out and told them not to touch my father. In the meantime mother had gone out through the grapevine arbor and on to camp where she reported their depredations to their white officers. Immediately two of them mounted their horses and came dashing up to the house. At the sight of them the negroes fled like chaff before the wind. That night the two young officers came to our house to apologize for the conduct of their men; . . . the soldiers annoyed us so much we were obliged to apply for a guard. A negro was sent us, he seemed like an old plantation darky, was polite and unpretentious. It did me good to see the white soldiers walk around the fence not daring to come in. We had the same guard on two or three times, he liked to stay with us on account of getting better fare than he received in camp.

Finally, mother took an officer and his wife to board with us, as she felt we would be more secure with them in the house. We liked them both very well, Mrs. Archer seemed a kind hearted woman, she came down stairs one night to give my brother some of her homeopathic medicine to stop his coughing, she had remedies for every ailment under the sun. Lieut. Archer decided he wanted his wife to learn to ride, so he procured a horse and proceeded to give her riding lessons. She soon learned to stay on. I think that was the main thing about horseback riding in those days. After a time they gave a little party and invited me to be present to meet some of their officer friends, strange but I had an engagement away from home that night. One day the lieutenant had a negro to weed our flower bed, this he effectually did by pulling up every plant of our cherished verbena.

After a time a Yankee Captain with about twenty men came near our place to camp. He ordered his men to tear down the cow sheds at the lot, father reminded him that the war was over and he had no right to destroy private property. He ordered his men to shoot the d—d old rebel; our boys came running into the house crying, "They are going to kill father." Brother Will knowing that trouble was brewing, had gone to headquarters to report. The man was arrested and his shoulder straps removed. He had the audacity to come and tell father that he had been the cause of him losing his position. He had to board with us until he could get away. Brother was wearing his gray uniform with yellow trimmings and C.S.A. buttons. An officer advised him to remove them as he was liable to have them cut off, rather than to be a source of trouble he had plain buttons substituted for them. In writing these details I am only telling what happened in our immediate vicinity, things were bad enough in town. I was told of a Captain Cleveland who had given them offense in some way, as punishment they cut a hole in the top of a barrel large enough to go over his head and made him march back and forth with it resting on his shoulders.

At this time too the negroes were very impudent, while walking in town I saw three women approaching side by side and knew by their looks they would not make way for me, I walked as near the edge of the sidewalk as possible and they shoved me off. A lady spoke to a negro about getting a cook. The darky replied, "You want to know who your next cook is going to be? You go look in the glass." The negroes soon found out that Southern white people were their best friends and their attitude changed accordingly.

For a while I taught a little school at home, father had built a room for the boys separate from the house and this was my school room. My pupils were brother Ed, Mr. Fromme's son and a drayman's little boy, also the Harrison boys who lived on the other side of the lake, they were Henry, Frank, Willie and Ben, they crossed in a skiff. The family was very unfortunate in losing the wife and mother with cholera, caught supposedly from the negro soldiers camped near Old Town, a great many of them died. There was one girl named Adaline, about thirteen years old at the time of her mother's death, and six boys. The girl was industrious and did all she could for the family but she must have had a hard time of it at best.

Soon after the war closed a good many people came to town and engaged in various occupations, others that had moved away on account of Federal possession returned. We scarcely realized at first that the "tragic era" was upon us and that for a number of years we should be under the yoke of Reconstruction. . . .

Now, one more story of Reconstruction Days, my sister-in-law, Gussie, had a friend in town whom she wished to visit and asked me to accompany her. We reached the house without molestation, after chatting a while we stepped out on the upper porch to look at a boat that was anchored in the bay on which Harriet expected to sail to Matagorda the following day; just as we turned back into the room we noticed a soldier had come up stairs and was about to enter. Harriet slammed the door shut and locked it. The man knocked violently at the door and insisted upon entering. Mr. Harrison came up the inside way and ordered the man to leave, by that time another drunken soldier had come up. Mr. Harrison pushed them down the stairway but they started up again using the most vile language I have ever heard. Mr. Prouty (who held some government office) was passing and heard the disturbance, he notified the officers and the men were taken away. We were a frightened set of girls and were almost afraid to go home by ourselves, we walked along the bay shore till we got opposite our home so as to avoid being near any camp. We heard the soldiers were sent to the Dry Tortugas which must be a dreadful place, almost as bad as Devil's Island, where Dreyfus was banished and lived for a number of years. Breaking into the house of a Union man probably made it worse for them. . . .

In July of that year yellow fever broke out in Indianola; we thought at the time it was brought there on a vessel by people who came from a fever-infested port, as the first person to take it was the drayman who carried their belongings up into town. It soon spread and there was scarcely a home that did not have one or more cases, it seemed to be more fatal with people who were not acclimated and there were quite a number of new residents. . . . I never had a list of all who passed away but there were many. I was anxious to go down town and visit some of my sick friends but mother begged me not to go, said she was afraid I would take the fever. I went to the cemetery, however, and located the graves of dear ones who had died. One day I was taken with a chill and my skin turned purple in spots, I sure enough had the fever, was quite ill for a week or more. Mother was my doctor and nurse too and a very successful one she proved to be, I was in low spirits over the loss of loved ones and scarcely cared to live. Father and brother Ed both took the fever but had it in a very light form and soon recovered, my dear mother was nurse through it all. . . .

In November of that year a young German couple came to Indianola and rented a house with the expectation of teaching music, in a short time the man died of yellow fever, the supposition was that the former occupants had the disease; it was very rare, in fact, thought impossible, for a person to have the fever that late in the year.

It took people a long time to find out that the mosquito was to blame, but "Knowledge is Power" and now we never hear of yellow fever epidemics in this part of the country any more. I am sorry to say, though, that mosquitoes still flourish in all parts of the coast country, after a rainy season there are millions of them but I guess they are the harmless kind, only their sting is just as bad as it ever was.

I have been asked the question: "Did many Federal soldiers die of yellow fever at Indianola?" The last two epidemics were in the years of 1862, 1867 and it will be remembered that the Yankees came there in December, 1863, and left in March, 1864. The statement about yellow fever raging there when the Yanks took possession was entirely without foundation as was also the manner of taking the place. Not a gun was fired and no Confederate soldiers were there.

After the war many negro soldiers died of cholera, some of them were buried at Old Town and a few in the cemetery at Indianola. A great deal of lime was used about their graves and in a few years their bodies were disinterred and taken to some national cemetery for final burial, I suppose.

Then and Now

Lines written during the visitation of yellow fever at Indianola, July 19, 1867:

A month ago our hearts were light,
Our words were gay; our smiles were bright,
We met together, laughed and sung,
All care upon the winds we flung.
We decked our hair with summer flowers
And danced away the fleeting hours,
Pleasure we sought for pleasure gained,
But now, oh now, we're sadly changed.
Sickness with polluting breath,
Has breathed and chilled our loved in death.
Nor age, nor infancy was spared,
But each its cold embrace has shared.
The forms that wandered by our side,
In all their strength and youth and pride,
Have gone from us forever more,
Death Angels steered their barks ashore.
The funeral hearse day after day
Carries our dead from us away,
Our well beloved, our darling dead,
Oh, in their deaths what bright hopes fled.
We cry, how long, Oh, Lord, how long?
Yet death with his sickle marches on
And in his tracks fresh victims fall
The earth seems one vast funeral pall.
Our hearts are sad, our pleasure o'er,
For those we love can come no more,
With restless fee we wonder 'round
And seek for rest but none is found.
With anguished voice, Oh, Lord, we cry,
Have mercy on our misery.

Oh, send us health and strength once more,
And comfort our afflications sore.

*   *   *

    After the war Eudora and her family continued to live in Indianola. While Eudora was visiting her brother Will on Wilson's Creek near Indianola, the 1875 hurricane hit. Indianola was flooded, and Eudora's father drowned. Her mother escaped by tying herself to a cedar tree.

    Eudora and her mother moved to the Abel H. and Jonathan E. Pierce ranch known as Rancho Grande. Eudora taught the children on the ranch. Later, Eudora and her mother moved to Ashby on Tres Palacios Creek, where Eudora built a house. In her memoirs Eudora states that she taught school in Matagorda County from 1875 through 1886. About 1906 she went to live on a ranch near Wimberley with her niece Maggie Kuykendall, who was a widow. Eudora acted as a companion to Maggie and as a governess to Maggie's four children. She lived out her life with the Kuykendalls, writing in her diary, composing poetry, and writing her memoirs. She was trying to get her memoirs published when she died in 1933 in the west room of the ranch house. Eudora was loved and respected by the members of her family. Her niece, Lamond Kuykendall McGhee, describes her: "She was a dear little old lady and exerted a great influence over many of us."

    Fifty years after Eudora died, a relative opened an old trunk which he found in the attic of the ranch house in Wimberley. It was filled with diaries, letters, and keepsakes. He surmised from reading Eudora's diaries and letters that she had been in love with a Union soldier. Several weeks after the trunk was opened, it was stolen, and it has never been recovered.

Amelia Edith Huddleson Barr

"It is the smell of yellow fever."

"I write mainly for the race of women. I am their sister, and in no way exempt from their sorrowful lot. I have drank the cup of their limitations to the dregs, and if my experience can help any sad or doubtful woman to outleap her own shadow, and to stand bravely in the sunshine to meet her destiny, whatever it may be, I shall have done well; I shall not have written this book in vain. It will be its own excuse, and justify its appeal." With these words, Amelia Edith Huddleson Barr begins her autobiography *All the Days of My Life*. This book is extremely interesting to the student of Texas history because Mrs. Barr spent twelve of the happiest and saddest years of her life in Austin and Galveston, and she records those years vividly.

In 1831 in Ulverston, England, the Reverend William Henry Huddleson and his wife Mary (Singleton) became the parents of a daughter whom they named Amelia Edith. The Huddlesons were rather eccentric, and Amelia grew up in a highly charged atmosphere of religion and mysticism.

When Amelia was sixteen, her father's health began to fail, and she went to the town of Downham Market, as she said, "to take my place among the workers of the world." Amelia became a teacher in a boarding school. A year and a half later she went to Glasgow, Scotland, to teach. There she met Robert Barr when she and a friend called on him in his office. Amelia, who claimed to be psychic, said of their first meeting: "It was a pleasant call, a fateful call, for I knew I had met the man whose fate—good or bad—I must share. A feeling of deep sadness overcame me. I said I was sick, lay down on my bed, and fell into a deep sleep." As she had predicted, Amelia married the handsome, wealthy young man in 1850. However, her strange reaction to their first meeting did indeed foreshadow events which occurred during their marriage. Although Amelia and Robert loved each other, their life together was plagued by periods of the deep sadness Amelia feared.

From Amelia E. Barr, *All the Days of My Life* (New York: D. Appleton and Company, 1913, 1923; reprint ed., New York: Arno Press, 1980).

For the first two years of their marriage, the two were bliss-
fully happy. Their first child was born, and Amelia was absorbed
with rearing her child and caring for her loving husband. However, tragedy entered the lives of the family when Robert en-
trusted a large part of his fortune to a friend, who betrayed him.
In her autobiography, Amelia, who knew nothing of the affair,
bitterly denounces husbands who do not confide in their wives:
"But when a husband says only, 'Yesterday I was rich, today I am
poor; you must do as well as you can,' his silence about his position has been not only cruel, but humiliating. He might make
such a speech to an affectionate dog." The Barrs decided to start
over in America; and soon after the birth of their second daughter,
Eliza, they left Scotland.

After short stays in New York City, Chicago, and Memphis,
the Barrs settled in 1856 in Austin, where they lived for a decade.
Amelia says of their stay there: "[In Austin] I spent nearly ten
years; and the first three or four of these ten were, in some respects, the happiest years of my life. Their very memory is a
blessing to this day, for often, when I am heart and brain weary, it
steals upon me, swift and sweet and sure as a vision. I smell the
China trees and the pine. I hear the fluting of the wind, and the
tinkling of guitars. I see the white-robed girls waltzing in the
moonshine down the broad sidewalks of the avenue, and the men,
some in full evening dress, and others in all kinds of picturesque
frontier fashion, strolling leisurely down its royally wide highway.
I am sitting in the little wood house, with its whitewashed ceilings
and unpainted stairway and one sits at my side, who left me forty-
five years ago. Oh, believe me! He who raised the shade of Helen
had no greater gift than mine!"

Amelia's joy was short-lived. With the Civil War came sickness
and death as two of the Barr's children, Ethel and Archibald, died
in infancy. The excerpt which is included here begins on June 24,
1865.

*   *   *

The sheriff read the Emancipation Proclamation. He read it with
no more ceremony than if he was giving notice of a forced sale of land,
or a new city ordinance about negro passes, or any other every day
occurrence. He was surrounded by white men, who listened without
interest or remark, and the negroes were shocked and dismayed. They
had been sure that the news of their freedom would come with the
calling of trumpets, the firing of a cannon, and the triumphant entry of

a victorious army. Robert said they were sick and silent with disappointment, and vanished from the streets. I went into the kitchen to tell Harriet. She was leaning against the open door, looking intently eastward. Freedom was to come from the east, and she was always listening and watching for its approach. Her child, a girl about a year old, was sitting on the floor playing with some empty spools. I had always thought her indifferent to it. "Harriet," I said, and she turned her eyes upon me but did not speak, "you are free, Harriet! From this hour as free as I am. You can stay here, or go; you can work or sleep; you are your own mistress, now, and forever." She stepped forward as I spoke, and was looking at me intently, "Say dem words again, Miss Milly!" she cried, "say dem again." I repeated what I had told her, making the fact still more emphatic; and as I did so, her sullen black face brightened, she darted to her child, and throwing it shoulder high, shrieked hysterically, "Tamar, you'se free! You'se free, Tamar!" She did not at that supreme moment think of herself. Freedom was for her child; she looked in its face, at its hands, at its feet. It was a new baby to her—a free baby. Actually the mother love in her face had humanized her dull, brutish expression. I said again, "You are also free, Harriet. You are your own mistress now. Will you hire yourself to me?" I asked.

"When dem Yankees coming, Miss Milly?"

"Nobody knows."

"How I free then?"

"They sent word."

"Mighty poor way to set folks free."

"Will you hire yourself to me, Harriet? I will give you six dollars a month."

"Six dollars too little, Miss Milly."

"It is what I paid your master."

"Thank de Lord, I'se got no master now. I 'long to myself now. I want eight dollars now. When a nigger free, they worth more."

So I agreed with the freed negro for eight dollars, but I noticed three days later, I had a fresh negro at one dollar fifty cents a day. Harriet had gone forever.

In this uncertain condition of affairs, it was perhaps astonishing they worked at all. In fact it was only the women who made any pretense of doing so, but they were generally mothers, and old master was the only sure provider for the children until the Yankees came. The men loafed about the streets, or made little camps in the corn fields, for the young ears were then ripe and milky and good to eat. But all were alike watching with weary impatience for the arrival of the military. . . .

Robert rented the Morris place, just back of the Capitol. I was delighted. I hated the house we were in, as soon as I heard of it; and we had nothing but trouble, while living under its roof. I thought perhaps our moving might make a break in the long roll of anxious days and nights, just as a nightmare is gone, the moment we stir under it.

The Morris place, to which I made all haste to remove, was almost in the center of the camp of the Sixth Cavalry, and their tents were all around our enclosure. A little behind them were the wigwams of the Tonkaway and Lipan guides, but I had no fear of either white men or Indians. And we soon found that we had come among the most courteous and friendly people. A little offering of cream and new milk opened the way for much mutual kindness; the officers came familiarly to our house. Colonel Morris had the use of our stable, and the girls had the use of horses when they wanted them.

I must notice here, that this kind treatment of "rebels" was not specially for our case. Almost as soon as the Sixth Cavalry arrived in Austin, its officers gave a Reconciliation Ball, and to their regular afternoon promenade and concert, there was a hearty welcome for all who chose to come. It was a great pleasure once more to feel myself surrounded by happy, hopeful people; the atmosphere around the camp was lighter and brighter than what I had been breathing for years, and my nature responded gladly to its stimulus.

Nevertheless, the half year following this removal was full to the brim of every sorrow that humanity can suffer. We were hardly settled when Lilly fell very sick with camp measles, and one after the other the whole family followed her. What we should have done without Dr. Bacon of the Sixth Cavalry at this time, I cannot imagine. He watched over every sick child with a care and tenderness that probably saved their lives. There were but few ladies in the camp, but those present were kind and sympathetic and Mrs. Madden, the wife of Captain Madden, helped me nurse through many critical nights.

During these hard nights of suffering and utter weariness, there was always the haunting fear of poverty. At first, after the break-up

Amelia Barr about the time of these memoirs. (*Courtesy Barker Texas History Center, University of Texas at Austin*)

Robert was not anxious. The three richest men in Austin, Mr. Swenson, Mr. Swisher and Mr. Raymond were intending to open a bank as soon as affairs would warrant the project. They had engaged Robert as cashier, and in the meantime he was putting the affairs of the Military Board in order for Major Pierce. But the Military Board work was now finished, and there was no prospect as yet for a bank in Austin. Moreover, word had just come that Mr. Swenson had gone into the banking business in New York. So we were anxious and uncertain, for with six children it would not be easy to move, as when we came to Austin with two. . . .

God accomplishes that which is beyond expectation. The next morning Robert got an offer from a large cotton house in Galveston, which he accepted. Of course this meant, that he must leave me and the children in Austin until October; before that, there might be some danger of yellow fever. But we both knew, that in the United States camp, there was every security, and that the kindness already given would not be withdrawn.

After a few day's preparation Robert went away one morning. We watched him until he mounted the last step, leading over the Capitol wall. There he stood a moment, and waved his hat, and we turned quickly into the house because it is not lucky to watch the traveler out of sight. And as I entered the sitting-room, the pendulum of the clock fell to the floor, and I picked it up and said, "It is ten minutes past eleven. We shall see that something will happen at that time." I was not worried about the circumstance. I merely thought it prefigured some unusual event.

The three months that followed were very happy ones. Colonel Morris sent the bandmaster to sleep in the house, and to watch the Indians, and I threw off all care, and gave myself and the children a holiday. All lessons were dropped, and the girls rode every day to their heart's content. I wrote cheerful, loving letters to Robert, and had cheerful, loving letters in return. And the weeks went quickly away, until the last one came. Then having sold all our furniture, and also the good cow bought with the Scotch pebble bracelet, I was ready to depart. Ten years previously I had come to Austin, and I thought it a city in a fairy land. I had seen every charm vanish away. It was a dead city that I was leaving. The dead houses and dead streets might live again, but nothing could restore unto them the glory of the past. I was not sorry to leave them. . . .

A little while before we reached Galveston, we had to cross a very long bridge or viaduct, connecting the main land with the island of Galveston. Over this viaduct the train moved very slowly. I looked at Alexander who was sitting on my knees, for I expected him to be full of interest and chatter, and I saw that his eyes had the most remarkable appearance. He seemed to be looking at an infinite, incalculable distance. He was evidently unconscious, and *I* could neither speak or move. Calvin was in the same trance. Mary and Lilly were gazing at the boy, but neither of them moved or spoke. Suddenly Alexander shuddered, and with a deep sigh was conscious, but he made no remark. At the same moment Calvin awoke to life, in the same manner, and none of us uttered a word. The boys were exceedingly sad, but neither of them asked a question, or made any allusion to their experience. The strangest, most sorrowful atmosphere pervaded the car, and I could scarcely move under the silent, somber inertia; but I expected the train to stop at any moment, and Robert would be waiting. This nameless, causeless, speechless dejection would be too cruel. It would never do, it must be conquered.

I made a great effort, and got the children to answer me in an absent-minded way, but when the train stopped, and Robert stepped forward happy and smiling, and stretching out his arms for Alice, we could hardly speak to him. For weeks and months we had all been joyfully anticipating this very hour, and when it came, none of us appeared to be even decently pleased. Robert was astonished but very good-natured, and pitied us because we were too weary for anything but sleep. But when I told him, a little later, about the kind of trance into which the boys had fallen at the same time, he was much troubled.

"Was it a trance, Robert?" I asked.

"It was vision," he answered sadly. "The same experience came to Ethel, the day before her death."

"And what is vision?"

"The cup of strength, given only to those who will need its comfort."

Then we were both silent, and for some time both unhappy, though we did not again name the circumstance.

We stayed in a boarding-house while furnishing our new home, and this occupied over two weeks, for Robert could not spare much time to assist me, though he had seen to it, that the house itself was spotlessly clean and in good order. The rest had to be mainly my work. Now, how is it, that the very same circumstances are not always equally pleasant? I could not but remember our happy furnishing in Austin ten years previously. What a joyous time it was! And there was nothing to prevent, in some measure, a renewal of this experience; there were even one or two things favorable towards making it a still more delightful one; for instance, we had more money to spend, and more certain prospects.

But it was quite different. Robert went about the matter generously and helpfully, and the result was a pretty, comfortable home, with which we were both pleased; but its making had not been the same delightful event that our Austin home represented. There had been no disagreement, no disappointment, not one untoward circumstance of any kind, *but it was not the same*! Why? We loved each other better than ever before; what had caused the change? *Ten years?* When I was alone, I could not help a few regretful tears, but alas!

> No tears can make the grass to grow
> On the trampled meadows of long ago.

Ah, if we had known that it was our last home making! The very last time we should talk together about chairs and tables, curtaining and china, how almost sacred these common household things would have become. I have not an article left of this furnishing, but a pretty Queen Anne cream pitcher. On leaving Galveston forever, I gave this pitcher to Mrs. Lee of that city, as a memorial of her great kindness to me in the most terrible hours of my life. Twenty years afterward, she sent it with a loving message back to me, knowing that it would be a relic beyond price. Surely the veil God draws between us and the future is a veil of mercy. If Robert and I had known it, how heart-breaking that furnishing would have been!

We took possession of our new home on the sixteenth of October [1867]. It was then in perfect order, and we made a gala meal of our first supper, at which all the children were present. Then there followed a half-a-year of days sweet as the droppings from the honeycomb. Lilly and Calvin were at good schools, Mary was studying music, and learning how to dance, and I was busy enough with my house, with the sewing for the whole family, and with giving Alexander his first lessons. Alice though near seven years old was yet too weak to be troubled. She had been born during the excitement and terror of the beginning of the war, and she brought with her—not the fervid spirit of the time—but its exhaustion and weakness. . . .

It was not until late in April that the first whisper of calamity came. We lived in a cottage belonging to Judge Wheeler, and standing next to his own house, and one evening he came over to smoke his pipe with Robert on our verandah.

"Barr," he said, "I hear a good deal of talk about yellow fever, and I dare say many people will be advising you to leave this house, because there is a meat market not far away, which will be sure to attract the fever. Don't you believe them. Sit still. You are as safe here as anywhere. We do not intend to move nor do the Dalzells, who have the next house to us."

During the following month the terror grew daily, and as the hot weather came on, we were sensibly aware of our too close proximity to the meat market. Robert was sure we ought to remove, and he came home one day delighted with an empty house which he had found. It was near the sea, and it had unusually large rooms, all of which had just been renovated, papered and painted. It is not great things, but trivial ones, which generally produce the most important and tragic consequences; and it was the fresh papering and painting that made me willing to go through another removal. Yet I did not inspect the house before moving into it; if I had, I am sure I should have hesitated about doing so, but the weather was hot and humid, and the road between it and the Wheeler cottage deep with sand. My feeling was about the change was really one of assent, rather than desire.

The place, however, appeared to be all that had been represented—roomy and clean, freshly papered and painted, and so near the Gulf that we could hear the waves breaking on the shore. But as I walked through the rooms, an indefinable repugnance took possession of me, and I asked Robert if he knew who had been living in it?

"I do not," he said a little tartly. "I never thought of asking such a question. Does it matter, Milly?"

"Yes," I answered, "it does matter a great deal. In spite of the fresh paper and paint, the air of these rooms is not clean. Wicked people must have lived in them."

Then he laughed, and said, "You are too fanciful. No one has lived in the house," he continued, "for a great many years. It was almost a ruin, when old Durr bought it. We are its first tenants since its restoration to a respectable dwelling."

I said nothing further at the time, but I noticed that when the two large lamps were lit in the parlor, they did not light the room. It remained dull and gloomy, and full of shadows, and an eerie feeling of fear and unconquerable depression dashed all desire to talk over our arrangement of the furniture; deny it as he would, Robert and the children were affected in the same way.

But the change was made, and the wisest plan was to accept it hopefully. I put up the white curtains, and white mosquito draperies as soon as possible, not only because they were necessary to our comfort, but because I hoped the profusion of white would relieve the gloom. I filled the rooms with flowers, I hung no pictures but such as were of light coloring and cheerful subjects, and when I had finished my work, I felt more satisfied with the place.

Then life settled into its usual routine, yet hardly so, for I was counseled against allowing the children to study during the hot months in which they were acclimating; and I felt little inclination myself for any duty that was not an imperative necessity. I sat drowsily within the open door hardly thinking. Life gradually became inertia. I laid down my book and needle, and the children played without spirit, or lay sleeping in any cool place they could find. In Austin the thermometer had often stood ten or twelve degrees higher, and not affected our work or spirits, but as soon as it passed ninety degrees in Galveston it became intolerable. And at this time the average heat, if I remember rightly, was one hundred degrees and upward.

Still I am glad now to recall we kept up as far as possible all our household ways and traditions. No matter how hot the morning or night, we never missed the usual family worship, and only in case of sickness, did I permit either myself or the children, to neglect dressing to meet their father for supper. I did not read so much aloud to them, for we were all too listless and anxious to care about imaginary sorrows, with so much real danger and suffering around. Sometimes, however, I took a little stroll with Robert to the beach, and sometimes even I went downtown with him as far as our grocer's. He was a Glasgow man called Shaw, and Robert had formed a warm friendship with him.

As the days and weeks went on, we could not escape the certain knowledge that the fever was steadily gaining ground. During the latter part of June the corporation were keeping large fires of tar burning all through the city, and the gutters had a horrible odor of disinfectants. Far and wide the lurid smoke of these fires darkened the hot humid atmosphere, and at night their dark and fantastic shadows, and the singular forms they took, seemed to prefigure and presage the fate of the doomed city. Here and there stores were closed, and frequently dwellings full of human beings were marked with the dreaded yellow cross.

At this time I had no great fear of the fateful sickness. However, towards the middle of July affairs were coming to a frightful crisis. The fever had at last reached the military camp of the United States soldiers, which was but a block or two behind our house. There were a thousand men in it, and every morning I saw long lines of carts filled with rude boxes and tarred canvas pass the house. They were carrying the dead to the long trenches made for them. In August the colonel of this regiment died of the fever, and not thirty of the men were alive to bury him.

There was nothing for the custom's house and post office to do, their doors were shut; the Strand, which was the principal business street of the city, was rank with waving grass. Its large warehouses, shops, wharves and public buildings were closed. There were half a dozen little places scattered about, that were still open, mainly for the sale of bread and drugs, but they had an air of hopeless silence and abandonment. A dreadful haze hung over the city, and the sea—a haze that appeared to be filled with the very odors of despair and death. I was glad when the corporation gave up all efforts at prevention. The fever was now far beyond it, and Galveston was strictly isolated from the living world. It had become a city of dreadful death.

Day after day and week after week the weather was of the same distresssing character—an hour or two of pouring, beating, tropical rain, and then an hour or two of such awful heat and baleful sunshine, as the language happily has no words to describe. These two conditions alternated continually, and the consequence was streets full of grass— this grass being literally alive with tiny frogs, frogs not bigger than a bean, but in such enormous quantities that pedestrians crushed hundreds under their feet with every step they took. I do not exaggerate this sickening plethora of life; it is impossible to do so.

One evening towards the end of August I told Robert we were out of certain household necessities, and asked if he knew how they could be procured. He answered, "Yes, Shaw told me if we wanted anything to knock at his house door, and he would give us what was required. I will go and see him after supper."

Then I pleaded, "Let me go with you, Robert. I want a walk so much." He entreated me not to go, but I was resolved to see with my own eyes whether things were as bad as reported, and after some demur he consented. So I walked down into the city with him. A walk through hell could hardly have been more dreadful. The beds of the dying were drawn to the open windows, and there was hardly a dwelling wanting a dying bed. The faces of the sufferers were white and awful, their heads covered with crushed ice. They were raving, moaning, shrieking, or choking with the appalling vomito. I covered my eyes, and clung to Robert, and finally asked him to turn back.

"We are nearly at Shaw's," he answered, "and you had better rest there half an hour. It will then be darker."

So he knocked at the door for admission, and one of Mr. Shaw's clerks opened to us. Robert asked for Mr. Shaw, and the young man replied, "He is in bed, very ill with the fever."

I knew it the moment the door was opened. A strong sickly odor, like nothing ever felt before, told me so. I said to myself on the instant, "It is the smell of yellow fever." And no one, I think, would have failed to give it its own dreadful name—that is, if they were in a situation where the fever was probable. There is no odor on earth to which it is comparable. The soul loathes, and sickens, and trembles in its presence; for there is no straighter or surer avenue to the soul than the sense of smell. . . .

One night in August, Robert brought home with him a Mr. Hall, an old Austin friend. They had some business to talk over, and when I saw their conversation was finished, I had supper brought in, and as we sat down at the table, Mr. Hall glanced around the parlor and remarked, "The old pirate's nest has quite a Barr-y look already."

"Pirate's nest!" I ejaculated. "What do you mean, Mr. Hall?"

"Well," he answered, "if devils haunt the places they made hells on earth, Lafitte and his men must be here. It is said that Durr's house was standing in the days when Galveston was called Campeachy, and was a haunt and home of the vilest men, pirates and murderers from

the scum of all nations, ruled by the infamous Lafitte. By the way, Barr,"
he continued, "Lafitte was a great slave trader, and he had a very convenient way of selling negroes, a dollar a pound for them, old or young.
If this should have been Lafitte's house, as I have heard some suppose,
it was originally painted blood-red and ———"

"Mr. Hall," interrupted Robert, "I think you ought not to mention
such things in Madame's presence."

"I beg Madame's pardon," he answered, "but I felt sure she had
already heard many incomprehensible things. To me they are hardly
so, for I know what fiends once made Galveston Island their home. Do
you think they have forgotten the place of their sins and cruelties? No,
Furies of ancient crimes are here, revengeful souls full of unsatisfied
hatreds. Perhaps they have been given a strange enlargement for some
reason, and that reason must be within the permission and mercy of
God." . . .

Sometime after midnight on the twentieth of August I rose from
my bed. I could not sleep; I was too restless and unhappy, but all whom
I loved appeared to be sleeping well. So I sat down in a rocking chair
facing the sea. This open window was however screened by the ordinary green blinds, made of thin slats of wood. All was quiet but the
dull roar of the sea, troubling the sad heart of the night with a sound of
vague anger and melancholy. I heard a faint stir among the leaves of
the Japonica hedge that surrounded the place, and I stopped rocking
and sat motionless listening.

Then there fell upon the closed blinds—on which my eyes were
fixed—a blow so tremendous, that I was sure they must be shattered;
but ere I could rise, another blow of less intensity followed, and then a
third not quite as crashing as the second. I never for a moment thought
the blows were given by any instrument. I was sure they were made
by a hand. I went to Robert's side. He was fast asleep. The children
were also sleeping. Then I understood. I prayed for God's mercy, but
God seemed far from me. Until the dim gray dawn I sat in troubled
thought, but when I heard Robert stir I told him what had happened,
and begged him to come to the window with me. I had been afraid to
go near it; I had turned my back upon it, but I was sure the blinds had
been shattered.

There was not a slat broken. But the thin strips of wood were
indented and showed painfully the full shape of a hand twice as large as

any human hand. Why were the blinds not broken to pieces by three blows from a hand like that? And how could the thin strips of wood be made to bend and take an impression? This evidence of physical force, made by some spiritual entity remained for every one to see, as long as I lived in the house. As to what came after, I know not. I never again went in sight of the place.

That day I noticed the leaves of the Japonica hedge had turned black, and were covered with a loathsome sweat or moisture, and Robert told me he had been with Scotch Brown to the camp to do something for a Scotchman ill there, and that they were shown the body of a calf killed one hour previously, and it was as black as a piece of coal. "I would not let the children go outside, Milly," he said, "the very atmosphere has the fever."

That night Alexander was taken ill, and before midnight he was delirious. The next day Lilly was sick, and the following day Mary. There was then no institution like the present trained nurses, but the Scotchmen of Galveston had formed themselves into a society for nursing each other, if attacked by fever; and Robert and Scotch Brown had been busily engaged in this work for some weeks. Now Scotch Brown came to our assistance. He went into the kitchen, and could cook a suitable meal if necessary. He kept the negro hired help at their duties, and no woman could have been more tender, more watchful, more ready to help and comfort. Lilly had not a very bad attack, but Mary came perilously near to the fatal end. But carefully watched over and nursed, they passed the crisis, and began to recover. The recovery from yellow fever is very rapid, but if a relapse should take place, the case is hopeless.

On Sunday, the sixth of September, Alexander, Lilly and Mary were apparently getting well as satisfactorily as we could expect. Mary looked white and frail; Alexander lay mostly on the sofa; Lilly, in spite of yellow fever, had her usual bright smile and cheerful voice; but, Oh, how happy we were to be able to gather at the dinner table! Very sparing was the food of the invalids, but they enjoyed it, and we had a pleasant meal. It was a very happy day, I remember every hour of it. It was the last day I was to spend with my husband and sons, but I knew it not. Surely, I thought, God had heard my prayers, and we shall be spared to thank Him. We did so together, as soon as supper was over, and the children with kisses and loving words went early to rest. Robert and I sat until late; Robert was very quiet, but I leaned my head against his shoulder, and we spoke tenderly and hopefully to each other of things past, and of things likely to come. And as I brushed out my hair, and coiled it for the night, I said cheerfully to him,

> God doth not leave His Own.
> The night of weeping for a time may last,
> Then tears all past,
> His going forth shall as the morning shine.
> The sunrise of His favor shall be thine and mine,
> God doth not leave His Own. . . .

The next day was the worst we had yet seen. It poured incessantly, and when the rain ceased at nightfall, it was followed by a fog so dense that it seemed palpable. Every room in the house was full of it, lights would hardly burn, and breathing was not easy. Robert and the children went early to bed, but I wandered about the different rooms, watching the sleepers. I did not feel very well, and was nervous and full of fears. When the clock struck twelve I was worse, and I concluded it would be well for me to try and sleep. But before putting down the lamp, I opened the Bible, for my father had often told me, to take a verse to bed with me to meditate upon, if I happened to be wakeful. It was a common, almost a nightly custom, and I followed it at that hour more as a habit than a conscious intent. So opening the Bible, as my fingers touched the screw of the lamp, my eyes fell upon these words, *Leave thy fatherless children, I will preserve them alive; and let your widows trust in me."* (Jeremiah, 49:11).

My first emotion was anger. I closed the Book hastily but did not put out the light. I told myself that I would not go to bed with that strange verse pealing in my ears. And I wondered at my opening on the book of Jeremiah; it was one book that we never read, either personally or in the family. Its pages indeed were fresh and white, while the Psalms and Gospels were well worn and discolored. All that splendid faith, which is exactly to the inner woman what courage is to the physical woman, had slipped away from me. Why was God so hard to me? I wanted so much a little verse of comfort, and I had been given an evil prediction. I cried very much as a sensitive child would cry, who thought its dearly loved father had been unkind, or indifferent to its distress.

I had said, I would not go to bed with the verse pealing in my ears, but the pain in every limb of my body grew constantly worse. I put my fingers upon my wrist, and found there that peculiar "bound" that says at every throb, *yellow fever*! I knew at last, that I was smitten with the fever. Then I called Robert, and was quickly in such physical anguish that I forgot all else; also a feeling of sheer despair took possession of me, and during the ensuing week I was only conscious of the agony of a thirst, which could not be satisfied but at the risk of the vomito. Robert put bits of crushed ice between my lips frequently, but they did not assuage the cruel longing for water. I was in an unconscious state wandering in "a desolate land, where the pains of hell get hold on me—a land of deserts and pits, a land of drought and of the shadow of death, that no man passed through, and where no man dwelt;" and into which neither husband or child could follow me; tossing, muttering, slowly parching and burning up, I lived on from day to day.

But He that "turneth man to destruction" says also, "Return ye children of men"; and on Friday, the eleventh, I became conscious of Robert at my side, and of the children passing through the room and coming to me. I could feel their soft kisses on my hands and face, and I finally found strength to ask Mary, "How are Calvin and Alice?"

"Calvin is sick, Mamma," she answered. "Papa put him in my room; he wanted to be near you."

"Very sick?" I asked.

"Not as bad as I was."

"Alice?"

"She has the fever very slightly. She is nearly well. Alexander also, but you, dear Mamma?"

"All is right."

The next day I was much worse. I could not move, and was barely able to whisper a word or two, and towards midnight Alexander had a relapse. Wringing his hands, and full of a strange reluctance, Robert went out into the dreadful night to try to find a doctor. What happened on that fateful walk, I may not write, but he brought back the doctor, who looked at the child, and then turned to Robert and said,

"You will be wanted soon, lie down and sleep. Oh, you must! You must! I will stay here until you awake."

I know not how long Robert slept. He threw himself on a sofa within sight of my bed, and appeared to fall into a deep sleep as soon as his head touched the pillow. Alexander begged to come to me, and the doctor laid him at my feet, and I felt with an indescribable thrill of love and anguish, his little hand clasp my ankle.

The clock had just struck three, when I heard Robert start suddenly to his feet and cry, *"Yes, sir!"* Then smiting his hands together as if in distress, he cried out still loudly, *"Yes, sir! I am coming!"* The doctor rose and went to him. "Barr," he asked, "what is the matter?" for Robert was weeping as men seldom weep—long moaning sobs, that were the very language of heart-breaking despair. "What is the trouble, my friend?" the doctor asked again, and Robert answered,

"My father called me twice, and I—I answered him. He has been dead thirty-two years."

"Well then, your father would only come for your relief and help."

"He came for *me*, Doctor; the summons was inexorable and sure."

"Let us go to the child. He is very ill."

I heard these words, and I felt at the same moment a tighter clasp of the small hand round my ankle, and Robert's kiss upon my cheek. Then the hours went slowly and cruelly by, and in the afternoon the beginning of the end commenced. But just before it, the child had another attack similar to the one he and his brother had shared on the train coming in to Galveston. He was quite unconscious, even of his physical agony, his eyes firmly fixed their vision far, far beyond any earthly horizon. His father sat like a stone gazing at him, and I could not have moved a finger, or spoken a word, no, not to have saved his life.

The trance lasted only a few minutes, but he came out of it laughing, and then asked in a voice of awe and wonder, *"Who is that man waiting for me, Papa?"* He was assured there was no one waiting, but he replied, *"Yes, there is a man waiting for me. He is in the next room."* Then his father noticed that his eyes had a new, deep look in them, as if some veil had been rent, and he with open face had beheld things wonderful and secret.

About seven o'clock they took him away from me into the next room. He clung to my feet, and begged to stay with me, and I—Oh, I strove as mortals strive with the impossible to speak, to plead, that he might remain! But it could not be. His father lifted him in his arms, and through the next five awful hours he held him there. No! no! It is not writable, unless one could write with blood and tears. At midnight it was over. But as his father laid down the little boy, Mrs. Lee went to him, and said,

"Calvin is very ill. Go and speak to him, while you can."

He went at once and put his arm under the sweet child, and spoke to him. And the first words the dying boy uttered were, "Papa, what is the matter with my brother?"

"He is very ill, Calvin."

"Is he dying?"

"Yes."

"Tell him to wait for me. I am dying, too, Papa! I cannot see you! I am blind! Kiss me, Papa."

These were his last words. He died two hours after his brother, and I do not doubt they went together; and they had "a Man" with them, who knew his way through the constellations. They would go straight to Him whom their souls loved. I was not permitted to see either of them, and on Tuesday afternoon they were buried. I heard them carry out the coffins; I heard their father's bitter grief, and I was dumb and tearless.

After they were buried, Robert came straight to me. "They are laid side by side, Milly, darling," he said. "Now *I also* must leave you. Forgive Robert all that he has ever done to grieve you." I tried to tell him that I had nothing to forgive, that he was always good to me, but he shook his head sadly, and continued, "O Milly, my love, my wife, farewell! I must go, dearest! I must go! O my dear, dear wife, farewell!" and I could only answer with low sharp cries. I had not a word for this moment. At the open door our eyes met in a long parting gaze, and then I remember nothing more, till it was dark and late, and I heard the sounds of men busy in the next room.

I never saw my husband again. On Wednesday he died. Thank God, he died as Calvin did, of general congestion. Death mounted from his dead feet to his heart, and head, with a swift sure pace, but he was really dying the last three days that he was nursing his dying sons. He fell on guard, and Death came as a friend to relieve him:

> "And so he passed to joy, through bitter woe,
> As some great galleon through dark may go,
> Where no star glimmers, and the storm wind wails
> Until the rose of Morning touch her sails."

Mrs. Lee stayed at his side until the last moment, and when all was finished, she came to me. "He has gone!" she said.

"I know," I answered. "He passed me as he went. There was *One* with him. I thank God! What time did he go?"

"It was just ten minutes past eleven."

Then I remembered the pendulum of the clock falling at ten minutes past eleven. And the memory gave me a sudden sense of comfort. Some wiser Intelligence than ourselves, had known even then, what was before us; had known when Robert left his home, that he was faring into the shadows in which his grave was hid. His death was not a blind hap-hazard calamity. It was a foreseen event, an end predetermined by Infinite Wisdom and Love. O mystery of life! From what unexpected sources, spring thy lessons and thy comforts! Whatever life was left in me was quickened by this blow. I felt it to the foundation of my being, and though I could not speak to those around me, I could to the *Divine Other* who was closer to me than breathing, and nearer than hands or feet. Instantly I found myself urging that almighty help.

"I cannot die now," I pleaded. "Oh, I cannot die and leave those three little girls alone—in a strange land, without money, without relative or friend to care for them! Oh, help me to live! Help me to live for their sakes! Not for thy sake, for thou can never see death! not for my sake, I am but as a dead woman now; but for my children's sake, help me to recover my strength! Help me, and I shall live."

In this manner I silently prayed, with all the fervor of which my soul was capable. And in that central tract of emotion where life and death meet, there are paths of spiritual experience remote and obscure, until some great crisis finds them out—experiences not to be unfolded save to that *one* Soul, and for which words—however wise—are impotent things. I feel this truth as I write, for I cannot find a way to explain the sure and certain influx of life, that came to me, even as I entreated for it. It came from no drug, no physician, no human help of any kind, but direct from the *Thee in Me* who works behind the veil, the *More of Life* in whom we live and move and have our Being.

I do not say that my prayer changed God's will or purpose concerning me. Oh, no! but God directed my prayer. He put my petition into my heart. The prayer was granted ere I made it. For if we do right, it is God which teaches us both to will and to do, so that every soul that cries out to the Eternal, finds the Eternal; I care not when, or where. God is not far from any one of us, and in every case he seeks us, before we have the desire to seek Him.

I had a full and ready answer to my soul's petition. I recovered rapidly, and in ten days was able to leave my room, and gather the salvage of my wrecked home around me. No doubt most of my readers have a keen and personal knowledge of that weight of grief, which hangs like lead in the rooms, and on the stairs, where the footsteps of the loved dead have sounded. They know what it is to come back from the grave of their love, and see his hat lying where he threw it down forever, and his slippers at the foot of the bed he died on. And, oh, what a multitude of mothers that no man could number, know what it means to put away the empty clothing that still keeps a heartbreaking look of the little form that moulded it—or the small worn shoes and stockings, the toys and books, that will never more be needed. Alas it is too common an experience to require words! This grief has but to be named, and at any hour thousands of heavy hearts can fill in all its sad details.

After the month of September the fever, for the very want of victims, began to decline, and about the middle of October there was a storm which shook Galveston Island to its foundation. The waters of the Gulf of Mexico and the Bay of Galveston met, and mingled, in the center of the city. There was a hurtling, roaring tempest around it, and a tremendous battle in the firmament above it. It was "a day of desolation, a day of darkness, of clouds and thick darkness;" and throughout the hours the storm gathered strength. All night the inhabitants sat still in terror, while the sea beat at their doors, and their homes rocked in the terrific wind.

After midnight, when the roaring and crashing and fury of the elements were at their height, it was easy to call to remembrance the magnificent description of just such a storm in Habakkuk, 3:5–12, and as the children drew closer and closer to me, I repeated what I could of it;

"Before him went the pestilence, and burning coals went forth at his feet . . . and the everlasting mountains were scattered, the perpetual hill did bow . . . I saw the tents of Cushan in affliction . . . Was thy wrath against the sea, that thou didst ride upon thine horses and thy chariots of salvation? . . . The overflowing of the water passed by:

Amelia Barr in 1880. (*From her autobiography,* All the Days of My Life)

the deep uttered his voice, and lifted up his hands on high. The sun and the moon stood in their habitation . . . Thou wentest forth for the salvation of thy people."

At the dawning, the tempest lulled off with mighty, sobbing winds; sullenly but surely it went, and with it departed entirely the dreadful pestilence. There was not another case known. The Lord had indeed arisen for the salvation of the city, and His angels had driven away the powers of darkness that had been permitted there for a season. Oh, then if our eyes had been opened! If we could have seen the battle in the firmament above us! If we could have seen "the Man Gabriel," or Michael "the great prince which standeth for the children of God's people against the evil ones," then, no doubt, we should have said with Elisha, "Fear not: for they that be with us are more than they that be with them."

*   *   *

In November, 1868, Amelia and her daughters left Galveston forever. The devastated family moved to New York City, and Mrs. Barr began what was to become a phenomenal career as a writer. Her first piece was a magazine article on "the breakup in Texas," for which she was paid thirty dollars. She says of the event: "I was astonished and delighted, but after a few moments I laughed joyously and cried, 'Why I can write three or four of those every week! . . . Is my work really going to be printed? Do you think I can write?'" She could indeed write and was soon supporting herself and her three daughters by writing magazine and newspaper articles. After publication of *Jan Vedder's Wife* in 1886, she became one of the most popular novelists in the United States.

In the years that followed, Amelia wrote at least eighty books and hundreds of short stories, poems, and essays. With her earnings she bought Cherry Croft, a beautiful house that overlooked the Hudson River. At the age of eighty-one she wrote her autobiography, *All the Days of My Life*, which many consider to be her best book.

Amelia Barr died in 1919 at the age of eighty-seven, a woman who had suffered much but had eventually attained great success in the literary world. An Englishman in New York once told her: "I know you by your Lancashire eyes, and your Lancashire color, and the up-head way you carry yourself." She answered, "No, sir, the up-head way I learned in Texas. It's an up-heart way, also. The up-head helps the heart, when the heart is dashed and down."

IV. Texas Sunshine: The Last Frontier, 1865–1905

During the Civil War and in the decade afterwards, much of Texas was a lawless land. Warlike Plains Indians returned to steal, kidnap, rape, and murder when forts along the western edge of settlements were abandoned. After the war an Indian "peace policy" allowed Indians to raid in Texas and then return to sanctuary on reservations in Indian Territory, now Oklahoma. The Comanches, Kiowas, Kiowa-Apaches, Cheyennes, and Arapahoes, most of whom had signed a peace treaty in 1867 with the United States, considered Texas to be a separate country not covered by treaty. From 1865 to 1867 at least 230 Texans were killed, wounded, or taken prisoner.

Other problems were created by bands of outlaws which flourished from 1865 to 1890. Also, vigilante groups, ostensibly created to bring law and order, themselves became little better than gangs of outlaws. Feuds broke out and increased the suffering of those who sought to remain neutral and law-abiding. Adding to the problem were Indians and Mexican outlaws who came north across the Rio Grande to raid and then fled to safety in northern Mexico.

To alleviate the suffering of the Texans, the Texas Rangers were reactivated in 1874. Luvenia Conway Roberts, the wife of a Texas Ranger, was given special permission to live in camp on the frontier and later wrote of her experiences.

On farms, ranches, and in small settlements other women were braving the dangers of the Texas frontier. For many years Ella Elgar Bird Dumont and Fannie Veale Beck lived in constant fear of Indians. Both these women lived in counties that were west of or close to the 98th meridian, which Walter Prescott Webb later designated as the Texas frontier.

Most of these women visited lawless frontier towns where outlaws were frequent visitors. Luvenia Conway Roberts faced greater danger in such a town than in the Ranger camp. As late as 1902 the leader of Mary Blankenship's group of settlers was killed by hostile ranchers who resented the incursion of what they called "nesters." Ella Dumont and Mary Blankenship also battled nature as they tried to make homes in the hostile environment of the dry, wind-swept plains.

In spite of dangers, hardships, and the deaths of husbands and children, these women made homes in the harsh land of North and West Texas. Their reminiscences, although tinged with sadness at times, are full of exuberance and pride in their accomplishments. They had come to a new land—a forbidding and strange land not easily tamed—and with their husbands had made homes for themselves and their children. The wind blew and they were beset by droughts and blizzards, but soon the sun shone on their crops, their cattle, and their children.

Fannie Davis Veale Beck

"When darkness came, everybody stayed indoors."

Fannie Davis Veale Beck wrote *On the Texas Frontier* so that her children who had been transplanted from "sunny Texas" to Iowa would know about their Texas heritage. She begins her autobiography by describing her ancestors, her "Grandma Hardin" and her mother Maria Lavenia Cresswell, who came to Texas with Stephen F. Austin's colony. Her father William Veale grew up on a plantation near Hillsboro, Texas.

Fannie's parents moved to Palo Pinto in 1863 when she was a year old. The open rangeland was shunned by most settlers because of the threat of hostile Indians in the area. At the time that the Veales journeyed to Palo Pinto, the Comanches were on the warpath, and the Veales heard stories of Indian atrocities which had occurred a few days earlier on the trail upon which they were traveling. The twenty or so families in the village lived in nearly constant fear of the Indians until the mid-1870's. In 1873 Fannie's cousin Jesse Veale was surprised by Indians while hunting, and his body was found "literally pinned to a tree with arrows."

In spite of danger from attack by Indians, Fannie had a happy childhood in Palo Pinto as she looked out "toward the blue, mist-covered mountains that almost encircled the little town." Fannie refuses to adhere to chronological order as she mixes description of everyday life with tragic tales of murder and mutilation.

*   *   *

For fear my children, and others who may read these pages, should get a mistaken idea of the sort of people who made up the community life of the farthest outpost of civilization on the frontier of Texas, let me say that it took courage of the very highest order and the stuff of which real heroes are made for men to face the dangers and privations of border life that civilization might be planted there and its borders ex-

From Fannie Davis Veale Beck, *On the Texas Frontier* (Saint Louis: Britt Printing and Publishing Company, 1937).

Henry and Fannie Beck with daughters Mary and Susie (on her mother's lap).
(*Courtesy Margaret Veale Beck Hays*)

tended to make homes for their loved ones. There were no induce-
ments, certainly, for idlers and cowards. Bad men there were a plenty,
as might be expected, who were attracted by the very dangers which
made for adventure and exploitation of their evil tendencies, but bad
men are to be reckoned with in any community and at any time. I
found a paragraph in an article I read recently, which explains very
well the reason why men pull up stakes and leave a comfortable home
in a civilized country to blaze new trails and establish homes in the
kind of places that Palo Pinto was sixty years ago.

Beaten paths are for beaten men. They would not have been paths if
others had not gone that way before, and those that go before usually take all
worth having. . . .

From the time I can remember anything about life in Palo Pinto,
the fear of Indians was ever present. Of course, the awful fear did not
affect us pioneer children deeply, but it was a deadly menace to our
fathers and mothers day and night. Every precaution for meeting this
dread emergency was taken. The houses were built of logs laid close
together so that an arrow could not penetrate them. The stables were
built just like the houses, with heavy padlocks to lock the horses in
every night, for a horse was an Indian's most prized booty. On their
raids on moonlight nights, they invariably carried off all the horses that
had been left outside locked stables, and those that they could not get
out of the stables they would shoot full of arrows, if they could find a
chink in the stable walls.

The houses were provided with heavy wooden shutters for doors
and windows, and these had padlocks for security at night. These
wooden shutters could be opened through the day for light and air, but
everything was closed down and padlocked at night. You young people
of the present time who must have so much fresh air at night would
have been in a bad way in those days; for you would have had to run
the risk of getting an Indian arrow along with your fresh air. When
darkness came, everybody stayed indoors. I can well remember with
what fear and trembling anyone who had to open a door at night did it,
and how soon he got it over with, and got out of sight of lurking savages. The water bucket was filled with water and brought in for the
night, and enough wood was stored inside the house if it was cold
weather; everything was made safe against going outside. The chickens

roosted in trees in the back yard and even though many times they set up a cackling and squawking, nobody ever dared to go outside to see what was the matter—nobody but Ma. One night, she stood it as long as she could. She heard an old hen squawking and fluttering; so she went out of the back door of the kitchen to help the old biddy out of her trouble. There were two live-oak trees in the yard, close to the kitchen, and the chickens were all roosting in these trees; as she opened the door, she heard, besides the noise the old hen was making, a swelling chorus of cackles and squawks from all the other chickens in the trees. As Ma stepped out between the two trees a big wildcat jumped out of one tree into the other, right over her head. She made a hasty retreat into the house, and the cat went on his way with the hen he had chosen.

As I have said before, no one ever dared to investigate any outside noises, like pigs squealing, or owls hooting, or even the meowing of a cat; for the Indians used such tricks as imitating animals to lure people out of their houses and kill them. The scream of a panther was one of the most common of Indian signals, and if there was an answering scream, it was a pretty sure sign that Indians were planning a raid. . . .

How anyone could endure life under such conditions! Well, of course, since the world has undergone three decades of changes since the far-away days of which I am telling, it would be impossible to expect Modern Youth to appreciate the testimony I am about to give, but, believe it or not, life was full of ambition then as now. The common necessities of life were hard to get, even if we had had the money for them. We were about as poor as "Old Mother Hubbard," for our cupboard was always bare, and we children usually had all the clothing we possessed right on our backs. But I can say that my childhood was a happy one and brimful of enjoyment, in spite of the handicaps of poverty and the ever-present fear of Indians. Not knowing anything about a better way of living, we children did not miss anything, and the few benefits that came our way were doubly appreciated. Our parents, of course, were the ones who really suffered, for *they* had left homes of safety and comfort "back East" that they might try their fortunes in a new country.

As I have already told you, John was the eldest boy in the family, and I was the eldest girl; so we were rather favored in being given the best of everything. If just *one* of the girls could have a new dress, or a

new pair of shoes, that one was I, and so with the boys. I can remember the pouting and tears when the younger ones were told to
"Never mind, your day will come," but "John and Fannie are the oldest
and they should have the advantage." Of course, such reasoning never
satisfied the poor younger children, and while John and I were rather
smug over our advanced age, we had to take all the slurs such an ele-
vated station carried with it in consequence, and listen to accusations
that Ma was partial (as indeed she was) and that we were nothing but
prigs. But don't get the exaggerated impression that I was well supplied with clothes. If there were new clothes, I was favored, but those
occasions were rare. One Christmas morning, for instance, while I sat
by the fire, waiting for breakfast, I looked down at my dress, an old,
faded, soiled calico that I had worn for so long that it was threadbare.
There was no unusual preparation for the day. Pa had gone to New
Orleans to help drive a herd of steers to market and would not be home
for several weeks. There was no cake, no pie. There were no clean
clothes for any of us, and, as I thought of this sad state of affairs, the big
tears dropped down into my soiled lap. When Ma came in, she said,
"Why, honey, what are you crying for?"

I said, "Ma, can I have a clean dress? It's Christmas, and I'm
ashamed of these old dirty clothes."

Ma said, "You know, my child, how sorry I am, but that is all you
have. I will wash it out tonight after you go to bed." But when she went
back to the kitchen, I slit the whole front into ribbons, just by running
my fingers down the folds. You see that even I, the favored eldest, was
often in a sorry plight for clothes. . . .

When a bunch of cowboys would come riding into town, they
always made a beeline for the saloon, and some one of their number would "set 'em up" for the crowd. This was also the signal for the
"hangers-on" and the "dead beats" to get in on the free drinks; for each
man, with reckless generosity, stood treats to all. Not till they had
spent all their money and were almost too drunk to ride would they
leave the saloon. Jumping on their cow ponies, they would go roaring
out of town, shooting their pistols as they rode. Of course, there were
some exceptions. Cowboys were not all reckless drinkers, but in the
very early days it seemed the only thing for them to do; for society was
not organized enough to make a place to take care of their entertainment, even if the cowboys had wished it. It was to the interest of the

saloonkeeper to be a good "pal" to the cowboys and have everything attractive and agreeable; so the saloon was their club, ready at all times for their entertainment and comfort. I am speaking of cowboys in the very early years, as I remember them, and I would not for the world give you a false impression about cowboys generally, but try to give you a picture of the "diamond in the rough" in those early days, as cowboys were so often spoken of in song and story. I have a high regard for all cowboys; I was brought up with them—went to school with them. A cowboy was my first beau, and I had other good friends, who were men of honor and integrity, whose lives were spent on the range, and I felt perfectly safe in their company. Many a night I have spent out on some lonely ranch dancing all night because the distance was too great to get back to town and there was no provision made for sleeping at the ranch. A group of us girls with our beaux would ride out on horseback, have supper at the house where the party was given, then dance the hours away until daylight, eat breakfast, and go home. John was usually along on these all-night parties, but I would have felt perfectly safe if he had not been; for a woman's honor was a sacred thing and sacredly guarded by these young gallants, even though they were lacking in a good many niceties demanded by polite society in later years. There was no chaperone except the hostess in the home where the dance was given. The young people paired off and rode in couples on horseback. There was no love-making, no drinking, no foolish and questionable conversation. We just had a good time, and felt none the worse for the all-night "carousal." One night our hosts were two brothers, bachelors, and we had to stay all night on that occasion. I remember that they cooked breakfast for us. There were about sixteen of us. They gave us soda biscuits, bacon, and coffee with no cream. As I remember, the men did not use sugar; so there was no sugar. But we didn't miss anything. We were young and we were hungry, and a long horseback ride was before us with our best beaux. We did not even mind that three or four of us had to the use the same cup, since, as our hosts said, they were "short on 'chaney'." . . .

At the time of the episode I am going to tell about (I think it was in 1873), Cousin Jesse Veale and another young man were hunting on Ioni Creek about twelve or fourteen miles from town. There were several hunters in the crowd. One of Cousin Jesse's brothers and a friend had become separated from the others. They heard the Indians coming, but they were surrounded before they actually saw the savages. The men put up a brave fight, but they were so outnumbered by the Indians that the two men running to escape and to get help from the rest of the party left Cousin Jesse where he had fallen, pierced by an arrow. He begged them to go on, as he was mortally wounded. When the others came up with the two who had been in the fight, they found Cousin Jesse literally pinned to a tree with arrows. He had sold his life dearly; for all the loads were discharged from his guns, which he had fired as long as his ammunition lasted. One Indian was killed and several wounded, as Cousin Jesse had fired several times after he himself was wounded.

I shall never forget the night he was brought home. Ma and Pa had to go to Uncle Bill's to help them get ready for the funeral. John was away at school; so Milton and I were left in charge of the other children. Sue was a little over a year old, and the others, except Milton and me, were small, and we ourselves were not grown-ups by a good many years. Ma and Pa had left as soon as they got the word about Cousin Jesse, and that was about dark. We had just finished supper, and they made preparations to go. Our house was rather isolated, for it was quite far out from the main part of town and was on a little creek. Our parents had told us there was no danger of the Indians that night because they would be far away, escaping from the vengeance of the posse out after them. But that did not make us feel any the better. We two older ones were in authority and we felt the responsibility of having five young chilsren to take care of through that long night. We nailed quilts up in the windows and stuffed rags into the cracks so that no light could shine through. We all slept in one room; that is, the others slept. Milton and I kept vigil by the fire, listening to every sound, imagining that every little noise we heard came from the terrible savages stealing upon us to massacre us. We suffered an agony of fear every time Sue, the baby, stirred; for we didn't want her to cry and let the Indians know there was a houseful of unprotected children for them to pounce upon. Well, that awful night passed somehow, and when morning came, bringing our parents back, my full heart responded as I threw myself into my mother's arms and cried with joy that we were safe, and all was well.

We all went to see Cousin Jesse and afterward went to his funeral. He had long, dark hair and clear, dark skin. He was finely proportioned and very tall. I had never seen a dead person before, and I had a feeling of awe and solemnity and a devastating sense of loss and grief that one so promising and so comely as this young man lying cold and still in death should be put into the grave and have the clods heaped over his coffin. . . .

The Indians continued their raids on white settlers until about 1875. The two stories I am going to tell now mark the last of their visits to the town. On this occasion the Indians selected our home, or rather our stable and yard, for their activities. Pa always kept one team of horses for both driving and working the field, where he raised his own corn and wheat. This was the same field I told about earlier, where I had to help the boys drop corn. I do not know how large the area was. I have no idea how many acres it contained, but it seemed, when I was trudging along putting the grains of corn in the rows, that there must have been hundreds of acres and that the corn rows were miles long. I am sure the field was really very small, for we kept only one hired man to tend it, and John's part was merely to take care of the horses, feeding and watering them three times a day, locking them in the stable at night, and tending them the first thing in the morning. This team was unusually good. The horses were large, evenly matched and young. One horse was brown and the other gray, and thus their names, Gray and Brown. We were very much attached to these animals and regarded them as valuable possessions. John had to get out before anyone else in the morning so that the horses would have time to eat their feed. The household was awakened on the morning I am writing about by John's running in from the stable, crying, "Pa, Brown and Gray have been shot. They have about a dozen Indian arrows sticking in their sides." The terrible news brought all the family tumbling out of their beds, some of us crying, while John told Pa how, when he unlocked the stable door, the gray horse was down and the other one was writhing in pain from the poisoned arrows. In a few minutes every man in town was there, and they did what they could for the poor horses. One or two arrows went so deep into Gray that when one of the barbs pulled out, a piece of the horse's liver was on the point. Poor Gray died, but the other horse lived. All the arrows were poisoned, and all that saved Brown was that the Indians could not get a good aim at him through the chinks in the logs. That was a sample of the mean, low-down tricks of Indians. If they couldn't get a horse, they always shot him. There were other horses stolen that night. The men of the town organized a posse and trailed the Indians out to a canyon on Ioni Creek. There were several Indians, and they had taken refuge in the thick brush in the bottom of the canyon. The men watched for several days and finally set fire to the cedar brakes. The Indians must have found a secret trail along which they escaped; for when the men went down into the canyon, the only evidence they found that the Indians had been there was a bloody trail where one of them had been wounded. One of our men got his face full of buckshot as he leaned over the rim of the canyon. This was unusual, for although some of the Indians had guns, they used bows and arrows as a general thing, especially when they were on a stealing expedition.

Despite the fact that Grant finally sent United States troops to the outlying frontier forts to protect white settlers, the Indians continued their raids up to about 1875. The Indians had been taken to the Reservation in what was then the Indian Territory, now known as Oklahoma, and the depredations were committed by roving bands of Comanches who had broken away from the restraints of Government discipline. One Sunday night, Pa and Ma had gone to preaching service at the Masonic Hall. We had no church buildings at that time, and no regular church services. The Methodist circuit rider came about twice or three times a year, and sometimes a Baptist preacher or a Hard-shell Baptist visited the town and preached for us. Everybody turned out to these services, saint and sinner alike. There were no denominational differences, no petty group prejudices, among those early congregations. They went to hear the Man of God tell them of a Heaven to be gained and warn them of a hell to be feared. Sometimes, indeed, most of the times, these messengers were crude and uneducated, and their message harsh and difficult, but the people were hungering and thirsting for the benefits of a Christian religion, and they were not critical, except occasionally, when a Hard-shell brother expounded too long, and, as sometimes happened, visited the jug too often and had to be put out or carried out. It was a night in early summer. John was home from Austin, where he had been attending school, and after supper, Pa announced that John and I should stay with the children while he and Ma went to church. So they left about dusk for the Masonic Hall. This was quite a distance from our house and stood on a hill east of town. This building, as I have said before, was used for a schoolhouse, also, for several years. In fact, it was the only place we had for public gatherings of any kind, until a more commodious schoolhouse was built several years later. (A cyclone destroyed the old hall several years ago.) Our house was a double log house, with a wide hall running down the center and separating the four rooms; there was a porch (or gallery) the entire length of the house, and there was a large yard enclosed with cedar pickets. We used the hall for many purposes, especially in warm weather. The four rooms opened onto it from the sides, and it was open to the gallery in front, with a back door leading into the kitchen. We had the dining table in the hall and ate all our meals there.

On this particular Sunday night, after the others had gone to bed, John and I took the lamp and our books and writing materials to the dining table in the hall. The night was so still that we could hear the least little noise outside. It was pitch dark, too, and we could not distinguish anything beyond the faint light from the lamp. We worked with our writing and reading a little while, and John got up to let the dog, a pup just a few months old, out of the room. As soon as it got outside the door, it began to growl and bark. It would run to the edge of the porch and then come tearing back. It kept that up until I was scared and John was provoked. So we shut the pup back in the room and went to bed. Pretty soon the folks came in. Pa insisted on putting his bed on the porch and sleeping there, as was his custom on hot nights. I heard all the commotion of his dragging the mattress out, Ma's protests, the little dog's continued tearing back and forth and barking his head off, and Pa's threats to "wring its neck." I had tried to tell John, earlier in the evening, that I could see something just beyond the rays of light from the lamp and near the porch. I *did* see several forms, indistinctly, of course, but he hooted at the idea. He said there was nothing out there to be afraid of, and the pup probably smelled some wild animal. Well, we slept a few hours that night when the dog quit barking. Pa always slept like a baby, and he probably dropped off while the pup was still yapping, but Ma said she lay trembling for hours, for she fancied she could see something moving around in the yard, and from the way the dog behaved, she felt that danger lurked out there in the darkness. It is a blessed thing that we are often spared the knowledge of the nearness of danger and death. When daylight came, we realized that we might all have been killed and scalped. We wondered why we were spared, for the yard was full of moccasin tracks, criss-crossed all over the place, and thickest near the porch where Pa and Ma had slept. I had some flowers growing in an old stump in the corner of the yard; they were pulled up and scattered on the ground. The mystery about the pup was cleared up by some of the men, who came as soon as the alarm was given that Indians had been to see us again. Indians have a satanic humor, and when the pup would run to the edge of the porch and bark they would try to catch him; then he would run back. Judging from the number of moccasin tracks, there were about sixty Indians in the raiding party that had chosen our place to reconnoiter. They had held a "caucus" in the calf pasture at the back of the stable, as was evidenced by the places in the sand where they had squatted for their pow-wow. They did not steal anything. They could have killed us all, for they had been around the place for several hours. A number of men got out after them as soon as they could the next morning, but the Indians had several hours' start and were never overtaken. This is my last Indian story, and this is the last time we ever heard of the Indians.

It was always a mystery in our little town why that band of sixty savages left our home and the little settlement without doing any mischief.

We had really lost our fear of Indians before the time they came to our place. The country was settling up, and detachments of U.S. soldiers were stationed at different places to protect the frontier; moreover, the Indians had been moved to the Reservation in the Indian Territory, and they were guilty of breaking their treaty when they left the Reservation. There were many tribes of Indians in Texas, some of which were hostile to each other and friendly to the Texans. The two I know most about were the Cherokees and Comanches, besides a friendly tribe on the Reservation at Fort Griffin, called Tonkawas. The Cherokees had been driven across the Red River, leaving the Comanches to kill and steal until the Texas Rangers were organized to patrol the frontier and prevent Indian atrocities. These Rangers were a fine class of men. They were experienced Indian fighters who had first been used to protect the settlements while the other men were fighting Santa Anna in the war with Mexico. They were paid by the State and were given the civil power of sheriff besides their military authority. In Indian times, their chief duty was to protect white settlers from Indian raids; later they aided in capturing cattle thieves and lawbreakers. . . .

The country developed rapidly after people got over their fear of Indians and many new families moved to town. More houses were built. A dry-goods and general merchandise store, a town hall, and new schoolhouse were added to the community. In any condition of life, where a group of people are gathered together, the need for food and clothing and services of the various professions are the constructive forces which build up a town; and pretty soon we had them all. We were so absorbed with the business of growing up, with adjusting ourselves to changing conditions, that we thought not at all of the great world beyond the blue rim of our own mountains. . . .

*   *   *

In 1877 the Veales moved to Breckenridge, Texas. A town of a few hundred people, Breckenridge was occasionally visited by the famous outlaw Sam Bass in disguise. Fannie, who was about sixteen years old at the time, soon met Henry Harrison Beck, a handsome bachelor nine years older than she. He owned the general store and several tracts of land.

After a long courtship the two were married in 1885. For the first three years of their marriage, Henry was constantly ill with "rheumatism and acute indigestion." The Becks lived on a ranch in Bosque County, and they finally found a doctor who administered a miraculous cure. From about 1888 until 1904 the Becks spent most of their time in Aransas Pass, Texas. In 1904 Henry decided to move back to his old home in Iowa, where he owned several farms. He planned to stay only "a few years." On March 3, 1935, Henry and Fannie celebrated their Golden Wedding Anniversary on the "*only* sunny day of the month, in Morning Sun, Iowa." Fannie had borne nine children and buried three, and she rejoiced in her six living daughters and many grandchildren. She remembered the dirty calico dress she had worn on that Christmas Day long ago in Palo Pinto, and she was especially proud of her fine chiffon gown, but she was most proud of "the fine looking man who would stand by her side."

Luvenia Conway Roberts

> "My friends thought I was courageous; in fact, quite
> nervy to leave civilization and go into an Indian
> country."

Luvenia Conway, who was born in 1849, was living in Columbus, Texas, when she met Daniel Webster Roberts. Thirty-three
years old at the time of his marriage in 1875, Roberts was a fine
specimen of manhood. Reared on the frontier in the Hill Country,
he had his first brush with the Indians in the Deer Creek fight in
1873. When the Texas Rangers were reorganized in 1874 to alleviate the suffering of the pioneers on the Texas frontier, Roberts was
asked to join Company D.

Roberts had served in the Rangers for about two years when
he began to think about resigning. In his book *Rangers and Sovereignty* he explains the situation: "Major John B. Jones . . . had an
'inkling' that Lieut. D. W. Roberts was intending to tender his
resignation, the purpose being to get married. The Major, in his
characteristic fine tact, broached the matter first, and in his keen
black eyes was a laughing twinkle that told me that he had antici-
pated me fully. He told me that he was in perfect accord with my
idea of getting married, but my resignation was not at all necessary, and to bring my wife on out to the company. . . . But a second consideration came to my mind, that I had been too hasty. My
intended bride had not been consulted, as to whether she would
come out among the red-skins or not . . . happily, she agreed to
the programme, and appeared to think it the climax of all the
romance she had ever indulged in."

So they were married. As Lou explains in her own book,
*A Woman's Reminiscences of Six Years in Camp with the Texas
Rangers*, she was very much in love with her husband and was not
about to be left behind in Columbus. Her husband planned to find
a place for her in the little town of Mason, located forty miles from
the Ranger camp, and to visit her whenever he could. However,
while Lou was staying in Mason, the worst part of the feud known

From Mrs. D. W. Roberts, *A Woman's Reminiscences of Six Years in Camp with the Texas Rangers* (Austin: Von Boeckmann–Jones Company, 1928).

as the Mason County War erupted at her doorstep, and she soon joined her husband at the Ranger camp.

Luvenia Conway Roberts begins her book with the newspaper announcement of her marriage.

*   *   *

Married September 13, 1875, Captain D. W. Roberts and Miss Lou Conway, the Rev. Dr. Archer officiating. The gallant groom and his accomplished bride departed on the train immediately after the ceremony. The best wishes of all attend them.

This brief notice appeared in the *Columbus (Texas) Times*. The clergyman had preached the day before, Sunday, at Osage, some distance from Columbus. He returned by train; there was only one train a day; as we were to leave on this same train the conductor obligingly held it while the minister came to the house and pronounced the words "until death do us part."

Captain Roberts commanded a company of Rangers stationed in Menard County, which was on the extreme frontier. His home was in Blanco County. He had been engaged in buying and selling cattle. At that time Columbus was the terminus of the railroad, and a good shipping point. It was during his visits to Columbus on business that we became acquainted.

My friends thought that I was courageous; in fact, quite nervy to leave civilization and go into an Indian country. But it did not require either; I was much in love with my gallant captain and willing to share his fate wherever and whatever it might be. Besides the romantic side of it appealed to me strongly. I was thrilled with the idea of going to the frontier, the home of the pioneer.

We came direct to the beautiful city of Austin. I had made trips to Houston, Galveston, and San Antonio—all located in a level country. The hills of Austin were beautiful, and, now since I have visited other States, I still believe that the scenic beauty of Austin and surrounding country cannot be excelled. . . .

While at Austin two Rangers came to take us to Menard. Except for my husband they were the first Rangers I saw; they looked formidable, armed with pistols and belts full of cartridges. Our mode of travel was by hack drawn by a pair of mules. Thus we set out on our bridal tour. I'm sure there was never a more delightful one, and there can never be another just like it. We spent a night at the old Nimitz Hotel at Fredericksburg, which became our regular stopping place as long as we were in the service. We were glad to lodge where we were served such excellent meals. Our next stop was at Mason, where my husband purposed leaving me while he went on to Menard and engaged board until he could arrange quarters at camp. In fact, he had not planned to take me to camp, thinking it was too rough a life for me. It was his idea to leave me at Mason and to visit me as often as he could conveniently do so. I had a different idea. I did not consider personal comfort, but wished to be with him. I think he was glad of my decision.

It was when he left me at Mason that my troubles began. Mason was settled up with well-to-do people who had built comfortable homes. Their principal business was ranching. We stopped at the hospitable home of Major Holmes. Captain Roberts had been away from his company so long that he felt he must proceed at once to camp. The ladies soon made me feel at home, and I was enjoying the novelty of living in a western town, ignorant of the danger to which I was soon to be exposed.

The "Mason County War" was in progress at that time. It was a feud between Germans and Americans. The latter were led by Scott Cooley. . . .

At the time of which I write the town of Mason was in a turmoil of excitement. Several men had been killed. The question in everyone's mind was, Who would be the next victim? I had no fear for my personal safety. But one evening the news was spread through the town that "Scott Cooley is in town." That report struck terror to the hearts of the people. They knew he had come to get his man. There was little sleep that night. Next morning, while at breakfast, we heard the report of a gun uptown. Rushing out into the yard, we saw two men, bareheaded, with guns in their hands, come toward us at full speed. We rushed into the house, locked the doors, and Mrs. Holmes and I went into her room, which had but one window. To our horror the men rode right up to the window. I looked for a place of safety, and the only one I could see was the space under the bed, which I pointed out to my hostess. She refused to take that shelter. She was looking out for the safety of her husband; I was looking after my own. Mrs. Holmes asked them what they wanted; they replied that they had come to inform Mr. Hester, who was Major Holmes' guest, that Scott Cooley had killed his brother. Now, I want to say right here that I did not go under the bed, and I hoped that Mrs. Holmes had forgotten my reference to the bed, but she not only remembered it, but told it. And some were unkind enough to say that "it was not a very dignified thing for a captain's wife to do," and that "a frontier woman would have suited him better for a wife." After having lived with the Captain fifty years, I am glad he did not think so.

I was very restless after having a gun pointed at me at such close range, and I confess that the western town of Mason suddenly lost its charm. It was altogether too unsafe a place to be. I concluded that Major Holmes' house in particular was in a very dangerous spot, so near the street that one might shoot into it without dismounting. I decided, therefore, to go to Mrs. Gooch's house, which stood some distance back from the fence, and any attacking party would have to dismount before coming to it. I was soon to discover that they could dismount. About four o'clock in the afternoon, while Mrs. Gooch and I were sitting in her room, we observed twenty men with guns coming down the road. Mrs. Gooch explained that they were Germans who lived in the country going home. But to our horror they dismounted and came toward the house. We locked the doors and ran into the dining room. Fortunately Mrs. Gooch's maid was a German, and was not afraid of her own people. She went out and talked with them. They told her that they were looking for Mr. Rank, a friend of Mr. Gooch's, who often stopped with him. The maid convinced them that he was not there, and they rode off. That was the second time I narrowly escaped being killed; at least, that was the way I felt about it.

My husband returned to Mason that evening. He found me eager to go on into the Indian country. But before dismissing the "Mason County War," I may state that twelve men were killed. . . .

My husband had been successful in finding a place to board until we could have quarters prepared at camp. The next morning we left Mason for Menard. We were going into a country where Indians raided, but I was leaving a country where white men raided. The distance from Mason to Menard is forty miles. There was only one house along the way, and there we had a good midday meal. When we reached Menard, one hundred and fifty miles distant from Austin, our wedding trip was completed. I can't imagine another more delightful. I have ridden in automobiles on highways, and have had a ride in an airplane, but they are not to be compared with that ride in an ambulance behind government mules. . . .

Menard is situated on the beautiful San Saba River. It contained only a few houses in 1875, and most of them were made of cedar pickets; had dirt floors and no spare room. We were fortunate to find one house with three rooms. The family that occupied it numbered seven, but they were kind enough to spare us one room. That was frontier hospitality. The room was small and had space for only one bed and a chair. It contained no window and no mirror. There was a wash basin on the porch that served for all.

The Rangers required only a few days to prepare quarters for us. About fifty yards from their camp stood a portion of a camp house. It had a shingle roof and a rock floor. It was converted into a kitchen, size twenty by twenty feet. Gunny sacks were tacked upon the walls. For our bedroom the Rangers built a room of logs with walls three feet high, on top of which they put a tent. It was provided with a fireplace built of stone. The floor was carpeted with gunny sacks. The kitchen also served as a storeroom. It was all so cozy. Here the newlyweds began housekeeping.

The camp was located in a fine pecan grove on the river about two miles below Menard. I wish I could describe that country as it was at that time. Beautiful nature had not been marred by the hand of man. It seemed to belong to the birds and wild animals; they were so abundant. There was game of every description. I had fished many times in the Colorado River and in Eagle Lake, but had never caught a fish. When I threw my hook into the beautiful San Saba almost immediately it was seized by a nice catfish. It was thrilling.

Another pleasure I had in anticipation was horseback riding. I had never ridden horseback at Columbus, but my sweetheart wrote me that he had a fine saddle horse for me. Before leaving that place, I had made an up-to-date riding habit which extended below the feet from half a yard to a yard. In 1875 no part of a woman's leg was visible. Looking back I recall a vivid picture of myself on my first horseback ride. Perched upon a sidesaddle, with a habit reaching almost to the ground, I set out. We rode along a trail through a thick wood. Captain Roberts led the way. Suddenly he stopped, drew his pistol and motioned for me to stop. I thought, of course, that we had come upon Indians. After he had fired the second time, I saw wild turkeys fly. We took two back to camp with us. What do you suppose happened to my riding habit passing through that brush? It was so badly torn that I had to cut off so much of it that what remained barely covered my feet. It was much more convenient, but it required great care not to expose an ankle, which would have been scandalous.

I was now a regular member of Company D, but entirely unarmed. I spoke to the Captain about how embarrassing it was not to have a gun and not to be able to protect myself in case of an attack. He immediately purchased a .22 caliber Remington rifle. I practiced target shooting with the Rangers, until I was satisfied that I could shoot as well as any of them, and could kill game, of which there was an abundance.

My ride through the brush showed that I did not have suitable clothes for hunting. I sent to Austin for a hunting suit made of heavy material, for I was particularly fond of hunting and fishing. I was warned daily of the danger of going too far from camp, but my interest in fishing caused me to forget about danger. On one occasion when I had gone some distance from camp, I discovered ten horsemen coming down the trail in single file. I had often heard that that was the way the Indians traveled. There was no doubt in my mind that they were Indians. I struck a bee line for camp, expecting every minute to be murdered. I knew it was useless to run, nevertheless I struck a lively gait. Looking back over my shoulder, to my great relief I saw them stop to water their horses. They were Mexicans. I had my gun by me, but it never occurred to me to use it in case of an attack. After that experience I was more careful.

Life in camp did not deprive me of visitors. The pioneer women came to see me and made me feel welcome among them. Many of them were educated and refined; those that had been deprived of those advantages nevertheless had hearts of gold. Friendships formed in those days have stood the test of half a century. There were some charming young ladies in Menard—every one of them a belle. There were about ten boys to one girl. Whenever Captain Roberts was called away from camp, I would invite one of the young ladies to stay with me. The Rangers paid them "much mind," and had many excuses for calling at our camp to get a look at a pretty girl.

The frontier people were not without their social pleasures. Amusements were not frequent nor were they elaborate, but they were enjoyed all the more because they came so seldom. I recall spending a very enjoyable day at a quilting bee. While the fingers plied the needle, tongues were equally busy. At noon all repaired to the dining room, which also served as a kitchen. The table groaned under the burden of rations tempting to the appetite. The feast lasted as long as we were there. When twilight began to fall the young men gathered in for a dance. And a dance it was. Few indulged in the round dance; the old time square dance was most popular. The table extended its inviting savor, and one could go in and help himself between dances. The beverage was steaming hot coffee. The dance lasted until daylight. Many came from long distances, and then it was an Indian country. I did not spend the night, for I had Ranger protection and went home at twelve A.M. . . .

The Rangers supplied me with various pets. Among them were squirrels, prairie dogs, a cub bear, a dog, and a canary bird. I enjoyed the bear while he was little, but he got cross as he grew up and I turned him loose. We were never dull in camp. Several of the Rangers were musical, and had their instruments with them. Captain Roberts was a fine violinist. A race track was laid out, and there was horse racing. Card playing was not allowed, and it was not done openly. Betting on horse races was permitted, but the Rangers ran their races for amusement. We had a croquet set, and that game was enjoyed.

After we had been in camp a few months it was decided to go up the river about thirty miles, which meant that far from any settlement. Going into that wild country exposed us to encounters with Indians. A strong guard—ten men—was taken along. That number had been victorious in their last fight with Indians, so we felt well protected. After we had made our new camp, and before we commenced to fish, it was agreed that we would not scatter and that everyone would keep his gun by him. Such sport as we enjoyed! As fast as a hook could be cast it would be caught up by a fish. I have often wondered whether a white man had ever fished there before us. We spent two pleasant days. No live Indians were seen, but we found the skeleton of a dead one where he had been buried in a crevice of rock. When we returned to camp, I felt that I had been on a scout, and I have always had a suspicion that it was so reported to headquarters, but this I do not know to be a fact.

Their encounters with the Rangers had taught the Indians to be cautious. Before the Rangers were stationed at Menard, the Indians raided every light of the moon, stealing horses and murdering anyone they met on their way out. Captain Rufe Perry commanded Company D during the first six months after it was organized. I must tell you what a brave wife he had. She visited him while he was encamped right on the trail where the Indians crossed the river. One beautiful, moon-lit night ten Indians passed right by his camp. She stayed there alone while Captain Perry reported the presence of the Indians to the main camp. That was a wife for a Ranger! Captain Perry detailed a scout, commanded by Lieutenant Roberts, to pursue the Indians. In the fight that ensued, Lieutenant Roberts captured the shield of an Indian chief who was killed. He presented it to his friend, Alex Casparis, whose widow still has it.

After this fight with the Rangers, the Indians were more cautious. They abandoned their favorite ford on the river. However, the news that Indians had been killed struck terror to the hearts of some of the more timid. The latter feared that the Indians would come in great numbers and murder all the whites in a spirit of revenge. They visited Captain Roberts and said, "Oh, Captain, the Indians will murder us all." He assured them that fear was the only thing an Indian could be taught.

A number of people came to camp to see the Indian prisoner. It was contrary to orders to take prisoners, but as Captain Roberts states in his book (Rangers and Sovereignty, pages 49 and 50), he could not kill a man even if an Indian when he was begging for his life. The prisoner suffered agony from fear while in camp, and his expression showed that he expected momentarily to be killed. At Austin the Indian prisoner was given a ride in a city carriage. He expressed his pleasure by repeating the word, "bonito, bonito." Within two years he died in the penitentiary of tuberculosis.

We had been in camp at Menard only a short time when a report was brought in that Scott Cooley was in the neighborhood. Captain Roberts at once detailed a scout, himself taking command. I was greatly alarmed. I knew Scott Cooley's reputation as a killer, and I could not believe that the Rangers would be able to arrest him without some being killed. Captain Roberts tried to remove my fears by assur-ing me that that class of men did not have true courage and that he had never found it difficult to arrest them. However, I was not easy until all had returned to camp. If Cooley had been at Menard he had made good his escape. False reports were not uncommon, due to unintentional mistakes. It still appears remarkable to me that during the entire period of Captain Roberts' command of Company D not one of his men was killed by Indians and only one (George R. Bingham) was killed by outlaws. . . .

We received orders to move. We were sorry to leave the camp where we had spent such a delightful time. But the company had orders to proceed to Laredo on account of some trouble with Mexicans. I was not allowed to go. It was a great disappointment. I accompanied the command as far as San Antonio, and was left there. I boarded at the Adams House on Flores Street. I realize now that I was exposed to great danger. The house was filled with tuberculars. We would sit in the living room, then called parlor, filled with tuberculars, and supplied with cuspidors. Two died in the house from that disease while I was there. How ignorant we were in "the good old days"!

After spending two months in San Antonio, I was delighted to receive a message from my husband telling me to join him at Sabinal. I took the first stagecoach out. Captain Roberts had come on in advance of the company, and we boarded in Sabinal until the Rangers arrived and established camp twelve miles below the town. Three families resided at Sabinal, so we were fortunate in finding a place to board. I was glad to get back to camp.

We found that a very different country from Menard. Game was not so abundant. Fishing was good, but not as good as at Menard. It was not the frontier that we loved so well.

Our camp was in a beautiful live oak grove, and there we spent the winter of 1877–'78. The Indians made no raids while we were there, but the Rangers had plenty to do running down outlaws. Many arrests were made. The wives of some of the married prisoners camped near us in order to be near their husbands. They were permitted to talk to their husbands only in the presence of a guard. The innocent suffered with the guilty. They may have been good women. It must have been heartrending to them to see their husbands in shackles. I pitied them. But nature is cruel, and they were victims of that law. In "the good old days" marriage was binding. A woman who valued her reputation would endure almost anything rather than be dubbed a grass widow. I believe in divorces, and am glad to see the change, but regret that they have become so numerous. . . .

Captain Roberts was ordered to take his company to Menard County and to establish his camp on the San Saba River five miles below Fort McKavett. Fort McKavett was located on the San Saba River twenty miles above our former camp. The trip from Austin to Menard was uneventful. On arriving at our destination, we pitched our tents under some beautiful oaks.

Up to this time we had had only one tent and a kitchen, but at Camp San Saba we were supplied a second tent, which because of its size the Rangers named the "elephant." We felt that our household was growing. The "elephant" I furnished as my guest chamber, and equipped it with army cot, washstand, a small table, and a mirror hung on the tent pole. Our kitchen was built of logs, with a tent for a roof. Both our tents were floored; we had outgrown gunny-sack floor covering. The two tents and kitchen were surrounded by a brush fence, with a whitewashed gate that looked quite imposing. The State furnished us a cook. The rations issued to the Rangers included only the substantials, but were of such generous quantity that we had a surplus to exchange for butter, milk, eggs, etc. Honey was obtained from bee trees. Game and fish were abundant.

The Rangers and the Yankee soldiers were now neighbors. The soldiers at Fort McKavett had never furnished protection against Indian depredations. Had they afforded such protection, Company D would not have been sent there. The soldiers did not go after the Indians the way the Rangers did. Their movements were military, regulated by a lot of red tape, and they couldn't catch them. The Rangers used no ceremony; they mounted their horses, ran down the Indians and killed them. The soldiers received thirteen dollars a month; the Rangers received forty dollars. When a soldier wished to quit the service before his enlistment expired the only way out was to desert; when a Ranger wanted to quit, his commander would readily give him a discharge on the ground that a dissatisfied Ranger was not efficient. Rangers had their hearts in the service; they were protecting the frontier of their home State. Soldiers and officers had no social intercourse; Rangers visited at captain's headquarters, and were frequently invited to a meal.

The officers at the fort were friendly, and one of them said to Captain Roberts, "Your fights here in the shadow of this post are so

Luvenia Conway Roberts stands at the corner of the tent that was her home in 1878. (*Courtesy Barker Texas History Center, University of Texas at Austin*)

humiliating that I feel like resigning." On my visit to the post I met my first house guest, Miss Cora Ogden of San Antonio. She was visiting her brother, who was sutler. She was a charming young lady. I entertained her by taking her hunting and fishing. There was always a Ranger who would volunteer to go with us, get the bait, and bait the hooks. We took a good many rides behind mules, and regretted very much that we could not ride horseback. Unfortunately there was but one sidesaddle and one habit available; it would have been impossible to have ridden a man's saddle without exposing an ankle. Some evenings we visited the main camp to listen to the string band.

The Rangers and the military exchanged courtesies in the following manner: The officers and their wives would drive down to our camp to listen to our string band, and we would go up and hear their brass band. . . .

The Rangers were kept quite busy during the summer, scouting for Indians. However, they found time to stage a minstrel performance at Menard. The citizens of that place were planning to build a church; the Rangers gave the play for their benefit. They cleared sixty dollars, which was the first cash contribution to the church building fund. My guest chamber was frequently occupied, for I enjoyed the company of young ladies. It was fun to visit the big camp and watch the rehearsals. The manager of the play was able to select some good talent. Sometimes the boys would attend a dance at Menard; on such occasions there was "rustling" for clothes. The Captain would sometimes lend a suit, and the others would invariably tell the girls about it. Practical jokes varied camp life. Even I caught the spirit. The Rangers were always on the anxious seat when the Legislature assembled to make the biennial appropriations. Would the appropriations for the Rangers be continued? Would they all be continued in the service? The mail was looked forward to with great eagerness at such times. Captain Roberts was away one day when the mail was brought. There was a letter to him from the Adjutant General. The Rangers came to me to know what the letter contained. I read it to them correctly that the appropriation had been made, but I added, "Discharge every man under five feet ten." Then there was some measuring. When Captain Roberts returned and read the letter to them, they knew I had manufactured that last statement, but they did not hold it against me.

Each quarter Captain Roberts made the trip to Austin for the
Rangers' pay, and I accompanied him. Most of these trips were uneventful, but they afforded enjoyable visits to our friends. But the trip
I am going to tell about now was different. It rained all day between
Mason and Fredericksburg. We found it impossible to reach the Nimitz
Hotel by night. As we knew of no place where we could find shelter for
the night we were worried. Fortunately, we met a man who told us that
at the end of the next mile we would find a trail which would lead us to
a house. It was dark when we reached the house. A woman met us, and
kindly consented to give us lodging. She at once began by apologizing
to me, or rather explaining why they were so poor. She said, "All my
children are gals. We might get along better if 'he' would stay at home
and work, but 'he' has to be gone away all the time preaching." The
house was one long room. It was occupied by two families. Each had a
separate fireplace, and each had several children. Our hostess prepared our supper by cooking some corndodgers in a skillet, and by
frying some bacon in the same skillet—the only cooking vessel she had.
She gave us some black coffee. The table seated four, which was our
number. After supper our hostess pointed out the bed we were to oc-
cupy, which was in a row with several others. There were no partitions
and no curtains. Undressing was a public affair. If the present style of
dress had been in vogue then, undressing would have been a simple
thing, but in those days we wore clothes. I managed the best I could.
Soon after we retired "he" came home. While "he" was partaking of the
evening meal "he" said, "I hear a lot about hard times when I'm gone,
but I never see it until I come home." It was with great difficulty that I
restrained myself from getting up and choking him. I wanted to say,
"You lazy, trifling thing; running around, eating hot biscuit and fried
chicken; and your family starving." I know our hostess served us with
the best she had. The condition of that poor family made a lasting
impression on my mind. Before women were emancipated, what dependent creatures they were! They had just what a man furnished
them. There were three grown women in that family. At that time the
only thing a woman could do was to teach school, if she had the education; if not, she could go to the kitchen and there compete with negro
labor. What a great and glorious change time has wrought! What a
wonderful age this is in which to live. We who have lived our lives and

are passing away according to the laws of nature rejoice in the great opportunities our youth of today are enjoying. . . .

Captain Roberts received orders to move his company to a point on the Llano River, four miles below Junction City. The people of that section were all our good friends. Junction City is located thirty miles southwest of Menard. . . .

Our camp was located in a beautiful live oak grove on the Llano River. The country is hilly. It was at that time on the extreme frontier. There were few settlements. There was not a fence in Kimble County. The first house to be built of lumber was on Farmer's Ranch, twenty miles above Junction. The lumber was hauled from Round Rock by ox teams.

The day before we reached our new camp four men were killed in Junction. I was very strongly impressed that we were in a bad man's country. My inclination to hunt and fish suddenly vanished. Camp appeared to me the safest place to stay. With Ranger protection I did venture to carry my laundry to Junction. I found it comprised a few log cabins, so frequently described as the home of the pioneer. On our way back to camp the boys told me that they had heard at the post office that the women washed on the banks of the river and that they had had several fights. It made me very uncomfortable to know that we were in a country where women fought. I renewed my determination to stay close in camp and to take up my embroidery to pass the time. A few days later I accompanied the Rangers, who were going after the mail, to bring back my laundry. I got out at the house where I had left the clothes; the Rangers went on to the post office. I walked boldly to the door, I might say fearlessly, without any premonition of the danger to which I was exposed. There were three women present, and as soon as I looked at them I saw their belligerent attitude. I was so taken by surprise that my voice may have trembled when I asked for my clothes. They said the clothes were washed, but that they would never wash for me again. Then they began to tell me their opinion of people who thought themselves better than other folks. They told me that they had been well raised, had always kept the best company, and continued for some time to pour forth a tirade of abuse, mixed with swear words, about stuck-up people. Money, they said, doesn't make anyone better. During all this time I had not said a word; I could think of nothing to say that would save me. But when they spoke of money, I said, "Surely, you are not mistaking us for rich people. Rangers are all poor." On hearing my reply they were mollified. There was a great change in their manner. They assumed a friendly attitude, and one of them asked me to have a "chaw." That placed me in an awkward if not dangerous dilemma. I was afraid to refuse for fear of giving offense. At that moment the Rangers drove up. I declined with thanks. I was glad to get back to camp. Later I learned that I had offended these women by not inviting them to visit me when I took the laundry down.

For nearly two weeks I stuck to my resolution to stay in camp, but the monotony of camp and the tempting attractiveness of the Llano River caused me to waver. I took my gun and went back to hunting and fishing, which were fine. Company could not be had; girls were scarce, and my acquaintance was limited.

Life was not monotonous for the Rangers. While the Indians had ceased to raid in Menard, they continued to depredate in Kimble. Besides hunting Indians, there was much police duty. We were not only in an Indian country, but also in the country of the bad man. The Rangers were continually making arrests, and invariably they would be "cussed out" by the wives. When the Rangers planned to make an arrest, they took station near the suspect's house the night before, and rushed upon it about daylight next morning before the culprit would have time to escape. The Rangers told the following joke on Captain Roberts. The Captain opened a door just as day was breaking; he didn't knock, and entered without ceremony. When he opened the door the wife confronted him. He said, "Good morning, Madam." She said, "Good morning, the devil," and began cursing him and his Rangers. It was not a pleasant business. There was no jail in Kimble County; prisoners were taken to Mason. . . .

While stationed at Junction on the Llano River in 1882, Captain Roberts resigned his commission in the Ranger service. It was with regret I parted from the Ranger camp where I had spent so many happy days. Camp life afforded many pleasures, which, coupled with duty and a determination to serve the people of Texas well and honestly, have caused us to treasure the memory of those years. The whole time that I was with the Rangers, not one time did I hear an oath or an ungentlemanly word spoken. The Rangers were always ready and eager to do us a service, and we are indebted to their kindness for many of the conveniences we had. Many of them have answered their last call, and in a short time Texas Ranger will be only a name, but they have given a meaning to that name that will cause it to live forever.

*   *   *

Lou Roberts obviously enjoyed her life with the Rangers, but her husband resigned after six years of service because of her poor health. The Robertses moved to New Mexico, where they lived for thirty years. In 1914 they returned to what Lou called "our beloved State."

At a reunion of the Texas Rangers, Lou Roberts was described by a reporter from the *Austin Daily Statesman*: "Mrs. Roberts is a lady of culture and refinement, and for three [six] years she was in camp with Capt. Roberts and his company on the extreme frontier suffering the hardships of a frontier life and braving the dangers of Indian warfare. Her womanly graces and indomitable courage were the admiration of the entire force of Rangers, and Company D, commanded by her husband, idolized her."

Ella Elgar Bird Dumont

"I wanted to be a sculptor."

"I wanted to be a sculptor." These poignant words reveal an underlying theme of the autobiography of Ella Elgar Bird Dumont. They express the frustation experienced by many frontier women as they lived out their lives amid incredible natural beauty but a dearth of man-made beauty. Most pioneer women expressed their creativity by rearing children, baking and preserving, fashioning beautiful quilts, and making good homes for their families. But Ella Dumont wanted more; she wanted to be a sculptor.

In addition to being talented, Ella was an amazingly strong and self-sufficient woman—a woman who lived in a tent and hunted buffalo; who lived for seven years on isolated ranches with no companions other than her two small children; who watched as her house was blown away by a tornado; and who buried three children and two husbands in the harsh soil of the Texas Panhandle.

Ella, who was born in Lee County, Mississippi, in 1861, learned her self-sufficiency from the women in her family. Her mother, Elizabeth Benson Elgar, was the refined and educated daughter of a merchant. Ella's father, Lewis Steptoe Elgar, died when she was eleven months old. After the Civil War, Elizabeth Elgar moved in with Ella's grandmother, Lucretia Benson, who was also a widow with several young children. Ella described her grandmother as a "shrewd, businesslike woman, industrious, and of great ability in the transaction of business."

The two women "took the Texas fever" and with other members of their family packed their belongings into covered wagons and spent two months traveling to Texas, arriving in Johnson County in 1867. During the next six years Ella's family moved several times before finally settling on the frontier in Young County, where they stayed in spite of many Indian raids in the area. Ella once said of her life: "Each time I moved, I moved west, finding more Indians, and more sparsely settled territory."

From Ella Dumont, "True Life Story of Ella Bird-Dumont, Earliest Settler in the East Part of Panhandle, Texas" (typescript), Barker Texas History Center, University of Texas at Austin. Copyright by Tommy J. Boley, used by permission.

Ella was just fifteen when Thomas Bird, a twenty-nine-year-old Texas Ranger, rode into her life. She describes their meeting: "My brother-in-law, Willie Fite, opened the door, and there I beheld, mounted on the most beautiful big black horse I had ever seen, a man, yes, a man, in full Western attire, that of a Texas Ranger, gallant, and brave in appearance."

Tom Bird was the son of a minister. He was from Blanco County and, like Daniel Webster Roberts, had received an engraved rifle from the Texas Legislature for his part in the Deer Creek Indian fight. Ella's description of the courtship is detailed and amusing as she tries to decide whether or not she wants to marry Tom. They did marry in 1876, and Ella's glowing descriptions of Bird throughout her autobiography indicate that the union was a happy one.

When the Birds were first married, they lived in the Ranger camp near Fort Griffin. After two months Bird resigned from the Rangers, and the young couple decided to make their living hunting buffalo.

*　　*　　*

We bade farewell to the settlements and bent our course for the wilds of the Texas Panhandle where buffalo, antelope, deer and many other species of wild animals roamed the prairie and breaks at will. We stopped overnight again at Fort Belknap where Mr. Alex Jones and little family of wife and two children joined us on the trip. We journeyed on a few days when the roads gave out; then we had to pick our way through the country as best we could. We crossed the Wichita breaks, came near turning over several times, but finally made it through. One man had gone that way before and had to take his wagon to pieces three times before getting across. Later, as time went on, we made a road through that way that was passable. We traveled on north about four miles and came to a big spring at the head of a creek that led back to the Wichita River. There was abundance of water here and plenty of fish lower down on the stream, so this was where we pitched our buffalo camp where Dickens joins Cottle County, December 28, 1876. We filed a claim on this land later and lived three years on it. This creek takes its name for us, being on the map "Bird's Creek."

Mr. Bird and Mr. Jones took a little hunt soon after we arrived and killed some buffalo, but first of all we had to build some winter quarters. Mr. Jones decided to build them a little rock house as there was

Ella Bird Dumont. (*From Carmen Taylor Bennett*, Our Roots Grow Deep, *by permission*)

plenty of material at hand already quarried naturally. He soon threw up the walls, chinked with mud and covered with dirt, all completed in three or four days' time. Our house was different. It was on the same order that most of the hunters used. They were called tepees made of buffalo hides. That was before dugout day. They were made as follows: first, we built a frame of small china poles, split some for rafters, no nails were used, rawhide strings instead. We took dried buffalo hides, tied the legs together and put them around the wall, wool side out, then another tier of hides over these in the same manner to break the joints of those underneath. The roof was made on the same order as the walls, tying down the legs all around the edges. The door was made of a frame of split poles with a buffalo hide stretched over it, legs tied inside. The little rock chimney with fireplace, which was crude, of course, came next. The floor was carpeted with buffalo hides, squared up to fit, wool side up. All was complete and a more clean and comfortable little home you could not find in any of the Eastern cities.

Mr. Bird was anxious that I should learn to use a gun. He wanted me always protected when he was away so he gave me his Winchester rifle, the one the state gave him. My, how I learned to love this gun as time went on. I still have it; no money could buy it. Mr. Bird and Mr. Jones began hunting regular now, most always took their wagons to bring the hides and such choice meats as was needed for our supply. They soon built a stack of buffalo hides which had to be freighted to Fort Worth, then to the market. There were a good many hunters in the country but far apart. Some had left as buffalo were not so plentiful as they had been. Nearly every afternoon when they came in off their hunt, Mr. Bird would give me training with my rifle shooting at targets. He said I was an apt scholar for which I felt flattered. Mrs. Jones and I also practiced together. She was learning to use a gun too. Sometimes we would go down on the creek and shoot turkeys.

There was one thing to which I was attracted most of all when we first arrived at this place. That was the gyp rock. This rock is just the same as marble with the exception that it is not quite as hard. About the first industry that took hold of me when we got settled was whittling and shaping things out of this rock.

I would often go out with Mr. Bird in the wagon on his hunts. It was wonderful to me to see them kill the buffalo. The method they used in shooting them was queer. The country was not altogether level prairie, and they could usually slip up in three or four hundred yards of them. When all was ready, they would shoot the one that seemed to be the leader. They never shot them behind the shoulder in the heart or they would pitch, buck around and break the stand. Always shoot far back in the body behind the ribs. This made them sick. They would hump up, walk around and lie down, then wait a moment until another led out. Shoot it, then another leader on and on until you had shot several. Then they would begin milling around and around. You had a stand on them. Then you could kill all you wanted.

There were many antelope and deer in the country. Herds of them would often play along ahead of the wagons. We never shot at them for fear of disturbing a bunch of buffalo that might be close around. . . .

We had been here about five or six months and supplies were running short. We had to make a trip back to the settlements for more. We had not had any letters from home since we left. We made the trip all right. We camped over night on Seymour Creek where the town of Seymour now is. Mr. Bird killed a large buffalo just about where the square is located there. We never thought then of its ever being a town. We stopped at Round Timbers and saw Bob and Ellen where they had moved. We stayed over night at Fort Belknap. They had just had a killing there. Mr. Martin, their only merchant, had been murdered. A bunch of drunken outlawed men of the country stood him on a box, shot it out from under him, then took him out that night and murdered him without any cause that any one knew of. We made our way on to Young County and found all well and glad to see us. Of course, we had wonderful things to tell them about the West, though everything seemed so changed except the home folks.

Several of the younger bunch had married and moved away. We only stayed three or four days, then loaded up our wagon and started for the wilds again. We made the trip in due time, found the little Jones family anxiously waiting to hear from the settlement. We were glad to get home again. This was our first and only little home, and we had learned to love it. It is truly said, "Be it ever so humble, there is no place like home." We were happy; it was a real little love nest. He was ever kind and good to me, and as the months and years went by, child wife, that I was, I grew and matured into womanhood and learned to love and even worship the only man I had ever loved in my life, as I had no father, or older brothers. I was contented, enjoyed my carving in the gyp rock, though I never neglected practicing with my rifle. I had begun to have confidence in my marksmanship; I hardly ever missed a shot. I was about ready to banter my husband for a shooting match, but I think he was prouder than I.

They were very busy hunting every day, most always brought in hides. I so often thought what a great waste and shame that all this splendid meat should be allowed to lie and decay on the prairie when it would have been worth millions of dollars to the people in the East. I believe though they claimed the Indians would never have been civilized had the buffalo remained here where they could be independent for a living. The hides had accumulated now till they must be freighted to market, so Mr. Bird and Mr. McSwain, a neighbor hunter, decided to make a trip to Fort Worth with hides. There was another family with us now. Mr. Jones' cousin, Bense Jones came up for a short time. It was cold weather now, Mr. Bird and Mr. McSwain loaded up their wagons with many buffalo hides. It is wonderful how many hides they could pack on one wagon without danger of toppling over. They were off early the next morning for their long journey. Mr. Bird hated to leave me alone, but I assured him I was not the least bit afraid with my old reliable Winchester always at hand and our camps were only a few steps apart. There were three camps now. I never got lonely. I busied myself mostly now with my carving in the rock. I enjoyed it so much. Little Porter Jones and I would take strolls down on the creek, pick up choice pieces of rock that worked beautifully, so many different colors and shades.

Mr. Bird and Mr. McSwain had been gone about three weeks. It was about time they should be coming in. Our supplies were running low. The two Jones men were out hunting most of the time. One day they came in with some news; they heard there were Comanche Indians in the country. They had been at some of the camps but were not hostile. There were about forty of them that had slipped out from the post and came down here hunting buffalo. The buffalo having been molested and so hard pressed by the hunters in Kansas and Indian Territory, they had migrated down in this part of the country. The buffalo were also being killed out fast here. The Jones men took a little hunt of two or three days up in Cottle County which was about fifteen or twenty miles away. We were a little uneasy about those Indians, so Mrs. Alex Jones insisted we three women stay together mostly through the day in their little rock house while the men were gone. I was the only one that had a gun. This was the third day since they had left. We were looking for them in most any hour. We were feeling pretty safe now. We were talking and laughing when all of a sudden the dogs set up an unusual raving and barking. We stepped out into the yard to see what was the matter and oh horrors, what do you think met our gaze? Those Indians were coming. They were within less than fifty yards of the house. We stepped back into the house. I hid my gun for fear they might get it, and so I could get it if needed. Mrs. Jones said she would stand in the door, and maybe they would not come in. They dashed up and were dismounted in a moment almost. The chief led the way to the door. Mrs. Jones did not move. He pushed her aside and six others followed him. Now imagine our plight. This house was about twelve feet square, two beds, five children, three women and seven Indians in it. We did not have standing room, nor could we understand a word they said.

The old chief was very friendly and tried to talk to us. He was dressed in citizens clothing; the others wore buck skin and were wrapped in blankets. They were very tall, large, ugly, grim looking fellows. Some were painted. There was one white man in the bunch. They used him for an interpreter, but it seemed he could not remember enough English to make himself understood very much. I think he must have been captured when a little boy and raised up by the Indians. He looked to be about twenty-five years old, with dark brown eyes, rather long curly brown hair and fair skin. He was dressed in their garb wrapped in a blanket. Had he been otherwise dressed he would have been a nice intelligent looking young man. What a shame his life was sacrificed to those wild creatures.

The object of their visit seemed mainly to trade clothing for groceries. This clothing was given them by the government of which they used but little, preferring to wear buck skin instead. Our grocery stock was short and we could not accommodate them much. They began prowling through the house as soon as they came. We did not know what they wanted until they found some groceries. Then they began showing us some clothes, holding up different garments, then pointing to the groceries. We understood but shook our heads; nothing doing. They kept on prowling and found my gun. They set up an excited palavering and talking; every one had to look at it. The chief took quite a fancy to it. He had a right new Colt 45 pistol. He offered it to me for my gun. I shook my head; he then began showing me the clothes he had on, first touching his coat, vest, shirt and so on. I did not understand him and did not make any reply, so he began laying off his clothes, one by one, and was taking off his shirt when Mrs. Jones and I looked at each other in helpless dismay. It was useless for us to offer any protest as to our right in the way of etiquette or in other words what seemed to be about to take place. Our language was dead to him but finally the truth dawned on Mrs. Jones just before it was everlastingly too late, and she said, "He thinks you have traded your gun for his clothes." I began shaking my head, saying, "No, no." He laughed and proceeded to put his clothes on again. She tried to explain to him why I would not part with my gun, that it was a present to my husband by the State. I wanted to add that it was given for killing Indians but thought it might be good policy to leave off that part of it; however, they did not understand anything she said. She also told them the men folks would be in that evening. She showed them their clothes to make them understand. They finally all moved out doors and sat down with some others beside the house and began talking in low and serious tones we thought. Mrs. Jones became very frightened and said she believed they were planning to kill us, but sure enough the Jones men came in that evening before they left. They had struck the Indian trail where they came into the road about one half mile from camp. Mr. Alex Jones said those women would be scared to death. He jumped out of the wagon and made for camp. He came in a dead run. He could talk Indian pretty well himself having lived near the Cherokees. He met them very friendly with a "How, how". The Indians seemed rather pleased that the men had come in, I thought. They wanted to trade with them. Bense Jones bought a good suit of clothes for about fifty cents worth of sorghum molasses. Alex Jones bought a nice dressed buffalo robe for about a dollar's worth of sorghum, also a fine green United States Indian Blanket, Macina blanket for the same above price in sorghum. They did not know what their goods were worth. They were soon ready to go and started to their horses. One old savage looking Indian came in, picked up my gun, offered me an old worn out vest he had on for it. I shook my head; he started off with it. I followed on after him shaking my head. He finally came back with an ugly grin on his face and handed it to me and they were gone. I have always believed that the chief of this bunch of Indians was none other than Quanah Parker.

It was now about five weeks since Mr. Bird and Mr. McSwain had left and we were uneasy about them. It had been very cold and a great deal of snow. They were due home in three or four weeks at most.

Every evening I would take long strolls over the hills through the scattering brush in the direction they would come, thinking I might meet them, but each time I would return alone, disappointed, and oh, so sad and uneasy. It had gone on this way another week or more. I was almost giving up in despair but would go one more time in hope of meeting them. I was about one half mile from home and looking away across the hills through the algeretta bushes about a quarter of a mile away. I saw two wagons, coming, jogging along. I knew it was they. Mr. Bird saw me at the same time. He stopped the wagon, got out and started toward me when he saw me start to run. We missed each other and had to hunt around some time before we met. I was laughing and he was crying. I had never seen him that way before. He was almost crazy he had worried so much. As soon as he could, he told me all the news that had reached Fort Worth while they were there: That there were nine hundred Indians up on Pease River not far from where we were. That they were killing women, children, all as they came to them, sparing none.

Of course they started for home at once, but they broke down two or three times and were snowed under different times, until they could not travel for several days. But it was a joyful arrival home to find we were all safe and well and unharmed. We certainly enjoyed the new groceries they brought. We had run out of bread about two weeks before they arrived, but where there is a will there is surely a way. Mr. Jones had a large box coffee mill. He staked it down to the ground so it could not move, and we ground corn on this for bread. Sometimes we ground peas for bread. We had plenty of meat at all times.

[Editor's note: After the buffalo herds were exterminated, the Birds led a nomadic life as Tom hunted antelope, deer, bears, and wolves and tanned and sold the hides. Ella earned money by making gloves and vests for cowboys. Since she was often paid with a yearling, the Birds accumulated a small herd of cattle. In 1881 their first child, Capp Jay, was born. Tom then began working as a cowboy on the Savage Ranch.]

My husband had been riding around and met some of the ranch-men. They were much in need of a hand and wanted us to move on the ranch and him to take a job as a line rider. He came home and we talked it over and decided to go. We had torn down our buffalo tepee house some time previous to this and moved in the old Bense Jones camp house, which was part rock and part dirt. We stored all our camping outfit and a box of large books which belonged to my father and which was priceless, also a box with all my carvings, now number-ing sixty pieces. They were priceless, too. We packed them all away, wired and nailed up the door securely, we thought. We did not expect to be gone more than three months at most. We started for the Savage Ranch, now Pitchforks Ranch. We arrived that afternoon without any trouble. Our little babe was now six months old and was quite a young cowboy. Everything seemed so strange and different to our past mode of living, though very quiet for a ranch. There were only three men on the ranch, my husband making the fourth. Women were scarce in this country at that time. They were more appreciated, I think, than in later years, when there were more. Those men were perfect gentle-men and treated me with the highest respect. They seemed rather pleased at my presence, I thought and tried to make everything as pleasant for me as possible.

The ranch house consisted of two large dugouts with no furniture whatsoever, except bedsteads and some benches. It was a camping outfit and nothing more, but this was customary; and no one expected anything better. The wealthiest cowmen's families lived in dugouts when they first came here.

It was rather lonely for me. The men all left early in the morning, each on his line, and did not return until late in the afternoon. There were no fences then. Each cattle range was laid off in so many sections, and each man had his own line to ride, throwing the cattle back in their own range and the other man's cattle back in their range.

One day after they had all gone, I was looking around the place and noticed some large sized goods boxes. We had been eating on two large benches, and I made my mind up that I would make a table. There were plenty of tools—saws, hammers, etc. The baby was asleep, so I went to work, and had good luck with it. Everything measured out, and by the middle of the afternoon I had a first class table on foot with a large drawer for cold victuals. For knobs on the drawer I sawed a large spool in two and attached them with two horseshoe nails in each, bradded on the inside of the drawer, and all was complete. I was rather proud of the job if I did do it myself. This same table was still in use eight or ten years afterwards.

That afternoon when the men came in, Mr. Sullivan was the first. He asked who had been there. I said, "No one at all." He asked, "Where did the table come from?" "I made it," I said. He laughed rather incredulously; he thought I was joking. I could hardly convince him I really did. He examined the drawer and everything and said it beat anything he had ever seen made by a woman. He went out and brought in Mr. Savage to look at it. He would hardly believe either at first. He said there was not a man in the country that could do half as good a job. They gave me such a "blow-up" I got rather plagued out and almost wished I had not made it. That evening when the others came in, I had supper on the table with a nice tablecloth on. They shied around as if they didn't know whether to come in or not, and Mr. Bird simply put on a show—at which he was an expert. He was such a tease and did so many funny, crazy things it made it more absurd than anything else. Everybody was dying laughing. I was so plagued and embarrassed I wished I had never heard of a table.

They had a round-up a short time after we were there. The men did most of the cooking. My job, they said, was to take care of the baby and put the finishing touches on the dinner. I suppose they were pleased with the dinner part of it, at least. Mr. Savage made me a present of ten dollars the next day for my services. Of course, this included my husband's help also. I liked the ranch life pretty well. It was not hard on me. They were all so nice and good to help around the place. I did not have dinner at all to prepare, but it seemed changes were taking place all the time. We had been on the ranch not more than one month when Mr. Savage sold out to D. B. Gardner of the Pitchforks Ranch today. . . .

We stayed there till the last of February when Mr. Bird decided we would leave the Pitchforks Ranch and go to the Ross Ranch. They wanted a family on a line camp and that suited us better; however, we liked the Pitchforks all right.

After a drive of about twenty miles, we arrived at the Ross headquarters. They were all strangers to me, but I rather liked the appearance of the folks and all the surroundings. Our camp was to be over on

Tongue River, ten miles north of headquarters. They did not have it finished when we arrived. Mr. Bird helped to complete it. I liked this camp. It was on and near the bank of the shallow river in a shady grove of cottonwoods. There were many interesting things here. We raised lots of chickens, kept cows, and had all the wild turkey meat we wanted, for the woods were full of young turkeys and of all sizes. There were lots of deer and antelope, and much wild fruit, plums, grapes, and berries, which were extra fine. I did quite a lot of preserving and canning. Mr. Bird dressed a good lot of deer hides. We bought a sewing machine and I made a good many pairs of gloves for the cowboys. I also made some buckskin pants and vests. I had many more orders than I could fill. My health was not very good at this time.

Mr. Bird had to make a trip to Seymour on business of some kind. He went by our old camp on Wichita where we had left our things; and, what do you think, when he came back, he told me everything we left there had been taken, the door was torn down, and even the cattle had been going in the house. All my carvings had been stolen, and no trace of them was ever found from that day until this. It almost broke my heart when I found out I had lost them. I simply lay awake nights and grieved about them. There was at least one year's solid work on them without any stops. There were sixty pieces in all; and it was all my first work and improvements. How I would like to have laid everything aside and worked in this rock and nothing else. I wanted to be a sculptor. It bore on my mind incessantly, though I said nothing about it to anyone, for I felt that we were not able to devote my time to something I could not see any profit in. Of course, I was inexperienced and knew nothing of Eastern life, arts, or any advantages in that line no matter how gifted I may have been. I was barred from any development whatever other than what I could just work out myself. Though I was never any hand to worry, I feel thankful I have always tried to make the best of life's possibilities; it is usually hard enough at best.

It was late summer now [approximately 1882]. We were preparing for a trip down east to my mother's; and right here I have another little secret to divulge—there was to be another baby with us. Mr. Brack Garrison was staying with us at that time, and we were leaving him to take care of things while we were gone. We were soon off to Young County and landed there without any trouble and found all well. It was such a pleasure and privilege to be with my mother again. It had been some years since I had seen her. We stopped with my grandmother mostly on this trip, dear, faithful friend she always was to the afflicted. To all the relatives she seemed as a magnet, to which they were all drawn in case of distress or affliction of any kind. Sister came down from Round Timbers a few weeks after our arrival and stayed two or three weeks with us. And during her stay on one eventful day there came to us the cutest little blue-eyed fair-haired six-pound girl imaginable. Her father said she was a perfect little nymph, a professional beauty. We named her Arra Jimmie. This was a part of both of our names.

We did not make a very long stay as cold weather was coming and we wanted to get home. Some of the relatives had been talking of moving to New Mexico, which made me a little uneasy as they all usually took the moving fever at the same time and that would mean to leave me behind. However, I gave it but little thought. We were soon on our way home, rejoicing that all was well with us and one more little sunbeam added to our little family.

We moved camp that winter and built another large roomy dugout farther up on the hillside a few yards from the old one, of which the walls were too sandy and inclined to cave in. From this new one we had a better view. It was fine winter quarters, well built, good fireplace, canvassed and papered all inside with carpet on the floor, and we had nice pictures and other fancy things on the walls. The door was hinged at the top when raised and fastened to the ceiling overhead. My husband often explained in a joking way that every night when the door was dropped, it trapped four birds, two old ones, and two young ones. This dugout was cut back in the hillside as most of them were, leaving only a small yard in front about ten feet wide with a deep canyon below, a narrow path leading out each way. Below and above, on the flats was the only pass way we had to the lots. When the cows came home, they had to pass right through the yard, and some of them were wild and rather vicious. Our little boy, Capp, often played out on this path and we had to keep watch for the cows. We had quite a little excitement one evening for a few minutes.

Mr. Bird's brother, Bill, was with us for a short visit. I was busy working on gloves. He and I were talking when all at once we heard Capp screaming at the top of his voice. He was about thirty yards down the road. When I looked out, the old blue cow, the worst one, was just passing the door. I made a dart, and out I went and took even breaks with her. Of course, it scared her, and she ran with all her might; but I stayed right by her side. It was a close race, but I won it and reached Capp just in time to save her from running over him. The next day some of the boys were speaking something about a horse race, and Brother Bill spoke up and said he would put Ella against any race horse they might trot out, that she went out at the door like a blue darter and beat that old blue cow a flat foot race of thirty yards fair and square. . . .

The boys often visited us from headquarters which kept us from being so lonely, but there were few women in the country. I was quite busy most of the time making gloves. We were saving up a little now. We were starting us a little bunch of cattle. I could not make gloves fast enough. They gave me five dollars for every pair. I made some for some of the boys who had small bunches of cattle and they gave me a yearling for each pair of gloves. Cattle was cheap then. Mr. Bird also bought a bunch from Mr. John Abbott. This gave us a little start by which I have profited all the way down until the present time. They have bought all the land we own today in the country. . . .

[Editor's note: The Birds lived on various ranches for five or six years. On a visit to Ella's sister in Seymour in about 1885, Arra Jimmie and Capp "took the fever." Capp survived, but Jimmie died. In 1886 another daughter was born whom they named Bessie Adell.]

Spring was near at hand now. Mr. Bird had been looking out for a location for us, a permanent home. He decided on a piece of land joining the Matador, twelve miles away. He built a large dugout with picket house in front and was going to use this for a barn and stables in the fall when we built a good house. So we were settled for a while. . . .

Our little bunch of cattle which numbered one hundred and thirty head then was still on the Ross Ranch and remained there for several years afterward. Mr. Bird worked through the range with the other cattlemen. We had been at this place some two years. Mr. Bird's health had been failing for some time; he had some very serious attacks of cramps, and the doctor said he could never survive another. He had wanted to move to the mountains of New Mexico so he decided to go out there and look at the country. The first of October he started on the long journey in a wagon. I dreaded so much for him to be gone from home for so long; it was so lonely for me and the two childen. Capp was then only seven and Bessie two years old but we made it all right. Mr. Bird was gone three months; it seemed ages. He was fully in the notion of moving to New Mexico next fall.

Mr. Jameson and Mr. Wells were our nearest neighbors. This was the same Wells we met at Otta. Mr. Bird had been home only about two weeks when he and Mr. Wells took a trip to Quanah for supplies and feed. The weather turned awfully cold, snowing and sleeting. They were gone several days when Mr. Wells came in, but Mr. Bird was not with him. They started out from Quanah together in the evening, he said, but became separated some way. He drove on ahead and finally camped, thinking Mr. Bird would come on, but he did not. The next morning he harnessed up, drove back a few miles, but did not find him so he came on home. He said he thought Mr. Bird must have gone back to Quanah for something which he spoke of doing after they had started home. The weather was still bitter cold.

We waited three days, then Mr. Jameson and Mr. Slaughter, the latter an old friend of Mr. Bird's, went in search of him. They rode until they came to Groesbeck Creek about twelve miles this side of Quanah. They first came in sight of his wagon where he had camped in the shallow flat bottom of the creek above the crossing. They did not suspect anything serious but rushed on; the first thing they beheld was Mr. Bird, lying on the side of a little bank. They thought at first he was asleep, but, oh, horrors, when they reached him, yes, he was asleep— his last sleep; he was dead. He had died all alone with no one to attend him. We believed he had an attack of the cramps. They searched everywhere around him; there were thirteen empty cartridge hulls in the spring seat. By these shots it seemed he was trying to attract the attention of Mr. Wells. A few yards back showed where he had turned his wagon around and started back to Quanah. It must have been dark for he missed the crossing, going above it and getting down in the bed of the creek. The banks were too steep to get out; it showed where he had cut his wagon around different ways but failed and had unharnessed his team, tied them to a tree on a hill. His bed was made but he was not on it.

Everything showed he was perfectly rational. It seemed his dog had gotten poison. A bucket of lard was sitting near where he had been doctoring him. The dog was a few steps away dead. The team was almost perished for water and feed. If the dumb brutes could only speak, revelations might be made that we have never guessed; but I believe my husband passed away the first night he was left alone, from the cramps. One of the men hurried to Quanah to give the alarm. They brought an ambulance out for him and carried him back to Quanah and prepared him for internment as soon as possible. They had no way of communicating with me and it was so far they could not wait, but the news came around by Matador and on to me by Mr. Fult Hardy. It was a shock that almost drove me insane. It was too bad to be true. It seemed that half my life had passed out. I could not comprehend it at first. My first thought was, oh, what would become of me, with no one but my two little children left me. It seemed the three months that he was away in New Mexico must have been intended to prepare me for this trial and to make me more resigned to my fate, and to know I could live alone. It may have helped some, but oh, I felt so desolate and lonely for a long time. The weary weeks and months that seemed to drag were almost unbearable.

*   *   *

After the death of her husband, Ella Bird remained a widow for nine years. For most of those years, she and her two young children lived on an isolated ranch. She earned a meager living by raising cattle and making fancy leather gloves and beaded vests for cowboys from neighboring ranches. Ella was known as one of the best marksmen in the Panhandle. Much of the food which she and her children ate was antelope and other wild game. Basically, however, the cowboys from the neighboring ranches who took care of her cattle without pay made it possible for her to survive. During her widowhood she was much sought after and received at least seventeen offers of marriage. The most devastating event of those years was the destruction of her home by a tornado. She and the children survived by hiding in a "flower pit," which was only three and one-half feet deep and had a glass top.

Nine years after her husband's death, Ella promised to marry August Dumont, a French-Canadian who was the postmaster, the sheriff, and a merchant in Paducah, Texas. Ella had known Dumont for twenty years, and he had patiently courted her for nine years. Shortly before their marriage, Ella fled to Dallas and obtained a job as a sculptress for a monument company. However,

Ella Elgar Bird Dumont about 1896. (*Courtesy J. Verne Dumont*)

she missed the West, and the beauty of her home drew her back to the Panhandle.

Ella and August were married in about 1896. They were happy and prosperous and lived in a big white Victorian house in Paducah, but tragedy continuted to follow Ella. One of the Dumonts' two sons died in infancy. Later, Ella's only surviving daughter was killed at the age of nineteen by a fall from a horse.

Ella Bird Dumont spent her last years in Paducah and became known as the "Mother of Cottle County." She summarizes her life in the Panhandle in the following words.

*   *   *

At times I seemed to stand and gaze on the progress of the country almost in wonderment. Only a little while ago it seemed when there were nothing but buffalo; then a space of time elapsed when there was nothing left but ourselves; yet we remained. This was a time ever to be remembered. There were months and months that I did not see the face of even one woman; next the cattle were being moved in, then the ranches, then a long space of time ere the farming and building of towns, schools, etc., began, and then the present. What a change! But this was a change I had longed to see, for I wanted my children to grow up with the advantages of a civilized country.

Mary Olivette Taylor Bunton

> "There were three other things on that old trail that disturbed my peace of mind—the Indians, the rattlesnakes, and storms."

Mary Olivette Taylor (c. 1863–1952) married her "girlhood sweetheart," James Howell Bunton in 1885, Mary, who was educated in exclusive schools in Austin and Elmira, New York, was described by her niece as a "society belle." Mary married Bunton in a ceremony in her parents' home. Her parents were Mary Helen (Millican) and Dr. Matthew Addison Taylor. Dr. Taylor was a wealthy and prominent Austin physician.

Bunton was a member of a respected pioneer Texas family. His father, John Wheeler Bunton, was a prominent rancher and lawyer and had served in the Third Congress of the Republic of Texas. James Howell had himself amassed a sizable herd of cattle, which he kept on a ranch near Sweetwater, Texas.

Shortly after her marriage, Mary joined her husband on his dangerous journey up the Chisholm Trail. Mary was one of the few women to participate in a trail drive, and her lively account in *A Bride on the Old Chisholm Trail in 1886* gives us a woman's view of such a trip.

*   *   *

My story of the old Chisholm Trail begins with my marriage, October 14, 1885. The winter that followed was a very severe one. Blizzards swept the great cattle states of the West and the Northwest. Thousands and thousands of cattle perished with the cold on the open ranges. You may think this story incredible, but it is a recorded fact in the weather bureau in Washington, D.C. These records tell of how the terrific velocity of the blizzards drifted the cattle on many of the ranches into sheltered places where they were actually piled to great heights, and were smothered and frozen stiff.

From Mary Taylor Bunton, *A Bride on the Old Chisholm Trail in 1886* (San Antonio: Naylor Company, 1939).

Mary and J. Howell Bunton in 1885. (*From her book* A Bride on the Old Chisholm Trail)

The wealthy cattle barons of Idaho, Wyoming, Montana, Nebraska and Dakota had their princely fortunes swept away in a single night. One of my fellow townsmen, Mr. Jesse Driskill, who built the famous Driskill Hotel in Austin and for whom the hotel was named, was at that time Austin's only milllionaire. Mr. Driskill had his ranches in the Black Hills of Dakota and the blizzards cost him his millions. The blizzards also robbed my young husband of his fortune.

However, the cattlemen were never whiners. Those grand old-timers were ever noted for their intrepid courage, and while they were dazed at first, when they did realize that their fortunes were gone and they had to make a new start in life, they, like the "Phoenix" of old, rose from the ashes of misfortune and began to look about for ways and means to recoup their losses. The cattle situation everywhere was appalling. Many conferences were held and it was finally decided that good money could be made buying cheap cattle in Texas and driving them north over the different trails to be sold to buyers who were re-stocking the great ranches of the North and West.

Mr. Bunton, after the greatest effort, succeeded in persuading Austin bankers to finance his gigantic undertaking and they did this without collateral. It was a hazardous risk for all concerned but they had unlimited faith in Texas and her opportunities and in him as a moral risk, so as soon as financial support was assured, Mr. Bunton lost no time in selecting experienced buyers and went with them into South Texas where cattle were bought and segregated. Cows, steers and yearlings were held on their ranches until whole herds could be assembled for driving over the Chisholm Trail to the Northern market.

While his plans were being successfully carried out in this part of the State, Mr. Bunton decided to go to his ranch, then near Sweetwater in Nolan County, Texas, where he had men gathering cattle to be thrown into the herds when they reached Sweetwater from the Southern part of the State. Mr. Bunton urged that I go with him to the ranch and I was delighted to have the opportunity. We had been married only two months and most of the time had been spent on our honeymoon in Chicago and Eastern points. I had never been on a ranch in all my life, so naturally, I was looking forward to my first visit with great anticipation as I had heard so much of the "Wild West," the "Great Open Spaces" and the fascination of cowboy life and their weirdly beautiful songs.

To add to my comfort while on the ranch, a small room of lumber was built and I was told that this was the first house of lumber ever built on Sweetwater Creek. It seemed that the living quarters on ranches in that section consisted of "dugouts" at that time. I wonder if any of you have ever seen, heard or read of a "dugout"? I never had until I first visited my husband's ranch. You may depend on it, I was shocked to find not only cowboys but large families living in them apparently comfortable and contented. Can you of this de luxe age imagine people living in dirt houses? That was what a "dugout" was—just a good-sized square hole dug back into the south side of a hill. On the north side of the room, a special place was dug out to be used as a fireplace. Just above this a round hole was dug through to the top of the hill for the smoke to escape, and the cowboys called it the dugout chimney. On the south side of the room was an opening without doors that gave light and ventilation. There were no windows in the dugout and only a dirt floor. In times of storm a wagon sheet or tarpaulin was fastened across the doorway. It was in such a dugout that the cowboys spent their time when they were not at work on the range.

If the weather was too inclement to work on the outside, the cowboys would bring in their saddles and bridles and grease them. When I asked them why they did this, they were too polite to laugh at my ignorance and just quietly told me that grease preserved leather and would protect it from the weather. The cowboys were expert in washing and mending their saddle blankets and their stirrup leathers. They also prepared and ate their meals in the dugout and, as there were no tables or chairs, they had to squat around on the ground to eat. They slept in bunks built on either side of the small dugout room or rolled up in their blankets on the floor or out in the open. Some of the dugouts had several rooms and were satisfactory homes, the largest room being used as a place to have their visitors.

The dugouts were recreational centers, too, and, on Saturday nights and Sundays, cowboys came from near-by ranches to visit. On these occasions, they would sit around the open fire and tell hair-raising stories of their riding, roping, and branding, or thrum their banjos and guitars and sing their beautiful songs of life on the range. . . .

Horseback riding, at that time, was one of the most fashionable accomplishments for young ladies and I was very fond of that sport. Even before my marriage I was a very good rider and it was fortunate for me that I had learned, for it enabled me to go with Mr. Bunton over the ranch or follow the cowboys over the range. I had the opportunity of seeing a "rodeo" every day as they were "breaking" wild horses for use on the trail.

We girls rode side-saddles in those days but, later on, I was the first woman to ride astride in our part of the State, and you may be sure it caused a stampede among the cowboys and the cattle. One "old-timer" near by observed me on that memorable first occasion, and rising in his saddle, with his long white whiskers flying in the breeze, his arms outstretched, exclaimed: "My God! I knew she'd do it! Here she comes wearin' the britches!" My own husband viewed me with surprise, but had no time to comment as he had to get busy and help round up the distracted cattle. Well, I galloped back home as fast as I could and that ended the initial display of my new riding breeches and boots which my mother had just sent me as a gift. . . .

I was just becoming accustomed to ranch life, to enjoy its novelties and to love its freedom when, late one night, a cowboy came galloping into camp and brought the news that three of Mr. Bunton's big herds were coming and that they were encamped just a few miles away. There was great excitement in our camp then and not a soul slept another wink that night.

Before day next morning, Mr. Bunton mounted his horse and rode away to meet the cattle and inspect the herds. He was gone all day and did not return till quite late that night. It was a new experience for me, as it was the first time he had left me at the ranch alone. As dark came on, I began to worry about him and imagine that a thousand things had happened to him. When he finally came and I saw a worried look on his face, I realized at once that something unusual had happened, and so it had. As soon as he could, he told me how sorry he was to have been so late returning to camp but that it had been unavoidable; that when he reached the herds he found that the general "herd boss" had been stricken with sore eyes on the way up and that the heat and dust of the trail had made the poor fellow almost blind. As the man was suffering such agony with his eyes, it would be impossible for him to have the responsibility of the cattle any further.

"What in the world are you going to do?" I asked.

"I don't know yet," he replied, "I have been in the saddle all day riding hard, going here, there, and yonder trying to find a man suitable for the place, but herd bosses are born, not made, and I have not even heard of *one*. It just seems to be up to me. I fully realize that with my little experience, I am undertaking a herculean task but I can find no other solution to my problem except to take charge of the herds and have the cattle driven through to market, myself. . . .

I was simply dazed with the news at first. Through no fault of ours, the blizzards had robbed us of our fortune and now, to have this calamity overtake us, to have my husband go, so soon after our marriage, on that long, dangerous journey and leave me, it seemed that the dreams of my life were shattered. As I sat there pondering over the seriousness of the situation, a bright idea flashed into my mind, and, after a slight hesitation, I said: "I do not want to stay in that little town of Sweetwater, and I am not going home without you." My reply was like a thunderbolt out of a clear sky. Mr. Bunton looked at me in amazement when I further said: "I know what I am going to do, and I guess you will think I am having a 'brain storm,' but I have already made up my mind. I am going up the trail with you."

As soon as he could get his breath, he said: "My dear, you know you could not do that. In the first place, you could not stand the hardships and, another thing, there are dangers on that old trail that you have never dreamed of. It will likely take us six weeks or two months to make this trip, and besides, I have never heard of a woman's going up the trail."

In my state of mind, his telling of the hardships did not faze me, for, as he said, I had never had to endure any, and as for the dangers I had never experienced any, so it seemed more like an interesting adventure to me than a thing to dread. His saying he had never heard of a woman going up the trail just made me eager and more determined than ever that I was going. To gain my point, I began to coax him into taking me, but listening to his better judgment, he said, "Please let's not discuss your going any further. It isn't either a safe or sane thing for you to do."

I was on the verge of hysteria when I thought of a woman's weapon— tears. So I then looked up at him with my eyes full of tears and sobbingly said, "Please take me. You could find a way if you wanted me to be with you. I remember your saying this morning that your slogan was 'where there's a will there's a way.'" He had never seen me shed tears and it was an entirely new experience for him, but it proved the "straw that broke the camel's back."

He hurriedly said, "Please don't cry. I thought you were only joking when you said you were going with me. It is true that I have always believed that one can accomplish wonders, if he tries hard enough, but you surely are putting me up against a hard proposition, and I don't for the life of me see how I can manage it." As I continued to sob a little, he said, "If your heart is set on going, I guess it is up to me to find the way." When he said this, I knew I had gained my point, so I looked up brightly and dried my tears and was soon happy again, while he rode away to attend to his duties around the herds.

After a little while, I heard Mr. Bunton coming back to camp, riding like the wind and once more I was frightened until I saw his face was all smiles. He called out to me, saying he had solved the problem.

"What do you have in mind?" I asked.

"Well, dear, it is this—you can start the trip with me, though I feel sure you will soon be sick of your bargain, and if you are, I can put you on the train at some point where the trail is close enough to the railroad for me to leave the herds, and you could go back home."

That settled the question, but I knew I would not be taking that train for home.

The news of my going spread like wildfire, even in that sparsely settled country and the very next day some of Mr. Bunton's friends, relatives and business associates came from Sweetwater to remonstrate with him. His oldest friend acted as spokesman and this is what he said: "Look here, young man, we have come out here to give you a talk straight from the shoulder, and we are not going to mince words with you either. To tell you the truth, the whole truth, and nothing but the truth, all of us think you have lost your mind. It's the craziest idea we ever heard of—your promising to take Mrs. Bunton with you on this trip up the trail. You ought to realize that she is too young, too inexperienced, and too unaccustomed to hardships of any kind to make such a trip, and she is a bride, besides. Why, man, even to let her start the trip with you will likely end in tragedy. Think it over, and you had better heed our warning." Then they made an earnest appeal to me, telling me that they were surprised that I would want to add the care of myself to Mr. Bunton's already too great responsibilities. I just couldn't see their viewpoint and so I told them plainly that while I greatly appreciated the interest they were taking in us and in our affairs, Mr. Bunton had promised to take me with him and I saw no reason why I should not hold him to his promise. I really thought it would be the thrill of my life to go up the trail with my handsome husband and I want to assure my readers that it was a thrill in more ways than one. Many times afterwards I thought in trembling remembrance how true was the saying: "Fools rush in where angels fear to tread."

Hasty preparations had to be made for my going, and of course I had "nothing to wear"—that is, suitable for living for weeks on the trail and traveling all the time. Mr. Bunton's cousin's wife gallantly came to my rescue, however, and I was soon outfitted with a dark green woolen cloth "riding habit" and several wash dresses of hers which fitted me perfectly. I also carried along one evening dress to be prepared for the social affairs of civilization when we reached the end of the trip.

In less than four days the three herds of cattle were thrown back on the trail and we started on that long, and to me, never-to-be-forgotten journey. The "chuck wagon" was loaded to the bows with supplies, camp paraphernalia and cowboy belongings, leaving little room for our baggage. We managed, however, to crowd in a suitcase and our blankets. One of the outfits carried a small tent. It was loaned to us and was stretched for our use at night. A tarpaulin was then put down with our blankets on that and we thus slept on the ground.

As the weather grew warmer, we abandoned the tent and had just the blue sky, spangled with millions of stars for our canopy, and the cowboys riding around the herds at night, singing their soothing songs lulled us to peaceful slumber.

There was a fine team of horses on the ranch but they were none too gentle, so in making preparations for my going on the trip, the question arose as to whether I would be able to manage this team if they were hitched to the buggy I was to drive. It was finally left for me to decide the matter. I was simply terror stricken for I had had very little experience driving a team. I was even shaking in my shoes. I knew, however, that I dared not show the white feather, for if I did they would probably brand me a "scared-cat" and likely as not, it would cause me to be left behind. So, I plucked up my courage and, though there was a lump in my throat, I managed to say, "Don't let that worry you; of course I can handle that beautiful team. Mr. Bunton ought to know that I am not afraid of horses." That settled the controversy.

Mr. Bunton realized that the trip would be a long hard one for me and he was determined to make it as comfortable for me as he possibly could, so a Concord buggy was bought. It was the finest buggy of its kind made at that time and was the last word in buggy comfort. It was the kind of buggy used by cattlemen generally for traveling long distances over rough roads. As Mr. Bunton's duties were very arduous on the trail, I had to drive or ride alone almost all the way.

Among a small bunch of horses which Mr. Bunton had purchased to use on the trail was a full-blooded Spanish pony, a beauty in cream color with long white mane and tail. As soon as I saw him I claimed him as mine, but Mr. Bunton doubted whether it was wise to buy it as its owner stated that no man could ride it as his wife had spoiled it from the time it was a colt and it was "mean as the devil." He said his wife was heartbroken to part with the pony but they just had to sell him. The pony was "bridlewise" and a woman could easily ride him when he was saddled. "Please, Howell, let me have that pony," I said, "He is such a beauty and just look how he eats sugar out of my hand!"

I guess when a couple is still newly-married and very much in love, if the wife should ask her husband for the moon and he could arrange to get it, he undoubtedly would do so. Anyway I got the pony and he proved a joy and was the best gaited saddle pony I ever rode. However, he would never let a man ride him or even catch him if he was loose. Every cowboy in the outfit tried time and again to conquer him but they gave up in despair. Finally, I laid the law down to them, one and all, that none of them was ever to get on his back again. When they attempted to saddle him for me to ride, he would paw, kick and fight every man that came near but the minute he heard my voice, he would neigh for me and as soon as I was in the saddle he was gentle and obeyed the slightest touch of my hand on the bridle. I had ridden him many times as much as thirty-five or forty miles on certain occasions and the going was so easy that I was not fatigued and my pony was none the worse for the trip. When I grew tired of riding horseback on the trail, he was turned in with the herd or attached to the chuck wagon as were the team of fine horses which drew the Concord buggy when I wanted a change.

Every morning during the drive up the trail, Mr. Bunton was up and in the saddle by daylight for he must ride ahead of the herds to find grass, water and bed grounds for his cattle that night. He had to look after the saddle horses to see that they were well cared for and never abused. Every few days he must count the cattle in the three herds to see that none was lost and no strays picked up on the way. He must use the maneuvering of a general to keep his small army of cowboys faithful to their herding tasks day and night, and above all, he had to be a diplomat to keep peace among them in the camps. As there were no towns or villages close to the trail, Mr. Bunton had to arrange ahead for freight wagons loaded with supplies for the various camps to meet us at designated points along the trail.

Naturally, at first, it was a hardship for me to have to sleep on the ground. Oftentimes I was afraid to go to sleep as I remembered the harrowing tales I had heard of snakes, bugs and crawling and stinging things that infested the woods or prowled around hunting their prey at night. I am ashamed even now to tell how it frightened me when I first heard the snapping and snarling and fighting of the angry, hungry wolf packs as they came closer and closer to our camp at midnight, searching for food. A panacea for my fears as I lay on my pallet at night was turning my face towards the sky, watching the stars. In my last year at school I had studied astronomy and knew quite a few of the constellations and where to look for them. The Pleiades were my favorites. Night after night, I watched them slowly rising through the mellow shade glistening like millions of fireflies tangled in a silver braid.

The first part of the trip was perfect in weather and in interest. It was a novel sight to see those immense herds of cattle slowly wending their way along the trail. Riding ahead of the herd I would turn in my saddle and look back, and it would look as if the entire face of the earth was just a moving mass of heads and horns. I traveled most of the time with what was known as the "lead herd" and camped with it every night. This one herd consisted of some several thousand head of heifer yearlings, all red Durhams of the same size, age, and color. They had been bought from the old Richard King Ranch near Kingsville, Texas, which is one of the most famous in song and story. The herd also had a record of being the largest one of its kind driven up the trail that year. It made a beautiful sight on the trail. To me, it looked as if a dark-red velvet carpet with its wide border of green grass was stretched just as far as the eye could see.

The old Chisholm Trail wound its way over the hills and through the valleys. Wild flowers grew in the greatest profusion everywhere and there were many rare varieties that I had never seen before. I was fond of flowers and it afforded me great pleasure and helped to while away the long, lonely hours to gather them in armfuls. Sometimes, I would fill my buggy and decorate my horses' bridles and harness with the gorgeous blossoms, then I would weave a wreath for my hair and a chaplet of flowers for my shoulders. I was young, romantic and imaginative and, having to ride alone so much I really fancied that the lovely flowers growing along the roadside knew me and would wave, smile and nod to me as I drove through them. Seated in my flower-bedecked buggy it was easy enough for me to pretend that I was taking part in a grand flower parade.

The cowboys felt sorry for me in having to spend so much time alone, so they humored my whims. If any of them chanced to pass anywhere near and see me arrayed in flowers as if a Solomon in all his glory, they would stop their horses, take off their hats and make me a sweeping bow, and as they bent low over their saddle horns would exclaim: "Hail to the cowboys' beautiful queen of the flowers!"

Another interesting sight on the trail was to see large herds of buffalo silently grazing on the distant plains or joyously galloping about in the full pleasure of their freedom. . . .

I wish I were gifted with my pen so that I might describe for you the magnificent ever-changing panorama daily spread out before me. How my eyes and ears were charmed with the sights and sounds of Old Mother Nature's handiwork! There were so many, many birds in the forest and I marveled at their songs and their varied and gorgeous plumage. I was always looking for the Bob-Whites calling from the tall grass or listening for the mocking birds singing their songs in the beautiful old trees. Ofttimes, leaving the trees, they would fly higher and higher while a trail of song floated back as if to cheer me on my lonely way, long after the clouds had hidden the birds from view.

Another fascinating sight was the great patches of wild berries ripening along the roadside. Early in the morning, wet with dew they would sparkle in the sunshine as if the fairies had sprinkled them with diamond dust. There were other beautiful things too numerous to mention, but, on the other hand, there is another side to my story of the trail. I was so afraid of the unknown wild animals, the queer sounds at night and the prospect of wild Indians roving near. I dreaded to hear the lonely hooting of the owls at eventide and, too, how frightened I was the first time I saw a sleek, spotted leopard stealthily creeping through the underbrush close beside me as I rode the trail! Ofttimes, my blood would run cold when I would be awakened just before dawn by the human-like screams of a panther calling to his dead mate which some ruthless hunter had killed.

There were three other things on that old trail that disturbed my peace of mind—the Indians, the rattlesnakes, and storms. The Indians were supposed to be peaceful, but every few days, "cattle barons" came from scattered ranches to see the herds and to look through them for stray cattle. On these rare occasions they would never fail to tell us of the cruelties and atrocities practiced by the Indians and warn us of their treachery.

These stories were brought home to me one morning, very forcibly, when riding along. I drew up at a small shack just off the side of the road where some saddled horses were tied to the trees and men were standing around in groups apparently in serious conversation. A woman's curiosity prompted me to stop and find out what was the matter. To my horror, I saw there a man, his wife, and a little child that had been murdered and scalped by the Indians and then dragged into the cabin, their blood still fresh on the doorstep!

There came a day on the trail when even the early morning was too hot for comfort. As the sun rose higher it grew hotter and hotter— the intense heat seemed not only to affect my nerves but to make my head ache and my eyes burn. The horses seemed harder than usual to drive and to keep on the trail. Finally, I was almost in a state of collapse. I wanted to get out of hearing of the lowing of the cattle, and the noisy cowboys slapping their leggings with their quirts, and whistling and calling to the cattle trying to urge the poor leg-weary things along, and keep them strung out on the trail. The dust was suffocating—my team of horses was restless and thirsty.

As Mr. Bunton kissed me good-bye that morning and reminded me of my promise not to get out of old Sam's sight, I answered him mechanically. However, as the day wore on I became obsessed more and more with the desire to get away from the disagreeable surround- ings, though I really didn't mean to break my promise. I unconsciously slackened my horses' reins when I thought I saw over a slight rise in the road ahead, a large group of trees. I thought how refreshing it would be to rest under the shade until the wagon came along, and I felt sure I would find water in the creek for my horses. Soon the team was traveling at a rapid clip—I suppose they had smelled the water—for I remembered that Sam, the negro camp cook, had told me that "old mother nature" had endowed horses with instinct and they could al- ways locate a stream of water when they were thirsty. It was not long until we reached the high bluffs and came in sight of a creek. I checked the horses' speed a little as we drove down the steep banks.

The water was up to the horses' knees and clear as crystal. At once the horses seemed to sense danger and began to paw the water and snort. They never even lowered their heads to drink. I tapped them with the reins to remind them to go on across, but, those blooded horses had more sense than I had, for in less time than it takes me to tell it, they had wheeled around turning in midstream and were run- ning up the bluff at breakneck speed. As they turned, I caught sight of five or six big Indian bucks grunting and wallowing around in the cool mud and water.

In the meantime, old Sam had missed me. My buggy tracks were the only clue he had to the way I had gone. He put whip to his mules and was coming to hunt me as fast as he could. The wagon sheet was flapping, the tin pans and plates were rattling and at every turn of the wheels the jolting was scattering everything loose out of the wagon all along the trail.

Sam said later that he couldn't see me sitting in the buggy for the cloud of dust that enveloped me—that he was praying with every breath, that God would let him save the "young Missus" from the In- dians, even if it cost him his life. Well, I was saved through the wise action of those fine horses but I'll never forget the fright nor the comic figure old Sam cut with his galloping mules and clattering chuck- wagon. . . .

You may like to hear some tales about the rattlesnakes we met on the trail, so I shall give you some of our experiences in that line, as my close association with ranch life and the tall tales told by the cowboys may have given me a little proficiency in that respect.

All Spring the weather had been very warm and rattlesnakes were to be seen and heard everywhere. I was almost afraid to walk around on the ground in daylight for fear of being bitten. I had to watch out every moment, for even as I rode along they would hiss as they lay alongside the road, coiled ready to strike. Giant rattlers, sometimes as many as six or eight by actual count would be coiled beneath the shade of the trees enjoying the sunlight and growing warmth. Once, a mother snake and her family of little snakes crossed the road just ahead of me, frightening my horse so that he came in an ace of pitching me over his head into their midst. One day, Mr. Bunton decided to count the cattle in the herd behind us, so I went with him. We were returning to camp, and, as usual after a day's trip we were tired and hungry, so we sat down near the chuck wagon and old Sam was serving us supper when one of the cowboys came up and kindly offered to spread our blankets for the night. It was a little too dark for him to see the ground plainly, so he spread the tarpaulin and blankets over a rattlesnake hole without knowing it. In the night, the snake, I suppose, got too warm or possibly hungry, so it crawled out of its hole, and as it could not get out from under the tarpaulin because of the weight of our bodies, it stretched its body full length between us. As usual, the next morning we were up before day, and as it began to get near daylight, I chanced to notice the ridge under our blankets. I spoke of it to Mr. Bunton only to be laughed at for my fears, and, to tease me, he asked me if my hair rope had lost its charm. He assured me the ridge was nothing more than a small branch of a tree that George failed to see when he spread our blankets the night before. His explanation failed to satisfy me, so I lingered around to see for myself, and sure enough, when the blankets were rolled away for the day, there we found his snakeship peacefully sleeping. We were so amazed and yet so thankful that he had not bitten us that we allowed that five foot diamond back rattler with its many rattles and a button to crawl back into its hole unharmed!

The season had been very dry with scarcely enough rain at any one time to lay the dust, but just after crossing the line into Kansas, we struck one of the terrible storms we had been hearing about. It was indeed one of the most terrifying electrical storms I have ever witnessed. We were out in the open without any sheltering walls or roof and we received full benefit of the performance. The clouds had begun to gather in the northwest shortly after noon. As the day drew to a close, the sky, as far as the eye could see, was inky black, with green and yellow streaks. Every few minutes, old Sam would look up into the clouds and, shaking his head would say, "De Lawd is sho aimin' to punish us dis night, and der's no tellin' what'll happen to us poor sinners before daylight." It was not until after dark that the thunder began to roar and rattle.

When the night shift reported for duty, Mr. Bunton put me in the chuck wagon telling me not to be afraid, that he would never be far from the wagon. Of course, I realized that his duty was to be with the herds to inspire confidence in his men, for the least thing will stampede a herd of cattle in a storm. It was not long before the rain began pouring torrents. All night long, Mr. Bunton and his faithful cowboys kept riding round and round the herd calling and singing to the cattle trying to allay their fears and prevent, if possible, a stampede that would have meant not only injury to and possibly the loss of some of the cattle, but the lives of some of his men as well. When the storm began, the air was so charged with electricity, the boys had taken off their pistols and spurs and had me take the steel hairpins out of my hair and the rings from my fingers. "You never can tell what these freaky Kansas storms will do," they said. "It is always wise to use precaution and be prepared for any emergency." Imagine me, if you can, sitting in that old chuck wagon, all alone with only the wagon sheet over my head to protect me from the fury of the raging storm which seemed to be growing worse and worse every moment. Sometimes the lightning would fall from the sky in fiery darts of flame; again, there would be a flash and it would look as if millions of fairies in glittering robes of fire were dancing in mad glee over the backs of the cattle and jumping from the horns of one steer to another. As I sat there, shaking with fear and a prayer on my lips, I was peering into the darkness, breathlessly watching and waiting for every flash of lightning, trying to see if the one I loved was still alive, and if the cattle were still there.

However, the longest night, no matter what its horrors, must pass. When daylight came at last, the storm was over, and just as old Sol began to peep his smiling face above the horizon, I was filled with new courage though it may seem strange after so much terror. By the close of the day, I had almost forgotten the dangers and horrors of the night just past.

Some days after the storm, Mr. Bunton decided he would drive on ahead of the herds to Coolidge, Kansas, to see what the chances were of his disposing of the cattle there. Coolidge, at that time, was one of the wildest frontier towns in the West. It had the reputation of being inhabited chiefly by bandits, gamblers, cow thieves, and murderers, but as we drove through its dusty streets, I was not one bit frightened, nor was I ever so much as thinking of the shocking tales I had heard. Instead, my heart was singing with joy, for, after two months on the trail, at last I would have a roof over my head, a good hot bath and a comfortable bed.

As we drove up to the hotel, we recognized men from home standing in groups on the sidewalk. As soon as they saw us, they came rushing out to meet us with open arms, shouting their welcome. I was fairly lifted out of the buggy and my feet never touched the ground while I was carried and safely installed inside of the hotel. Every step of the way, those gallant cattlemen in loud voices were proclaiming me as the "Queen of the Old Chisholm Trail" and that night at a great impromptu feast and ball at the hotel, I was wined, dined and toasted and made to feel like a real heroine in a great western story.

*   *   *

After returning from the trail drive, the Buntons moved to Mary's father's ranch in Dimmit County, near Eagle Pass, Texas. Mary enjoyed living on the ranch even though at one time her life was threatened by Mexican outlaws.

In later years, Mrs. Bunton lived in Austin, where she was a prominent member of society. At times she would be called upon to recount her experiences on the Old Chisholm Trail. In a preface to *A Bride on the Old Chisholm Trail in 1886* Mary Connor Cook describes one such occasion: "The story is told with such perfect poise and in voice low-pitched, yet so perfectly modulated that it reaches the farthest away in a crowded auditorium; told dramatically because it is dramatic, and made to live for her hearers it is still so vivid in her memory."

Many people implored Mrs. Bunton to write a book on her experiences on the ranch in Dimmit County, but she never did. Mary Taylor Bunton died in Austin in 1952 at the age of eighty-nine.

Mary Alma Perritt Blankenship

"We had plenty of time to be still and know God. He was our nearest neighbor."

"My determination to rise above my childhood portion as an orphan since four years old [was] teamed with Andrew's frugality and inherent love of the land. . . . we knew that with the earth bringing forth such increase, the Lord willing, we would some-day be big farmers." The spirit expressed by Mary Alma Perritt Blankenship in the above quotation was typical of that of pioneers who were willing to undergo danger and hardship to make better lives for themselves and their children.

Allie, as Alma Blankenship was known, and her husband Andrew moved in 1902 to the Staked Plains, one of the last areas of Texas to be settled. They faced the hostility of big ranchers, lived in a dugout, and burned cow chips for fuel in order to obtain the most valued possession of the pioneers—land. When Andrew traveled to the courthouse in Lubbock to file their claim, Allie, their baby, and the young son of a friend stayed on the land alone.

Mary Alma Perritt, the daughter of Mary Ann (Richards) and William Wallace Perritt, was born on May 4, 1878. Her parents died when she was four years old, and she and her younger brother and sister were reared by their grandparents, Elander Caroline (Cooper) and Stratford Wade Hampton Richards. The Richardses had lost their plantation and slaves after the Civil War and had adopted a nomadic lifestyle, with Richards serving as a traveling Baptist minister and Mrs. Richards working as midwife and pre-scription druggist.

Allie met Andrew Wesley Blankenship while she was working for his family near Stephenville, Texas. Andrew's father was a friend of Richards, and while Richards was leading a revival, the two men agreed that Allie would spend three weeks with the family. Blankenship jokingly told Allie that she could have the pick of his seven boys, and she took him up on his offer.

In her later life, Mrs. Blankenship began writing her "most

From Seymour V. Connor, ed., *The West Is for Us: The Reminiscences of Mary A. Blankenship* (Lubbock: West Texas Museum Association, 1958). Reprinted by permission of West Texas Museum Association.

Mary Alma Perritt in 1895. (*Courtesy Wesley B. Blankenship*)

memorable experiences and endearing thoughts" on scraps of paper. After the death of her husband in 1952, she moved to the home of her daughter Doyle Blankenship Thornhill, and the two of them began to organize the memoirs as Allie continued to add to the collection. The two women wanted to finish the memoirs so that they could be included in an exhibition called "The Saga of the South Plains," which was held in 1955. They succeeded, but Allie died suddenly a few days before the exhibition.

Mary Alma Perritt Blankenship's memoirs were later published by the West Texas Museum Association in Lubbock under the title *The West Is for Us*. The warmth and energy of this pioneer woman shine through as she shares her life with the reader.

*   *   *

While awaiting our land to come on the market, we learned something of the way of life on the plains. We continued living in our wagon, as did the others, using Ward Jarrott's dugout as our community house. I was the only woman and had the only child in our group. The other women of the strip had decided to wait until the land was awarded and the three months allowed to set up a homestead had passed before they moved out.

Andrew and I broke up a small spot and planted a feed crop at Ward's after the snow melted away. Mail was distributed here and all passers-by stopped.

Jim Jarrott, who had surveyed our strip and staked the land, was notified that the papers were being mailed from Austin, so we made ready our wagons after three months' delay, and waited for him to lead us to our four sections, lost in the tall grass to all except himself. Those who were to claim land were to move some possessions on to the land and file at this time. The filing had to be done at Lubbock where there was a court house, several stores, a hotel, and a wagon yard.

Those filing on April 24, 1902, with Andrew and Jarrott were Lee Cowan, John Doyle, Walter Frazier, Solon Cowan, and G. M. Royalty. John Doyle filed for Louise and Florence Watkins.

We loaded, ready to leave Ward's at 5 P.M., Jim leading us. We drove to the west end of the long strip and came east through each man's claim, hastily pitching up a tent and camping outfit in the black winter night.

Since my baby and I were to be the only ones on the strip while the men were away for filing, I took Brock Gist, an eight year old boy from the Terry County bunch for company. They unhitched our wagon, pitched our tent up on a hill and Andrew rode Snide to Lubbock leaving us Old Duggan tied to the wagon wheel, a shot gun, and a five gallon keg of water. We watched the men ride away into the darkness, knowing that we were to be on our own until they returned.

I did not unload the things into the tent, but continued to live in the wagon, as the tent was only pitched on two poles, and waved wildly in the night wind.

It is needless to say that I was too scared to sleep, as the three of us and the shot gun occupied the same feather bed. By the time the anxiously awaited sun arose, I was up looking long and hard in all directions to locate some landmark. We only located the windmill 1½ miles to the north, where the boy was to take our horse to water later in the day. Not a neighbor's tent could be seen. They had blown flat, but still marked the spot of a settler. We could see nothing but thick winter grass, scattered mesquite, bear grass, and cat claw bushes.

We cleared off a spot of grass with our grubbing hoe, built a fire from dry mesquite limbs and cooked our breakfast. After a colorful prairie sunrise, the boy rode off alone toward the windmill to water our only horse. I took my baby in my arms, leaned against the wagon, the gun close by, and watched him all of the way there and back. The trip seemed longer than the two hours.

Soon after he returned, we noticed several horseback riders in the direction of the mill. They were probably attracted to us when they saw the boy and horse at the mill. When they failed to come to our wagon, but circled around us in the distance, and off, we knew that they were no friends. Brock stood holding the gun, which was as long as he was tall, and leaned against the wagon wheel, watching their strange behavior. This display of unfriendliness had come sooner than we had expected. The rest of the day was spent in anxious anticipation.

Our chores were limited, so we became idle and ill-at-ease. We soon had the opportunity to display our gunmanship and courage, when five small coyotes came out of a hole only about 50 feet from our wagon and started a lonesome chorus, as only coyotes can. I stopped their singing with a blast from the shotgun, but did not make a kill, as all scampered away and out of sight.

The second night brought us even less sleep as the coyotes came back to serenade us from the darkness, and the high wind flopped our tent and rocked our wagon. Upon arising the second morning, we discovered that the howling coyotes had dug under our chicken coop in the tent and slipped off with two of the five hens I had brought for a start.

The strange acting cowboys did not come back to kill us during the night, as we had expected, but they made the same ominous ride around us the next morning. Then we began to look wishfully in the direction that the men had ridden away, and hugged our gun more closely. There was not even a trail in the grass that could lead us to anyone for help. We didn't even know from what direction we had come, only the direction the men left. We were expecting a showdown just any time, but were determined to stand our ground. In my prayers I reminded the Lord that He had delivered Daniel from the lions den and I was accounting Him "faithful to make us a way of escape" if bad came to worse.

Lubbock was a day's horseback ride, and we measured space then not in miles, but by a day's ride. We knew something had happened when the men did not show up by dark on the second day.

When the men got to Lubbock they heard whisperings about others going to file on the promised land, so they slept in the court house just to be "on hand." The stage from Big Spring bringing the filing papers in the mail did not arrive as expected. This caused another day's delay, and another night in the court house, sleeping on saddle blankets with the saddles for a pillow.

The mail arrived with the papers on the third day. They were signed and mailed back. There was still to be uncertainty, however, until we received our award notice card from Austin, saying the land would be ours after three years of "living up the claim."

By the time the men rode out of the open prairie, the cold blowing wind had whipped our tent off its poles and it lay in a defeated heap on the grass. But the boy, horse, shotgun, baby and I had defied all scares and still had enough enthusiasm to shout with joy when we saw the horsebackers coming straight toward us, instead of mysteriously around. We laid our gun down.

The men thoughtfully laid plans together before departing, as our get-togethers were to be few and far between. We grieved to see the men who had brought us here, leave us alone now, taking the brave little boy, who had become a man in the three days he had stayed with Wallace and me. Boys became men at an early age in this frontier.

When we were left to root-little-hog or die, we set out to fill our needs from the new land. Necessity became the mother of invention as we took our wagons and team to the ranch windmill to solve our wood and water problem. In a round-about way we had been sent word not to water at the windmills. We realized that our settling meant an intrusion upon the cowmen's grazing range, but we had staked our lives here in the midst of their domain without even a fence to mark our own ground, and had no choice but to trespass as we gathered dry cowchips for wood and watered the horses and carried out water from their wells. How true was the expression: "the windmill draws our water and the cows cut our wood." The lowly cowchips around which I at first tip-toed and raised my skirts held a place of high esteem.

We found that the mesquite trees, which were to feed our hungry stove, grew so far underground that it took one hour of digging to recover a grub large enough to cook a meal. However sooner or later these must be grubbed out before we could plant our field, so we killed two birds with one stone, and they did supplement the prairie wood (cow chips) which burned up hurriedly, and the precious coal which had to be freighted from Big Spring, 110 miles away.

We had brought enough 12-inch boards tied on our wagon to box up a four-foot side-wall around our tent, making it a higher ceiling and warmer. Inside we set up our bachelor stove with the drum oven, table, chairs and the bedstead for housekeeping and moved out of the wagon home. . . .

I was happy to see other women moving in after the three months grace and I was happy to have them stop for a visit of a night or sometimes a week. We felt the absence of life on the great plains and were always starved for company and thirsty for conversation. John Doyle married Louise Watkins, and they stayed with us much of the time.

On August the 25th the men had all pitched in to help us dig the "dug-out" for our sod house. They had been staying at our camp several days when the men became worried over Jim Jarrott's not returning from Lubbock as scheduled. He was then three days late, so John Doyle and Griff Hiser rode to Lubbock to see about him. They went around the road by Copeland's place, thinking that he might have come by there with some mail or freight.

They did not find him at Copeland's or on the road to Lubbock, where his family was staying at the Nicolette Hotel. Nor was he to be found in Lubbock. He had left his family three days before in his wagon and was to return by the ranch trail, which was a cut-off trail. Tension rose among his friends and family when they discovered that he had left his gun on the dresser in the hotel room.

Following the ranch trail toward the strip, the two men located his team grazing around the twin windmills, three miles north of our camp, the harness hanging on the windmill tower, the wagon nearby and Jim's body floating in the shallow surface tank, face down.

They awakened us about 10 p.m., telling us that the windmill where we had gathered our wood and watered our teams had become the scene of this tragedy. It looked as if Jim had been shot in the arm and right side with a rifle by someone ambushed in the windmill tower, where empty shells were found. There was evidence from the bloody trail that he had fallen or jumped from his wagon and run toward the tank dam for cover, falling into the water. The murderer then unloaded his gun into Jim's back. All of the men went to the scene, taking sheets in which to pick up and wrap his body, leaving the baby and me frightened and alone on the prairie.

A passing cowboy testified later at the hearing that he took the harness off the horses, hung them on the windmill, turning the animals loose, without even seeing the slain man's coyote-eaten body in the shallow pond. This murder was confessed by Jim Miller in 1933 upon his death in Oklahoma.

We became more concerned about our safety now, expecting to be wiped out any time. Our gun and Bible became the family altar as they lay side by side upon the same table. It was a familiar sight to see seven or eight "hog legs" laying around any nester's dug-out shelf, when just that many men would be our guests.

Instead of being scared off our claims—if such was the purpose of the foul murder—we became more intent and closely allied in our fight for survival. The name Jim Jarrott became a legend among us, and his martyrdom served to spur us on. We were determined not to pull up stakes and retreat back to the east.

Jim Jarrott's widow, who is now Mrs. M. D. Abernathy, and their children, Dick, John, and Bessie, (now Mrs. John Vickers) carried out the tradition of the frontier their husband and father had settled and given his life for, by living out their claim in the same dedicated spirit that had motivated their loved one.

In time our differences with the big ranchers dissolved, love overcame fear, and our tensions gave way to harmony. We came to understand and to believe that "the West is for us and not against us."

Our next home was considered a half dug-out or a story and a half. It was one 16 foot square box room built over a 14 foot dug-out, high enough to leave windows in the dug-out room. This sod room was a comfortable bedroom, the dirt floor padded with grass and covered with my hand loomed rug. We sometimes shared this with a water dog or lizard. Our cooking and eating were done in the upper room above the dug-out.

The winters were severely cold so we learned to stock up well on food for ourselves and plant plenty of bundle feed for our stock which we stored in the stack lot. Snow covered the ground for weeks at a time. The fourth winter (1905) we ran short of coal, grubs and chips and had to burn corn for heat, which we gathered from the tops of the stalks left sticking out of the deep snow. The snow covered our feed stacks until the cows could walk over them and the fences and go where they pleased. The horses wore icicles on their foretops and manes, and the men came in with icicles hanging from brows, whiskers and mustaches.

That winter, Andy (as he was affectionately called by our friends) went on a freighting trip to Big Spring for supplies and his team got away from camp, causing a delay in his return. I had watched and worried several days about his delay. The great danger in traveling was a runaway team or the horses's getting loose from their hobbles at the camp. I had been making a lighthouse for him night after night by hanging a lighted lantern high in the windmill tower, as we did to guide the ones home who were out after dark. "Josh" Spires came by late one afternoon looking for a lost cow and I sent him on the trail to see if he could locate Andrew. Just as "Josh" went over the hill he saw the wagon coming and gave me the happy bandana handkerchief sign, and went on his way.

We would lose stock occasionally in the cold blizzards. They soon tramped out trails to the north and south of the pasture, as they walked to the north line to meet the blizzard and drift southward, single file, tails to the wind. After they reached the south fence, they would stand against it until the wind changed, sometimes freezing to death. After the thaw, the carcasses were skinned, and the hides were stretched on the fence to dry for selling to A. E. Shireman, the hide man, or tanned for making raw hide harness, rugs, and chair bottoms. The horns were polished for gun and hat racks. Not one hide was wasted even if the hair had slipped. We pioneers had to hold fast to everything useful if we were to survive.

Lightening struck a fence during one storm killing 50 head of cattle standing on our north fence. What a skinning!

We climbed the windmill tower to look over our herd in bad weather and good. We could always spot a cow and new-born calf off to themselves from that height. Then came the trip on horseback to bring the calf home across the saddle in front of the rider, the bellowing mother following close behind. We also used the windmill as a signal tower to call the hands in to dinner by hanging the cup towel high in the air.

We studied the sky for weather signs, planted and cut our cattle by the moon signs, predicted the change of seasons by the flight of the wild geese, told time of night by the cock's crow, time of day by the sun, and a wet spell by the falling of the smoke. We had no thermometer, but knew it was zero when we had to break a hole in the ice two or three times a day for the cattle to drink. In the winter most of the heat went up the stove pipes and the summers were always cool with the wind blowing across the green prairies. We spent most of the summer outside, moving our beds and rocking chairs out on the east porch for the season.

In the spring the green prairies were enriched with white and yellow buttercups, covered with red-orange Indian blankets and high-lighted by the "candlesticks of God" (bear grass), blighted only by the blooming loco weed. The whole family, armed with hoes, combed the prairies chopping up every loco weed that raised its grey head. The loco caused the stock to become dopey and unmanageable, wandering aimlessly until they died or had to be shot.

The worry of winter was prairie fires and in the summer it was the motionless windmill, that threatened to let our stock tank and water barrel dry up. Only once did dry weather cause us to drive our cattle to New Mexico for grass and home again after the rains.

Years were measured in the succession of seasons. Everything terminated in the spring, summer or fall, the winter being a dormant season. Spring brought planting, round-up and calving time; summer brought cultivating, canning, dipping and branding time, highlighted by the Fourth of July picnic and camp meeting; fall brought the busy time of reaping our increase. The winter brought a time of rest to land and man, but meant the eating up and feeding up of what we had stored up. We marked the past by seasons as: that first winter, second summer or third fall, and so on to another cycle of seasons. . . .

We had plenty of time to be still and know God. He was our nearest neighbor.

Although the neighbors' places were beginning to show up in the shimmering mirage of distance, as their trees began to tower above the new homes, we felt the absence of homefolks. My brother was hunting for a place to settle with his large family of children, so we promised to give him one quarter of our land, to have our kin near us. He brought his family out with the intention of staying, but soon "threw-it-up" and went back from whence he came. We made the same offer then to Andrew's folks, only to be told they would not have the whole country and live the isolated pioneer life.

There were times before we became completely happy on the prairie when our loneliness would almost panic us into going back. We looked over the prairies, sprinkled with cattle, swimming in the deceitful mirage which threatened to engulf us, and wondered if we were the only people inhabiting the earth. But we knew that to attain our goal, we must "forget those things behind and reach forth unto those things which are before." . . .

Our rainy days in the winter were spent toasting our boots at the open oven of the kitchen range, dipping ashes, stoking the fire, playing dominoes, parching peanuts, popping corn, chewing, smoking and dipping snuff. We worked at carding cotton batts, quilting, patching, and tall tale swapping. We often had company or went visiting on such days, as this was the only time we had to pay back visits outside of

visiting that was done when the men swapped out work. In later years
I laid down my snuff box and picked up cigarettes. . . .

We learned to overcome the besetting sieges of loneliness and to
evaluate our blessings and opportunities in the early days. The pioneer
woman of the prairie soon sacrificed her femininity as she laid away her
frills for the plain living, and took upon herself the yoke beside her
husband as team mate and companion, forever at his side whether it
was on a saddle, cultivator, go-devil, binder, pulling a cotton sack,
hunting, pitching bundles, or stacking feed, and all of this in addition
to the housekeeping and preserving food. Our day was from daylight
till dark. But what a thrill to Andy and me to have been two of the few
who blazed the trail for the multitude that followed.

Many mornings we took cotton sacks to the field and sat down
on them waiting until it became light enough to see our cotton. The
children were used, when old enough, as hands at whatever there was
to be done. We were known as little men with only four sections to
our name, but we were continually grateful for our stake. My determination to rise above my childhood portion as an orphan since four
years old, teamed with Andrew's frugality and inherent love of the
land, which he inherited from his Indian maternal ancestry, made our
eventual success a sure shot. America Jane Jefferies, his mother, was
part Indian.

We realized when we beheld our first small white cotton patch
and strong stalks with heavy heads of feed that this would ultimately be
our stronghold. We did not possess the grass spread to bear the brand
of big ranchers, but we knew that with the earth bringing forth such
increase, the Lord willing, we would someday be big farmers. We dedicated ourselves then and there to this purpose. We became rooted
and grounded in this faith in the plains, and had only to cast our bread
upon the waters to reap our promised return.

More and more sod has been put into cultivation until the cows
have been pushed off the caprock into the brush and the breaks and
farther north on the plains. Hardly a milk lot has been spared around
the present day farm home. The sod shanty has turned into the most
expensive and extensive homes in the country. The esteemed windmills have gone to stays, giving way to the electric pumps that flood
our one time pleasant pastures with water, turning them into busy,

Andrew (Andy), Wallace, Mary Alma (Allie) Blankenship, in front of their first real house, 1907. (*Courtesy Wesley B. Blankenship*)

friendly fields of grain for food and cotton for clothing. We don't watch the clouds sipping water from the ground and wonder when we will get it back again, and the prairie doesn't have to pray for rain any more. . . .

And now we are living another life divided for awhile. Andrew has gone ahead of me this time, pitching his tent in another new world, but I shall wait patiently for my call, taking advantage of "Grace." The Lord, who has guided, guarded and directed us here will surely prepare for old pioneers green pastures in the new frontier. Andrew died three days before his 80th birthday, December 11, and I am 74. We again shall have the thrill of pioneering another life together, when I shall have joined him.

*   *   *

Allie joined her beloved Andrew on September 11, 1955. Andrew had lamented the loss when the Depression forced the Blankenships to turn their beautiful ranch into a cotton farm. But they had been successful in creating a good life for themselves and their children. The little orphan girl who had been a sharecropper with her young husband died a wealthy woman, rich in love as well as gold. The American Dream was once again realized on the Staked Plains of West Texas.

References

Mary Crownover Rabb

Bailey, Ernest Emory, ed. *Texas Historical and Biographical Record.* Austin: n.p., n.d.

Barkley, Mary Starr. *History of Travis County and Austin, 1839–1899.* Waco: Texian Press, 1963.

Branda, Eldon, ed. *The Handbook of Texas.* Vol. 3. Austin: Texas State Historical Association, 1976. S.v. "Rabb, Mary Crownover."

Brown, John Henry. *Indian Wars and Pioneers of Texas.* Austin: L. E. Daniell, n.d.

Crawford, Ann Fears, and Crystal Sasse Ragsdale. *Women in Texas.* Burnet, Tex.: Eakin Press, 1982.

Phelan, Macum. *A History of Early Methodism in Texas, 1817–1866.* Nashville, Tenn.: Cokesbury Press, 1924.

Pickrell, Annie Doom. *Pioneer Women in Texas.* Austin: E. L. Steck Company, 1929; reprint ed., Austin: Pemberton Press, 1970.

Rabb, Mary Crownover. Biographical folder. Austin History Center, Austin Public Library, Austin.

———. Family papers, 1823–1922. Barker Texas History Center, University of Texas at Austin.

———. *Travels and Adventures in Texas in the 1820's.* Waco: W. M. Morrison, 1962.

Sinks, Julia Lee. *Chronicles of Fayette: The Reminiscences of Julia Lee Sinks.* Ed. Walter P. Freytag. La Grange, Tex.: n.p., 1975.

Thrall, Homer S. *A Brief History of Methodism in Texas.* Nashville, Tenn.: n.p., 1889.

Webb, Walter P., and H. Bailey Carroll, eds. *The Handbook of Texas.* 2 vols. Austin: Texas State Historical Association, 1952. S.v. "Rabb, John."

Wharton, Clarence R. *Wharton's History of Fort Bend County.* San Antonio: Naylor Company, 1939.

Mary Sherwood Wightman Helm

Helm, Mary Sherwood Wightman. Biographical folder. Barker Texas History Center, University of Texas at Austin.

———. *Scraps of Early Texas History.* Austin: n.p., 1884.

Jeter, Lorraine Bruce. *Matagorda Early History.* Baltimore: Gateway Press, 1974.

Pilgrim, T. J. "First Sunday School in Texas." In *A Texas Scrap Book*, pp. 69–76. Comp. D. W. C. Baker. Austin: Steck Company, 1935.

Webb, Walter P., and H. Bailey Carroll, eds. *The Handbook of Texas*. 2 vols. Austin: Texas State Historical Association, 1952. S.v. "Helm, Mary Sherwood Wightman," and "Wightman, Elias R."

Ann Raney Thomas Coleman

Coleman, Ann Raney. "Journal" (typescript). Barker Texas History Center, University of Texas at Austin.

———. Papers, 1810–92. Barker Texas History Center, University of Texas at Austin.

Creighton, James A. *A Narrative History of Brazoria County*. Waco: Texian Press, 1975.

Golson, Josephine Polley. *Bailey's Light: Saga of Brit Bailey and Other Hardy Pioneers*. San Antonio: Naylor Company, 1950.

Holley, Mary Austin. *Mary Austin Holley: The Texas Diary, 1835–1838*. Ed. J. P. Bryan. Austin: University of Texas Press, 1965.

King, C. Richard, ed. *Victorian Lady on the Texas Frontier: The Journal of Ann Raney Coleman*. Norman: University of Oklahoma Press, 1971.

Strobel, Abner. *The Old Plantations and Their Owners of Brazoria County, Texas*. Houston: Union National Bank, 1926.

Dilue Rose Harris

Carrington, Evelyn M., ed. *Women in Early Texas*. Austin: Jenkins Publishing Company, 1975.

Crawford, Ann Fears, and Crystal Sasse Ragsdale. *Women in Texas*. Burnet, Tex.: Eakin Press, 1982.

Harris, Dilue Rose. "The Reminiscences of Mrs. Dilue Harris," *Quarterly of the Texas State Historical Association* IV (1900): 85–127; 155–89; VII (1904): 214–22.

Houston Post, April 4, 1914.

Looscan, Adele B., "Harris County, 1822–1845," *Southwestern Historical Quarterly* XVIII (April, 1915): 399–409.

Webb, Walter P., and H. Bailey Carroll, eds. *The Handbook of Texas*. 2 vols. Austin: Texas State Historical Association, 1952. S.v. "Harris, Mrs. Dilue (Rose)."

Wharton, Clarence R. *Wharton's History of Fort Bend County*. San Antonio: Naylor Company, 1939.

Rachel Parker Plummer

De Shields, James T. *Border Wars of Texas*. Tioga, Tex.: n.p., 1912.

———. *Cynthia Ann Parker: The Story of Her Capture.* . . . Saint Louis: n.p., 1886.

Fehrenbach, T. R. *Comanches: The Destruction of a People*. New York: Alfred A. Knopf, 1974.

———. *Lone Star: A History of Texas and the Texans*. New York: Macmillan Publishing Co., 1968.

Parker, Daniel. Papers, 1836–1910. Barker Texas History Center, University of Texas at Austin.

Parker, James W. *Narrative of the Perilous Adventures of Rev. James W. Parker . . . to which is appended a Narrative of the capture and subsequent sufferings of Mrs. Rachel Plummer. . . .* Louisville, Ky.: n.p., 1844; reprint ed., Palestine, Tex.: n.p., 1926.

Peckham, Howard H. *Captured by Indians: True Tales of Pioneer Survivors*. New Brunswick, N.J.: Rutgers University Press, 1954.

Plummer, Rachel. *Rachel Plummer's Narrative of Twenty One Months Servitude as a Prisoner among the Comanche Indians Written by Herself*. N.p., 1838; reprint ed., Austin: Jenkins Publishing Company, 1977.

Red, William Stuart. *The Texas Colonists and Religion, 1821–1836*. Austin: E. L. Shettles, 1924.

Richardson, Rupert Norval. *The Comanche Barrier to South Plains Settlement*. Glendale, Calif.: Arthur H. Clark Company, 1933; reprint ed., Millwood, N.Y.: Kraus Reprint Co., 1973.

———. *The Frontier of Northwest Texas, 1846 to 1876*. Glendale, Calif.: Arthur H. Clark Company, 1963.

Speer, William S., ed. *The Encyclopedia of the New West*. Marshall, Tex.: United States Biographical Publishing Company, 1881.

Webb, Walter P., and H. Bailey Carroll, eds. *The Handbook of Texas*. 2 vols. Austin: Texas State Historical Association, 1952. S.v. "Parker, Cynthia Ann"; "Parker, James W."; "Parker, John"; "Fort Parker."

Wilbarger, J. W. *Indian Depredations in Texas*. Austin: n.p., 1889; reprint ed., Austin: Pemberton Press, 1967.

Mary Ann Adams Maverick

Chabot, Frederick C. *With the Makers of San Antonio*. San Antonio: n.p., 1937.

Crawford, Ann Fears, and Crystal Sasse Ragsdale. *Women in Texas*. Burnet, Tex.: Eakin Press, 1982.

Green, Rena Maverick, ed. *Samuel Maverick, Texan: 1803–1870*. San Antonio: n.p., 1952.

Maverick, Mary A. *Memoirs of Mary A. Maverick*. Ed. Rena Maverick Green. San Antonio: n.p., 1921.

Maverick, Maury. *A Maverick American*. New York: Covici, Friede Publishers, 1937.

McLemore, David. *A Place in Time: A Pictorial View of San Antonio's Past*. San Antonio: Express-News Corp., 1980.

Sexton, Irwin, and Kathryn Sexton. *Samuel A. Maverick*. San Antonio: Naylor Company, 1964.

Speer, William S., ed. *The Encyclopedia of the New West*. Marshall, Tex.: United States Biographical Publishing Company, 1881.

Webb, Walter P., and H. Bailey Carroll, eds. *The Handbook of Texas*. 2 vols. Austin: Texas State Historical Association, 1952. S.v. "Maverick, Mary Adams."

Mathilda Doebbler Gruen Wagner

Cade, Winifred, ed. *I Think Back: Being the Memoirs of Grandma Gruen*. San Antonio: n.p., 1937.

Gideon, Samuel A. *Fredericksburg: A Little German Town in the Lone Star State*. Fredericksburg: Gillespie County Historical Society, n.d.

Ragsdale, Crystal Sasse, ed. *The Golden Free Land*. Austin: Landmark Press, 1976.

Silvia King

Rawick, George P., ed. *The American Slave: A Composite Autobiography*. 19 vols. 1941. Reprint ed., Westport, Conn.: Greenwood Press, 1976.

Yetman, Norman R., ed. *Voices from Slavery*. New York: Holt, Rinehart & Winston, 1970.

Rebecca Ann Patillo Bass Adams

Freestone County Historical Commission. *History of Freestone County, Texas*. N.p., 1978.

Strobel, Abner J. *The Old Plantations and Their Owners of Brazoria County, Texas*. Houston: Union National Bank, 1926.

Woods, Gary Doyle. *The Hicks-Adams-Bass-Floyd-Patillo and Collateral Lines, Together with Family Letters, 1840–1868*. Salado, Tex.: Anson Jones Press, 1963.

Eudora Inez Moore

Indianola Scrap Book. Victoria, Tex.: Victoria Advocate Publishing Company, 1936; reprint ed., Port Lavaca, Tex.: Calhoun County Historical Survey Committee, 1974.

McGhee, Lamond Kuykendall. Interview, May 4, 1984, Wimberly, Tex.
———. Letter to Jo Ella Exley, May 5, 1984.

Malsch, Brownson. *Indianola: The Mother of Western Texas*. Austin: Shoal Creek Publishers, 1977.

Moore, Martha L. Interview, April 30, 1984, Bay City, Tex.

Robertson, Connie Moore. Interview, February 24, 1984, Wharton, Tex.

Stieghorst, Junann J. *Bay City and Matagorda County: A History*. Austin: Pemberton Press, 1965.

Webb, Walter P., and H. Bailey Carroll, eds. *The Handbook of Texas.* 2 vols. Austin: Texas State Historical Association, 1952. S.v. "Indianola, Texas."

Wimberly View, October 1, 1981.

Amelia Edith Huddleson Barr

Adams, Oscar Fay. "The Novels of Mrs. Barr," *Andover Review* XI (March, 1889): 248–68.

Adams, Paul. "Amelia Barr in Texas, 1856–1868," *Southwestern Historical Quarterly* XLIX (January, 1946): 361–73.

Barkley, Mary Starr. *History of Travis County and Austin, 1839–1899.* Waco: Texian Press, 1963.

Barr, Amelia E. *All the Days of My Life.* New York: D. Appleton and Company, 1913, 1923; reprint ed., New York: Arno Press, 1980.

————. Biographical folder. Austin History Center, Austin Public Library, Austin.

————. Biographical folder. Barker Texas History Center, University of Texas at Austin.

————. Letters, 1861–1916. Barker Texas History Center, University of Texas at Austin.

Bicknell, Percy F. "The Crowded Life of a Woman of Letters," *The Dial* LV (August, 1913): 76–77.

Blake, Horace Everett. "Mrs. Barr and Her Story," *The Bookman* XXXVII (August, 1913): 617–21.

Eby, Mary Howard. "The Novels of Amelia Barr." M.A. thesis, University of Texas, 1943.

Gideon, Samuel E. *Historical and Picturesque Austin.* Austin: Steck Company, 1936.

Graham, Philip. "Texas Memoirs of Amelia E. Barr," *Southwestern Historical Quarterly* LXIX (April, 1966): 473–98.

Hawthorne, Hildegarde. "Amelia E. Barr—Some Reminiscences," *The Bookman* LI (May, 1920): 283–86.

"An Industrious Life," *Nation* XCVII (August 14, 1913): 144–45.

Johnson, Allen, ed. *Dictionary of American Biography.* New York: Charles Scribner's Sons, 1957. S.v. "Barr, Amelia."

Kirk, John Foster, ed. *Supplement to Allibone's Critical Dictionary of English Literature and British and American Authors.* Philadelphia: J. B. Lippincott and Company, 1900.

"Mrs. Amelia Barr, The Novelist," *American Review of Reviews* LIX (May, 1919): 548–49.

Myers, Robin, ed. *A Dictionary of Literature in the English Language, From Chaucer to 1940.* Oxford: Pergamon Press, 1970.

Sweetser, Kate Dickinson. "Amelia Barr and the Novice," *The Bookman* LVIII (October, 1923): 172–78.

Webb, Walter P., and H. Bailey Carroll, eds. *The Handbook of Texas.* 2 vols. Austin: Texas State Historical Association, 1952. S.v. "Barr, Amelia."

Fannie Davis Veale Beck

Beck, Fannie Davis Veale. *On the Texas Frontier.* Saint Louis: Britt Printing and Publishing Company, 1937.

Clarke, Mary Whatley. *The Palo Pinto Story.* Fort Worth: n.p., 1956.

Hanna, Betty Elliott. *Doodle Bugs and Cactus Berries: A Historical Sketch of Stephens County.* Quanah, Tex.: Nortex Press, 1975.

Richardson, Rupert Norval. *The Frontier of Northwest Texas, 1846 to 1876.* Glendale, Calif.: Arthur H. Clark Company, 1963.

Luvenia Conway Roberts

Pickrell, Annie Doom. *Pioneer Women in Texas.* Austin: E. L. Steck Company, 1929; reprint ed., Austin: Pemberton Press, 1970.

Roberts, Daniel Webster. Biographical folder. Austin History Center, Austin Public Library, Austin.

————. *Rangers and Sovereignty.* San Antonio: Wood Printing, 1914.

Roberts, Mrs. D. W. *A Woman's Reminiscences of Six Years in Camp with the Texas Rangers.* Austin: Von Boeckmann–Jones Company, 1928.

Webb, Walter Prescott. *The Texas Rangers: A Century of Frontier Defense.* Boston: Houghton Mifflin Company, 1935; reprint ed., Austin: University of Texas Press, 1965.

————, and H. Bailey Carroll, eds. *The Handbook of Texas.* 2 vols. Austin: Texas State Historical Association, 1952. S.v. "Roberts, Dan W."

Ella Elgar Bird Dumont

Bennett, Carmen Taylor. *Cottle County, My Dear: Where the "Pan" Joins the "Handle."* Floydada, Tex.: n.p., 1979.

————. Interview, September 4, 1983, Lubbock, Tex.

————. *Our Roots Grow Deep: A History of Cottle County.* Floydada, Tex.: n.p., 1970.

Dumont, Ella. Biographical folder. Barker Texas History Center, University of Texas at Austin.

————. "True Life Story of Ella Bird–Dumont, Earliest Settler in the East Part of Panhandle, Texas" (typescript). Barker Texas History Center, University of Texas at Austin.

King County Historical Society. *King County: Windmillls and Barbed Wire.* Quanah, Tex.: Nortex Press, 1976.

Lee, Ernest, ed. "A Woman on the Buffalo Range: The Journal of Ella Dumont," *West Texas Historical Association Yearbook* XL (October, 1964): 146–67.

Long, Mr. and Mrs. T. E. Interview, September 3, 1983, Paducah, Tex.

U.S. Department of Commerce, Bureau of the Census. *Eighth Census of the United States, 1860*, Itawamba County, Miss.

————. *Tenth Census of the United States, 1880*, Cottle County, Tex.

Mary Olivette Taylor Bunton

Austin Public Library. *Austin and Travis County: A Pictorial History, 1839–1939*. Austin: Encino Press, 1975.

Austin Statesman, October 15, 1885.

Barkley, Mary Starr. *History of Travis County and Austin, 1839–1899*. Waco: Texian Press, 1963.

Bunton, Mary Taylor. Biographical folder. Austin History Center, Austin Public Library, Austin.

————. *A Bride on the Old Chisholm Trail in 1886*. San Antonio: Naylor Company, 1939.

King, Dick. "Two Austin Women and the Chisholm Trail," *Cattleman* LXII (November, 1975): 62–68.

Pickrell, Annie Doom. *Pioneer Women in Texas*. Austin: E. L. Steck Company, 1929; reprint ed., Austin: Pemberton Press, 1970.

Sweetwater Junior Historians. *Early Days—Nolan County: A Book of Readings*. Sweetwater, Tex.: n.p., 1975.

Taylor, T. U. *The Chisholm Trail and Other Routes*. San Antonio: Naylor Company, 1936.

————. "Honeymoon on the Old Cattle Trail," *Frontier Times* XIV (October, 1936): 1–4.

Wilson, Richard W., and Beulah F. Duholm. *Bunton-Buntin-Bunten-Bunting, Including Family of President Lyndon Baines Johnson*. Lake Mills, Iowa: n.p., 1967.

Mary Alma Perritt Blankenship

Connor, Seymour V., ed. *The West Is for Us: The Reminiscences of Mary A. Blankenship*. Lubbock: West Texas Museum Association, 1958.

Graves, Lawrence L., ed. *A History of Lubbock*. Lubbock: West Texas Museum Association, 1962.

Rathjen, Frederick W. *The Texas Panhandle Frontier*. Austin: University of Texas Press, 1973.

Terry County Historical Survey Committee. *Early Settlers of Terry: A History of Terry County, Texas*. Hereford, Tex.: Pioneer Book Publishers, 1968.

Index